Everyday thanks-giving

Interactive photobook with gratitude-enhancing ideas

Positive self-talk series 2

Author and Photographer: Beatrix Csinger, C.H.H.C. (Certified Holistic Health Coach) and certified early childhood educator

THIS BOOK BELONGS TO:_____

I am grateful for who I am and who I am becoming.

Copyrighted © 2020 By Beatrix Csinger

All rights reserved. No parts, segments or illustrations of this publication may be copied or reproduced by any means or in any forms; nor transmitted or distributed without the permission asked prior in writing from the publisher/author, except for brief quotations by a reviewer.

Disclaimer

The information inside this book, in the section "Gratitude-enhancing ideas" related to the book' is based on the author's own experiences and researches. Every effort has been made to describe activities and instructions clearly, therefore, the author and the publisher cannot offer any guarantee or accept any form of liability for damage, injury, or illness that might be caused to the reader following these instructions.

Table of Contents

Everyday thanks-giving 1

Other books published by the author 4

Why is this book different from other books? 6

Everyday thanks-giving 7

Acknowledgement 113

About the Author 114

Upcoming books 114

Other books published by the author

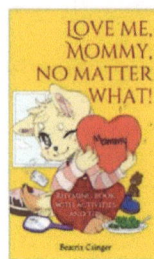 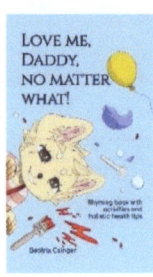 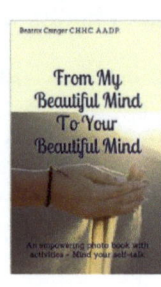 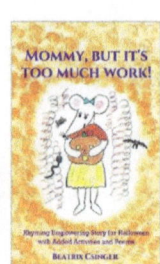

Beatrix Csinger has combined her knowledge and expertise on the areas of early childhood, self-growth, holistic health, psychology, arts and crafts, poetry and rhymes composing, healthy cooking, and photography to create books for readers of various ages and to help families and individuals on the path towards a healthier and more fulfilling life.

Praises for these books

Incredible eye-opener
June 18, 2019
Format: Kindle Edition
I've been taking care of my baby cousin for the past month, and I can say this is way more than a children's book. The story at the start coupled with great illustrations elicits such empathy that really made me reconsider how I treat her when she is most troublesome. The great number of creative tips in raising a child and thought-provoking explanations that make up the rest of the book is beyond helpful! It does not just say what to do to help a child's beautiful self to emerge, but how to do it and why. There are several examples of ways to interact a growing child of varying ages. There is no shortage of creativity in this, especially for someone like me who struggles in that area. It is amazing! I plan to turn to this book again and again as I watch cousin grow.

Beautiful book from a beautiful mind.
September 4, 2019
Format: Kindle EditionVerified Purchase
I'm really enjoying this beautiful book and the activities in it. Nowadays, most people run around with cluttered minds filled with stress, worries, unresolved ideas, and other dominant thoughts. This occupies valuable mind space that limits the capacity for problem solving, idea generation, and clear thinking. This book is vital for overwriting the funky programming most of US inherited and equip us with the right messages for our subconscious mind and activities to do after to really have us do some inner work. I'm loving it so far and I'm pretty sure you would too. I highly recommend it!

Excellente read
September 5, 2019
Format: Kindle EditionVerified Purchase
I loved this book is like a balm for the soul, it feels like meditation while going through the pages. So many positive and inspirational messages.
The poems are beautiful. The author is also a great photographer

Beautiful photos

September 13, 2019
Format: Kindle Edition
I really enjoy this book, I love the beautiful photos. Highly recommended.

Put this gem in your collection pronto!
May 18, 2019
Format: Kindle EditionVerified Purchase
This book brings to light one of the most profound concepts in regards to our children as well as humanity as a whole! I love the way Beatrix weaves the truth of a child's incalculable value into a rhyme. As the father of three daughters, I learned early on in parenting, that the worthiness of my girls, and likewise all of us, is inherent and not tied to any certain action, skill, ability or function. That they deserve the entirety of my love simply because they are brilliantly and uniquely them. It's such a joy to see this truth shared in such an easily understandable format. Thank you Beatrix!

Why is this book different from other books?

This book is a combination of beautiful and intriguing photography, eye-opening ways to become more mindful and appreciative and extra suggestions how the reader can expand on practicing gratitude for everyday and special events and items.

This book is about sharing photos that were taken by the author throughout years to show the beauty all around us.

This book is filled with activity ideas for adults and children that promote bonding with family, and exercising self-love.

This book is a gentle guidance towards practicing living in the present and making the best out of each moment.

Everyday thanks-giving

Have you ever tried to consciously direct your attention towards what you can be thankful for instead of what is still missing from your life? As a child and teenager, I used to focus on what went wrong, what was "bad" or undesirable for me and I remember suffering a lot emotionally. When I've begun my studies as a holistic health practitioner in New York, the whole world has shifted around me and inside me. It was and it's been ever since the most profound experience in my life. The holistic approach to my life, to my body and health, to my relationships with people, food, challenges, work and studying, and much-much more has opened countless doors for me, and opportunities by great numbers have started to flood my days to create my own happiness.

Thanksgiving has been celebrated on the last Thursday of November, every year, since Abraham Lincoln's time. It's a national holiday in the United States of America. Originally, it was a harvest festival. In 1941, Roosevelt has signed a bill that Thanksgiving would fall on the fourth Thursday of November every year whether it's the last or not the last Thursday in November.

This is the time when families and friends gather together to spend a wonderful time having a great feast of stuffed turkey with cranberry sauce, mashed potatoes with gravy, pumpkin pie, corn and green beans. It's to be grateful for what we have.

The big question is why to feel and behave this way only once a year?! What really sets the tone of the day, what really generates solid results in every area of life is what we do on a regular basis, not what we do once in a while.

Let me ask you this. Do you feel nice when you feel grateful? Does it make you feel small or big as a person? Does it motivate you to go after your dreams? Does it elevate your mood? Does it generate extra mental and physical energy inside you? Does it allow you to connect more deeply or more superficially with others, the Creator and yourself? Do you feel like smiling when you are thankful? There are so many more questions that I could ask. This is the time to become a little more self-aware, dear Reader. I know when I focus on all my gifts I've received and I am able to enjoy (and I am not talking only about materialistic gifts), I feel like flying. I feel absolutely light and energetic. It's like a tingle and a rush of wonderful energy through my body and mind.

I've created this book for You, decorated it with my own photos to guide you towards enhanced gratitude-attitude, to open your eyes, heart and mind for all the beauty around you, to trigger ideas in your head so you can develop things further for your loved ones' and your own benefits.

Let me elaborate a little on a fantastic tool for developing a more positive and appreciative mindset towards life. Photography is one of my passions. As I've begun taking photos in increasing number of subjects around me, I've noticed the huge power of this hobby. When you take a photo, what do you do? You must focus in the moment, on your subject. Your mind can't be wandering around and about the laundry of the past or the worries of the future. You are living where you're supposed to: in the present! The more you are able to pull that off, the happier and more powerful you'll start feeling. Yes, I am talking from personal experience, and I can't emphasize enough how amazingly this has changed my life.

Here's another point about photography. When you take pictures, you start noticing details that went kind of unnoticed before. These details might not always be beautiful, but they are certainly widening your knowledge and experience regarding things. Through my own photos, I've started understanding what life is all about, how blessed I am, and we all are, how my life is filled with opportunities to create, build, grow and love, and how breathtaking my life is indeed. Breathtaking … with every breath I am taking.

So, dear Reader, please join me on this special journey to explore your soul, heart and mind. Leafing through this book, but also with a great focus on its content, you'll begin discovering more about yourself, your desires and preferences, and maybe even your fears. That's OK, too. Knowing your fears will allow you to deal with them properly.

Most of all, the pictures in this book and the words are there for you to realize how fascinating our world is, how exciting your days could be if you let them be, if you learn and get into the habit of observing and receiving things that way. I'd like to bring it to your attention that it's probably one of the best presents you can give your children as well: educate them about becoming more grateful every single day. I know what you might be thinking. What if my life is really hard and full of suffering? How could I be thankful then? I've got these questions from a great percentage of my clients. It might sound corny but there is always something in every situation to be grateful for, no matter how horrible it is. It's just the programming of the brain usually prevents us from noticing it or wanting to notice it. Often, it leads back to feeling guilty or ashamed by feeling thankful for a particular thing in the midst of unfortunate happenings. Remember, if your mind was programmed that way, most likely in your childhood, then it can be re-programmed as well. No programming is ever final.

There have been numerous studies about the connection between gratitude and happiness/health. With the title "How gratitude changes you and your brain" there was an article written a couple of years ago, supported with a study, how being grateful impacted the participants' mental health more positively. "Does gratitude writing improve the mental health of psychotherapy clients? Evidence from a randomized controlled trial" – it was published in the Journal of Psychotherapy Research in volume 28, 2018, issue 2. The findings were so promising.

Those participants who have written gratitude letters for weeks or months have experienced improved mental health compared to those who have received only counseling and/or have written down only negative experiences.

So, what can we be thankful for anyway? Should it be only great things like becoming famous, or earning millions, or enjoying impeccable health and fitness level, or having a faithful and loving spouse? Frequently, most people feel grateful for the big accomplishments and gifts only. How often do you meet the phrase "Don't take it for granted!"? Familiar, right? What I've observed through years of practicing that even when I am doing my part of gratitude writing, I still find that I take certain people or things for granted. Some things would slip by always. Oh, wait a second. I am choosing right now and here a different word instead. The word "always" can become a dangerous word because just like the word "never" implies there's no between, no exceptions, and nothing breaks the rule. I wouldn't want to give such commands to my cells, right? Do you see how one word, one thought can make a profound difference? Imagine when your mind is filled with tens of thousands of thoughts daily of which a large percentage is just repeated from the days and weeks before and many of them are negative! Boom! A real downer. However, we all are so powerful and we can decide at any given moment to change our thoughts. Isn't that so amazing? Back to the previous line of thoughts: "Some things would slip by always." I correct it: Some things have slipped by up until now, but from now on, I can choose a different approach or technique.

So, how do we get to the point of not taking anything for granted? Practice, practice, practice. This isn't that kind of practice that ends when you have done this or that much. It should be – and that's how it's worth doing it – done every day for the rest of our days. Writing it down is definitely the best way to confirm it for ourselves, to imprint it more deeply into our hearts and brains, and also, to focus on it 100%. I have gratitude journals, two of them. One, I use for general thankfulness what I have been feeling thankful for daily, like my cozy, comfortable home, or food on my table daily, and so many more things. The second one is for events, people and things that are specific for that particular day. If you think it would take too much of your time to write into an appreciation journal every single day, let me show you a different perspective. 10 minutes of writing would take up less than 1 % of your day! If you read studies or articles on what a great positive impact daily gratitude can bring into your life, and try it out for yourself for a couple of weeks too, it's easy to see the priceless value of this daily habit inserted into your schedule.

Now, please allow me to show you a bit what you could be grateful for and feel free to translate it into your own reality. We are all unique. Whatever doesn't exist in your life at the moment, and it's included in this book, I'd recommend considering the probability for your life or the actual existence of it in someone else' life who is important to you.

Let's float into the experience now... allow your eyes and mind truly enjoy the images.

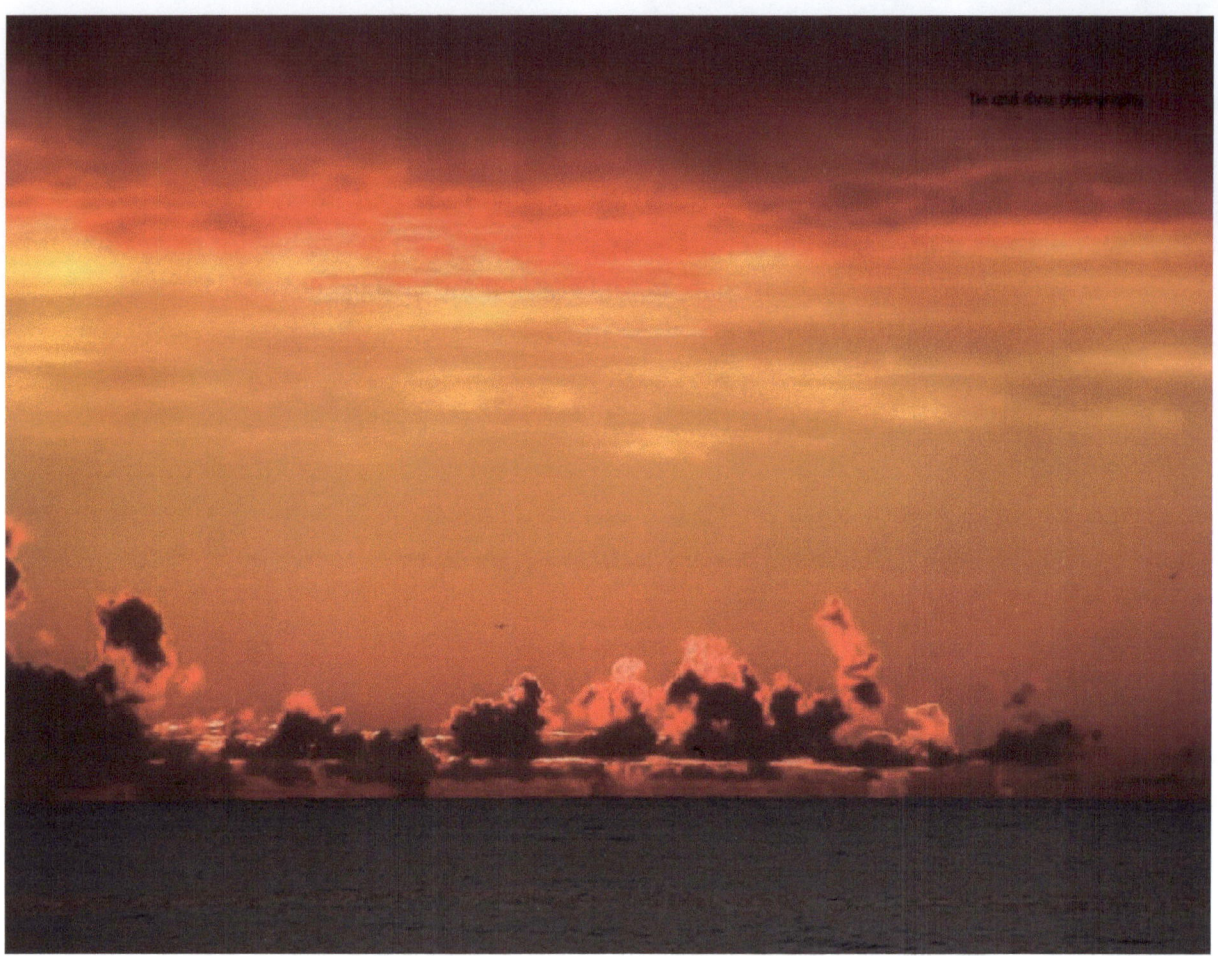

I feel absolutely grateful for the gorgeous sunrises I can observe on the sky. Those mesmerizing colors and hues, that clean feeling when I walk on the beach at this time of the day. It's so pure, clean energy. It fills me up with such a great mood. I walk on the wet sand, bare foot, enjoying the light breeze or the wind. Whether the sky is covered with clouds, or just a few or none, each sunrise is beautiful and unique. Each sunrise brings dozens of new opportunities to me to smile, to love, to give and share, to create and to enjoy. Isn't it so incredible what a colorful picture nature paints for us almost every morning to start the day with?

Gratitude-enhancing ideas: take time once or twice to sit out on a great spot where you can observe the sun rising really well. Take an easel or pad with you, paint and paintbrushes and re-create this magical experience on paper or canvas. If you aren't interested in using paint, how about making art with crayons or pencils? The key is to create through your own heart and mind, whatever captures you, for yourself or others, as you wish. Taking pictures of these magical moments and then arranging them into special photo albums are other ways you can appreciate sunup more deeply. It can inspire you to use the color scheme of sunrise to dress up your bedroom, prepare a delicious, fancy dessert or salad, or sew a dress. Let it grab you, take you away a bit…

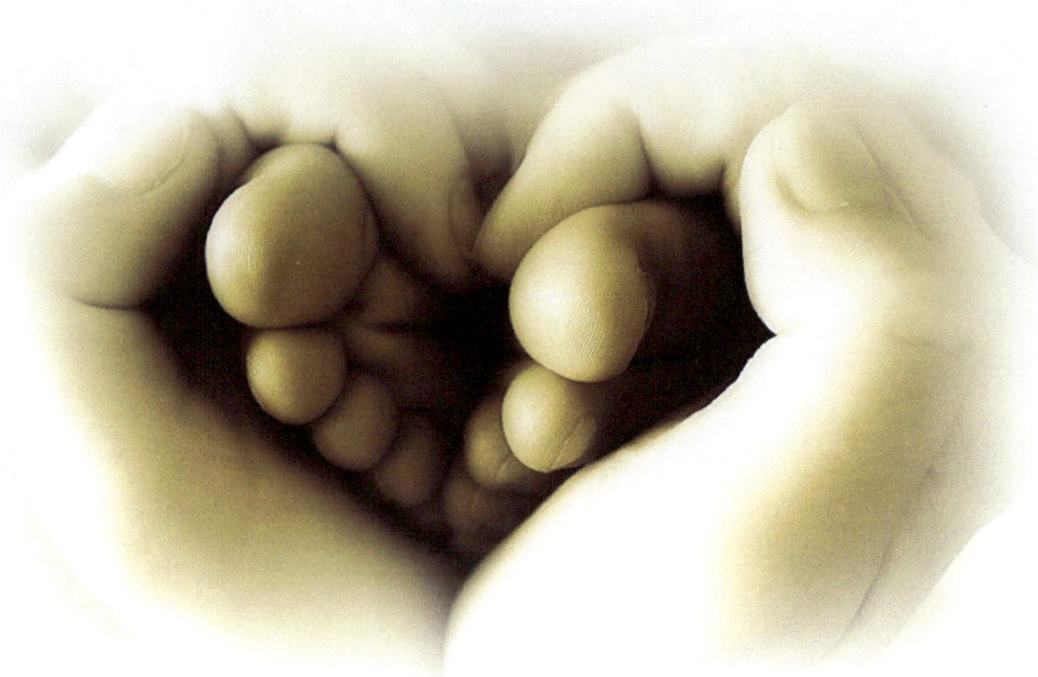

Do and show photography

I feel so very grateful for my children. I recall a variety of memories when they were babies. I realize that being a parent is probably the hardest job of all and we do so many things for our children with the best intention, yet often we feel unsatisfied with the results. I know it's absolutely challenging and generates a mixture of emotions, however, having a child is one of the most miraculous and amazing life experiences there are. I feel extremely thankful for this experience, for the opportunity to contribute to a better world through raising my children in a particular way, for the power and responsibility that show me I am trusted and capable, and for the heartwarming and soul-flying memories we create along the way together as a family.

Gratitude-enhancing ideas: gather photographs of your children. Stitch the edges of the pictures with embroidering threads doing blanket stitch. For a simpler photo box, you can use six photographs. For a more complex but also more 3-dimentional box, you should create a plain box first from plain cardboard sides (or patterned ones), then attach the photos on the outside in bent form. You can attach the sides by lacing the stitches together. Other projects: make little books for your young children from construction papers and with their added photos of silly faces, or composing rhymes or a story under the pictures, teaching about colors in different languages, etc. One of my favorites is making finger puppets from colorful felt, and gluing faces of family members and friends onto them. It's a blast. Children truly seem to enjoy whatever is about them, and people and objects that are important to them. Through a puppet play, you can learn a ton about your child's thoughts and emotions regarding their lives and people they are in touch with.

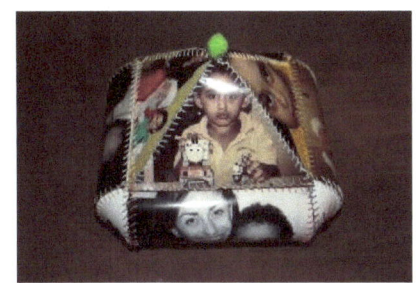
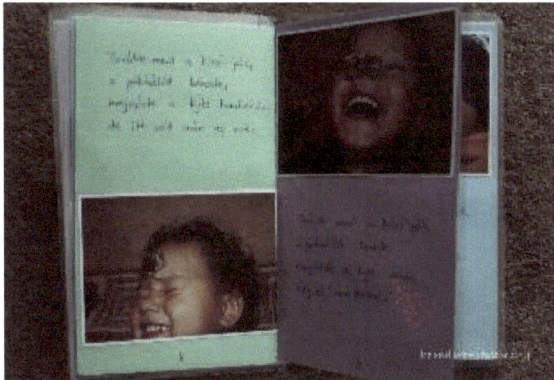
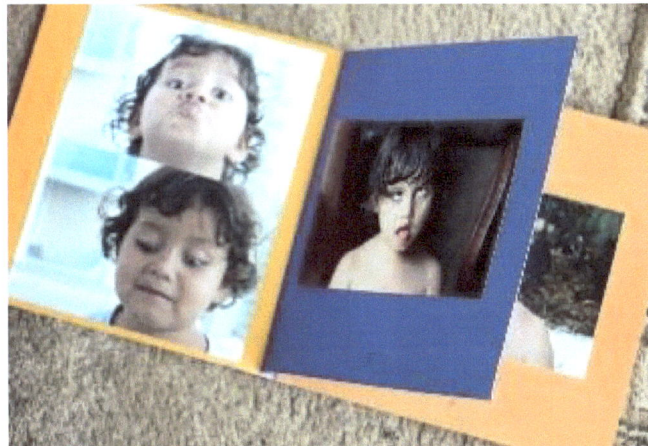
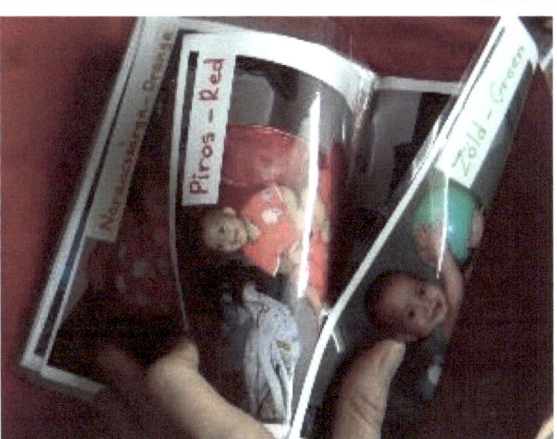
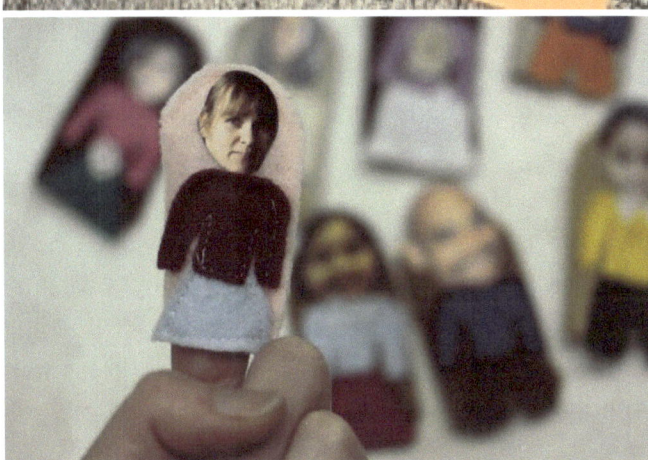

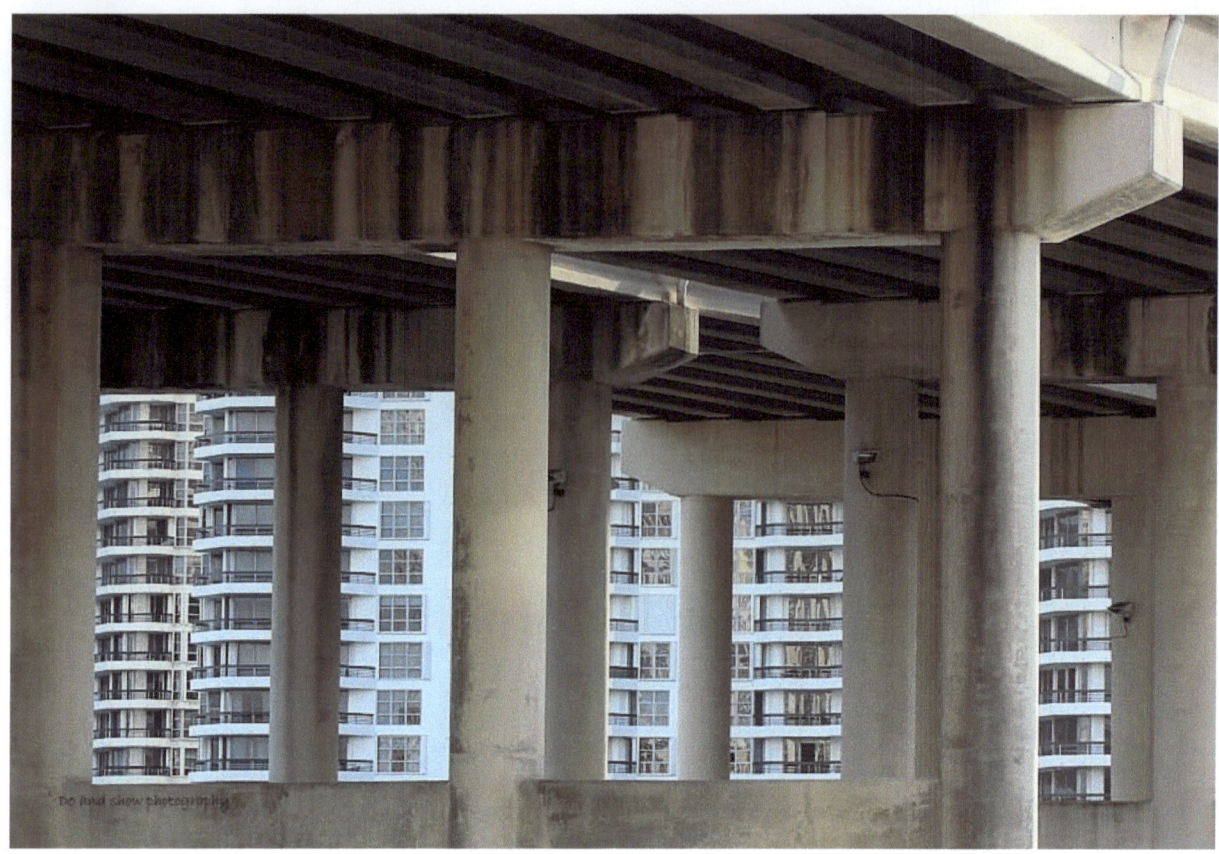

 I feel very blessed for having my cozy home, and all the buildings in the world that provide a shelter for families. Isn't it wonderful how safely now we can live even in high skyscrapers? I am very grateful for the knowledge and work of all the architects and construction workers, all the experts involved in creating these magnificent towers and buildings, therefore beautiful cities for us, humans. What's even more amazing that many of them truly care about the environment and work hard on producing newer and better materials and construction details in the area of green architecture.

Gratitude-enhancing ideas: a great time to construct with your child or nephew/niece to gain more appreciation of this type of blessing. Let your inner child have fun! Use various building materials, even unconventional ones, like toothpicks, pencils, playdough and erasers to join sticks, bottle caps, and much more. Create art! Frame it if it's flat or use strong glue to make it a permanent piece. I have endless fun photographing interesting buildings and structures from unique angles. You can collect photos of such as well to start appreciating them even more.

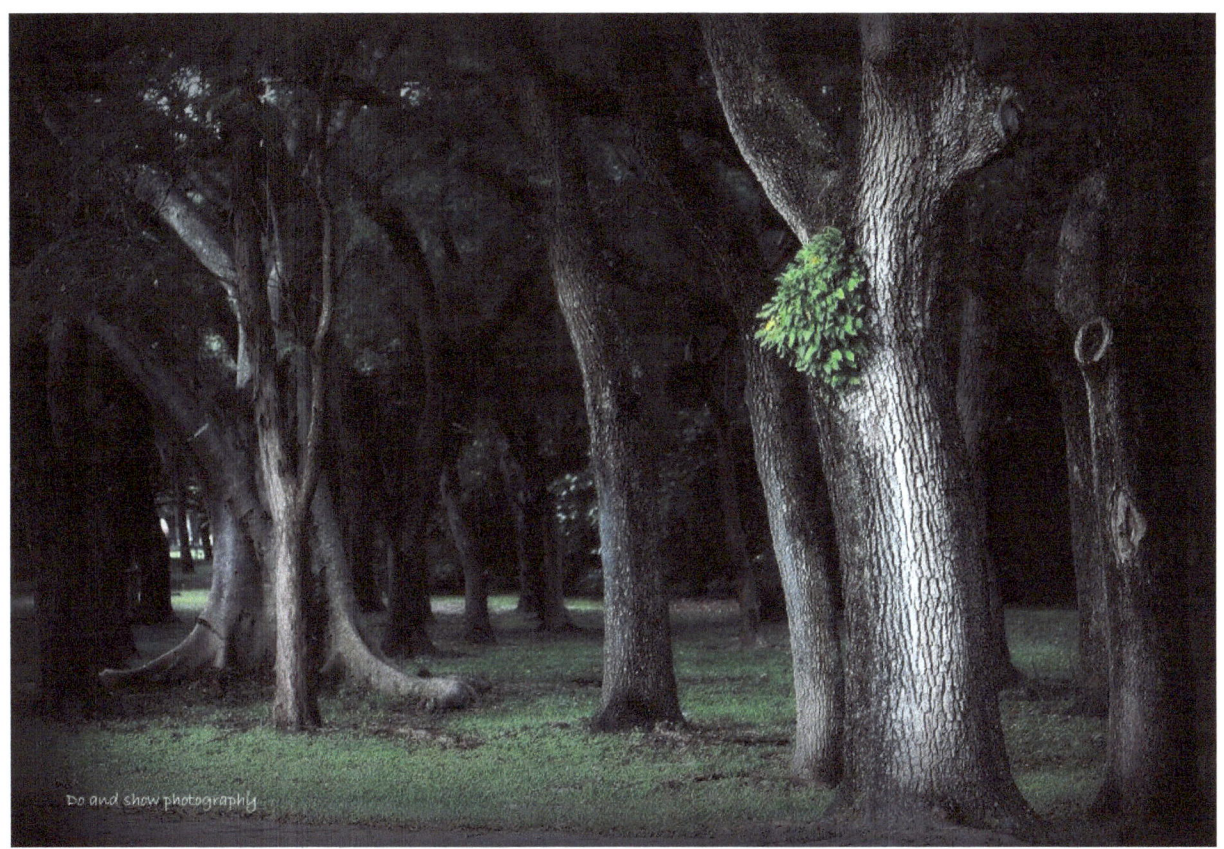

I am extremely thankful for parks where I can take a stroll with my loved ones or alone, I can clear my head and gather my thoughts, I can take some light exercises and inhale fresh air. Isn't it lovely how in the middle of a city we can enjoy nature? Those old trees, that green grass and birds chirping to remind us how beautiful our world is indeed. It's nice to see the squirrels hopping around looking for nuts. What a great relaxation time we can have often nearby our work or home!

Gratitude-enhancing ideas: craft stores sell adorable wooden birdhouses that are waiting to be painted and utilized. Think of all the fun you could have with your little ones or yourself. Then add seeds and tie them on trees in the park or in your backyard. You can also create one from scratch recycling used materials and containers. It's a terrific quality time to spend with loved ones.

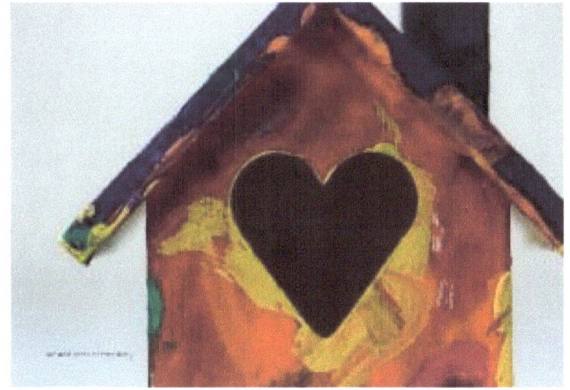

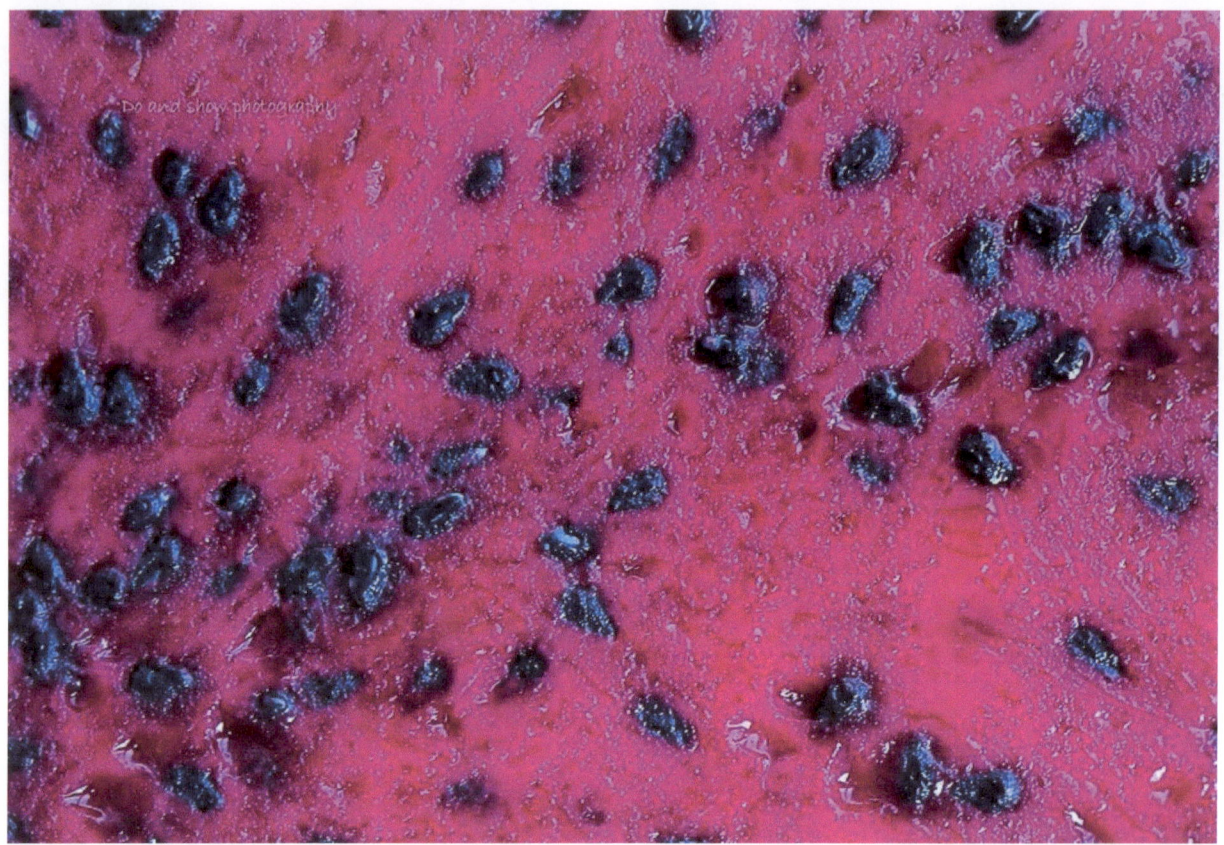

Look at this incredibly vivid color! It's a picture of the flesh and seeds of a dragon fruit. I feel so very thankful for all the seeds and their absolutely fascinating divine wisdom and programming to grow into life-giving plants. How amazing is that in our world we have numerous ways to spread seeds around to ensure plants are growing and dying trees are replaced!

Gratitude-enhancing ideas: collect some seeds from fresh fruits, engaging other family members too. Plant them into small clay pots or containers. Many of them will grow when being watered regularly and left near a window or outside in pleasant weather. It's a wonderful way to teach children about how to take care of living things. Another idea is to join those who have started planting trees to be part of the solution in order to re-forest. I've always loved making seed-boards for my students. I gathered different kinds of seeds. I attached them onto cardboards using wide clear tape. I added their names underneath. I also put seeds in varying numbers to practice math.

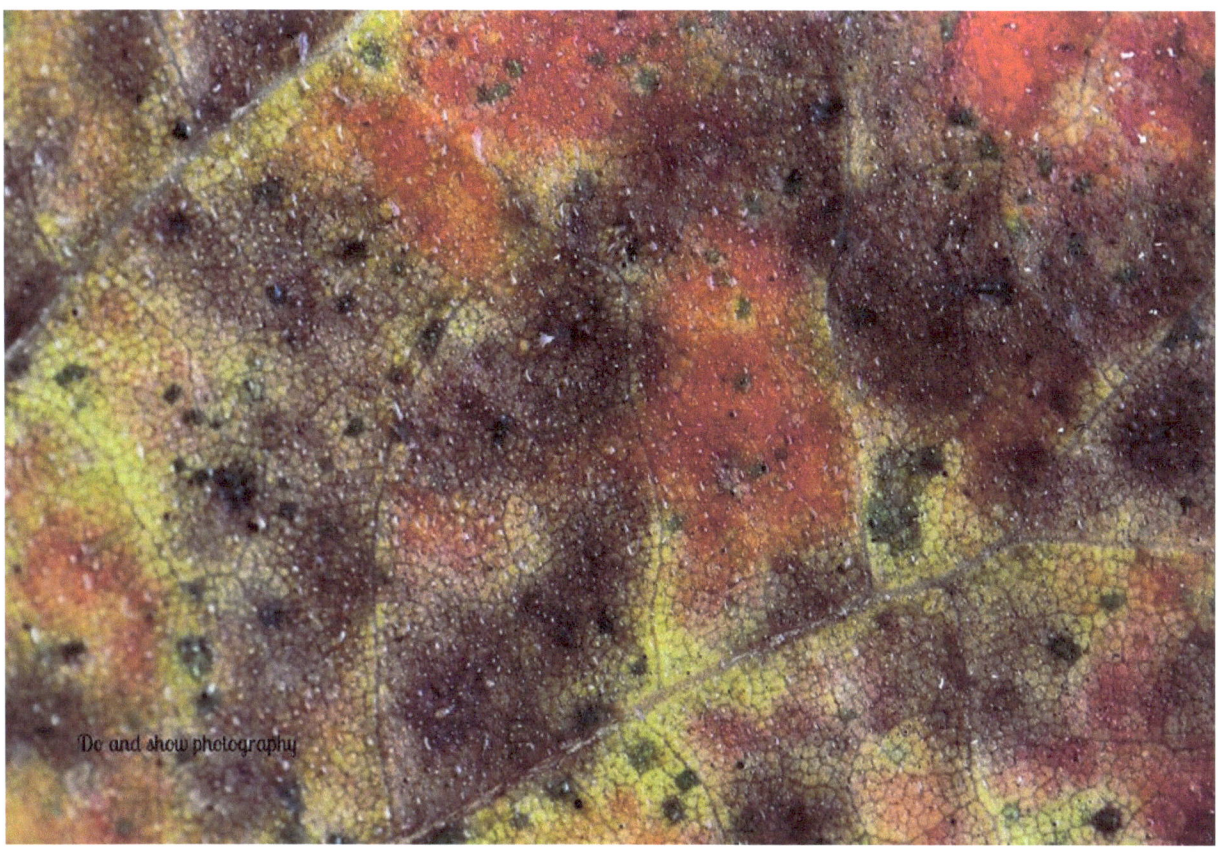

I am very grateful for the autumn leaves. They are such eye-candy! Nature is showing us change may be difficult sometimes but it also can be a really beautiful transition. As the weather begins to cool down and we've got to wear our warmer clothes, it's time to adjust and find new ways to connect with our loved ones and ourselves too.

Gratitude-enhancing ideas: gather autumn leaves and create some art. Your children can enjoy this activity with you while you can share more information about the changing season. Leaves can be dry-pressed, then used for hand-made cards, or the cover of a journal. You can paint them, then print with them onto a canvas to decorate the walls of your home. If you use dye for clothing, why not to create an autumn shirt for every family member? I still have my leaf-collection from 2nd grade. We needed to do it for science class. I gathered leaves of fruit trees and vegetables from our garden. It's kind exciting to realize that they are over 30 years old. Fun projects aren't just for youngsters. I have been creating all kinds of art pieces and projects ever since I was a child. I have to admit it keeps me so excited and entertained, so alive.

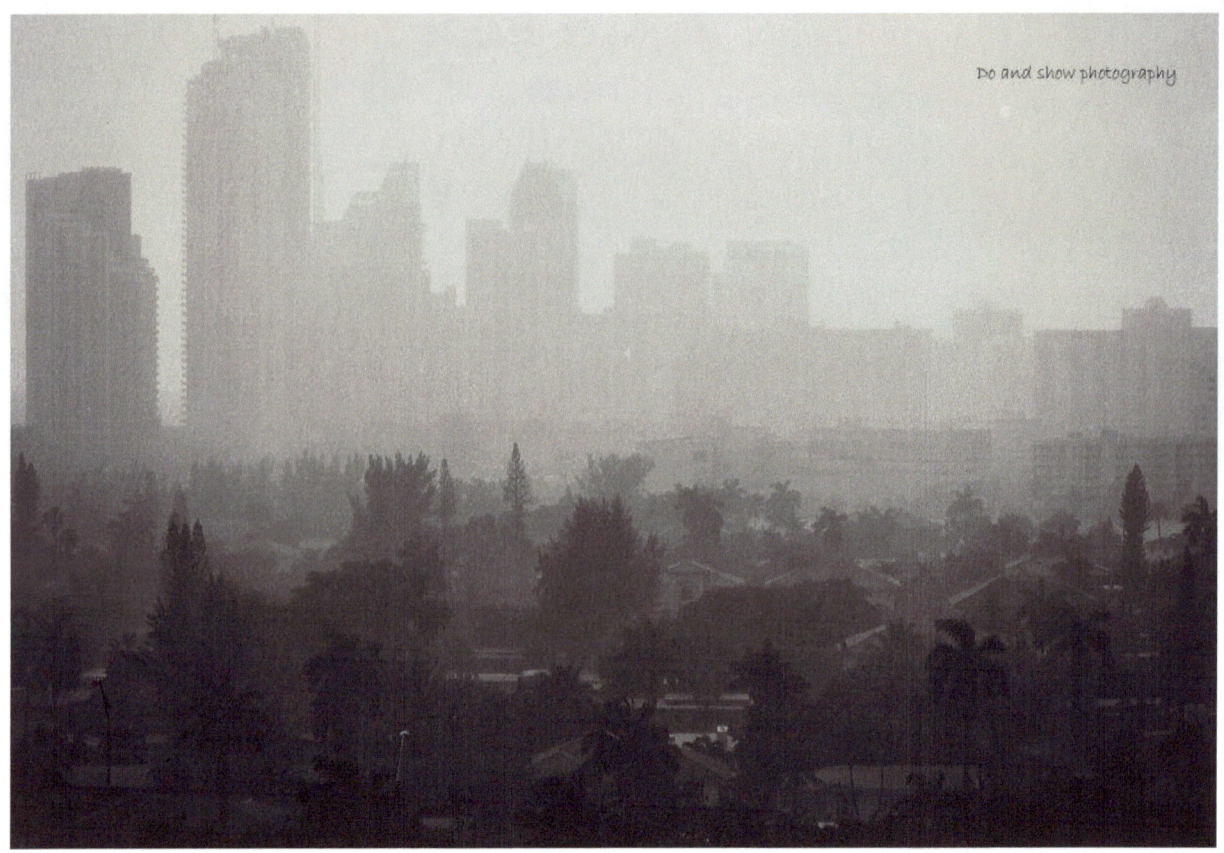

I feel absolutely grateful for the rain, the refreshing, cleansing and life-supporting rain. I can feel how the thirsty plants are absorbing the water and how countless animals enjoy the rain itself or the puddles and elevated water levels that remain afterwards. How cozy a rainy day can be, right? Sipping a hot tea while curled up in a soft armchair with an exciting book is such a lovely way to spend a rainy day. The waterdrops wash away the dust and dirt and make the air smell good. Very importantly, the rain helps to put out fires that firefighters may be struggling with. In a summer shower, it's so much fun to jump in puddles with my child and entertain my inner child as well.

Gratitude-enhancing ideas: during rainfall, sit with a loved one in the car or in a place where there are large windows or ceiling windows. Consciously devote some time for just being there, relaxing, and watching and listening how the raindrops pattering on the glass. Snuggle with your loved ones, go down memory lane, enjoy. Maybe you'd like to also invest in a rainstick. Rainsticks are long, hollow, wooden tubes with seeds or beans inside that generate the sounds of falling rain when turned vertically. Use visualizing the falling rain as a method to wash away negative feelings and thoughts, or even pain. It's definitely worth a try. It's been working wonders for me.

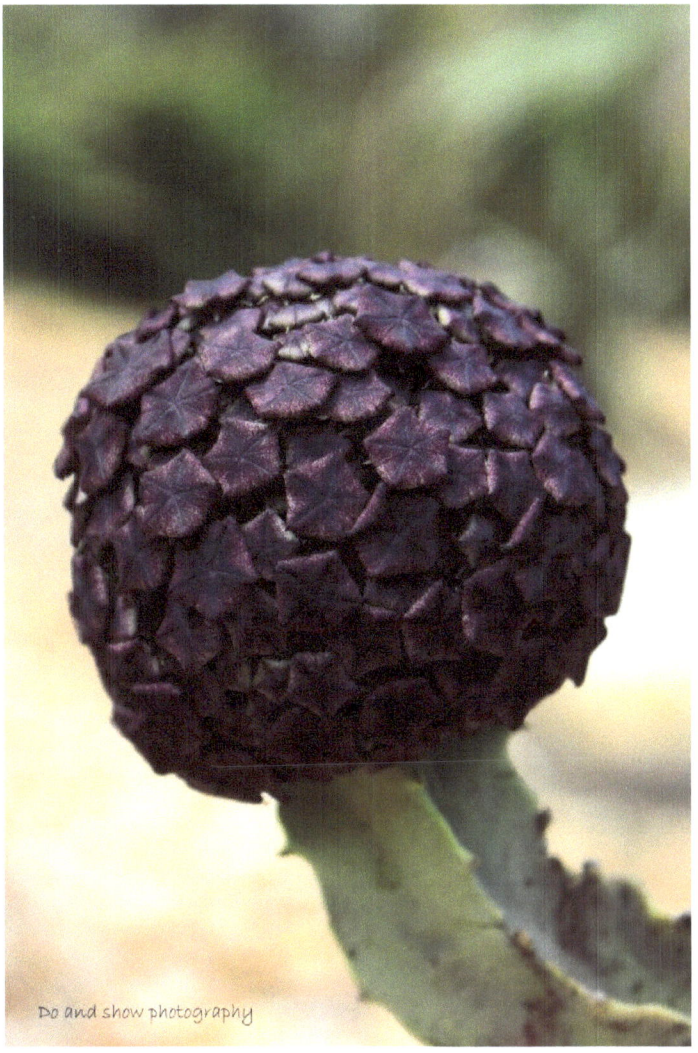

I feel so very thankful for the mesmerizing flowers, their various colors and shapes, scents and sizes. It's amazing how they change a plain street or park into a picturesque scene. It's fascinating that no matter how many flower species I have seen and taken pictures of, I keep encountering new ones on and on. And we have different flowers for different seasons! In fact, on the winter, we can admire the frost flowers on the window pane.

Gratitude-enhancing ideas: besides planting flowers in flowerpots or window boxes, how do you feel about creating a book of flowers, for example, using your own photographs? Taking pictures is an excellent way to pull you back into the moment and shift your focus on every day beauty. To take it one step further, you can look up their names and information about them, and add all this to your picture book.

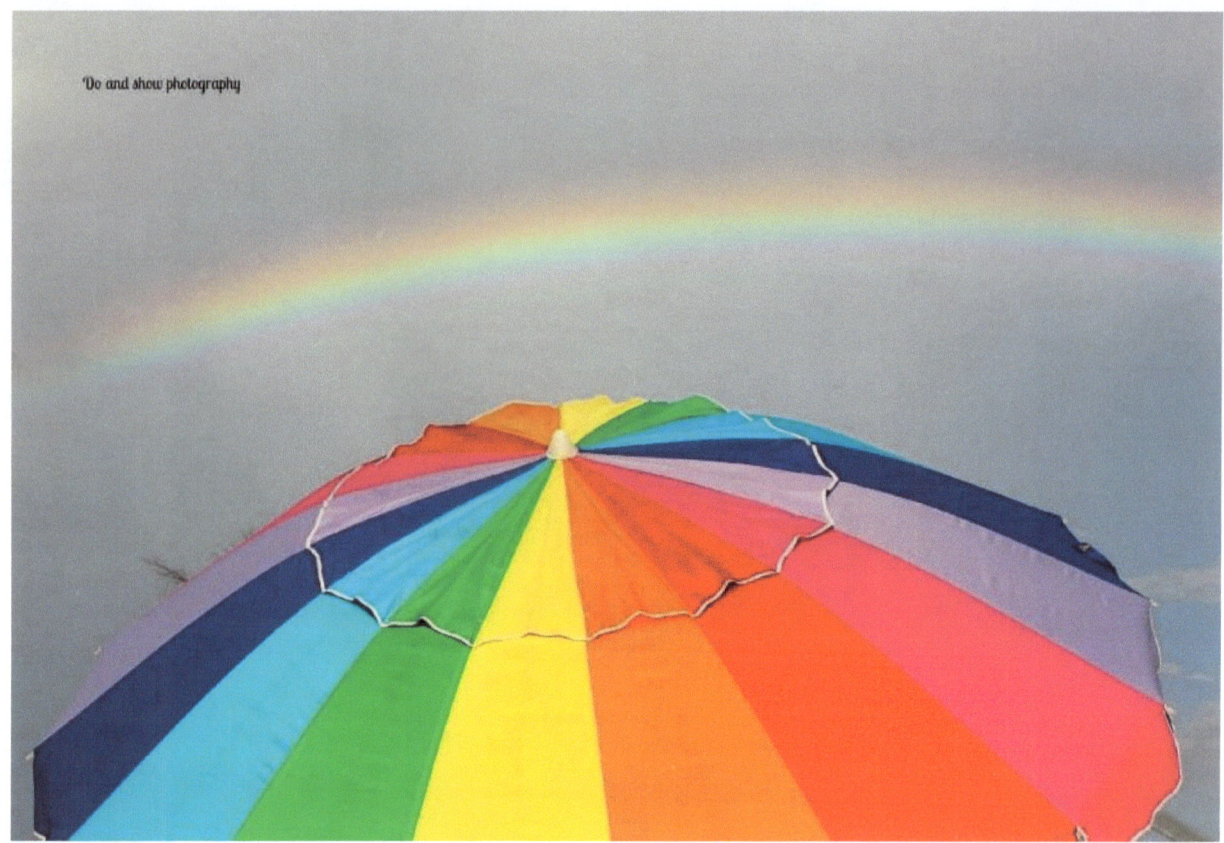

I am so very grateful for the rainbows on the sky and around waters. What a gorgeous arch to inspire us to stop for a few minutes and give ourselves to the moment. Rainbows aren't only for the children's eyes. I always feel excited when I see one. This rainbow on my picture has colored the sky above us on a beach in Florida. Then I saw the rainbow-colored beach umbrella right under it. I felt so much gratitude for this picture that it came together like this.

Gratitude-enhancing ideas: since rainbows are short-lived, remind yourself to stop and enjoy these moments, if you can. Take a picture of it. Realize how incredible it is that the colors are always lined up in the same exact order. Are you ready to have a silly fun for yourself and your family? Cook rainbow pasta or bake a rainbow cake with colorful layers. If you love jello, layer different colors in cups or a large tray, then cut them up into cubes. Take time to truly be in the moment and enjoy the results using all of your senses.

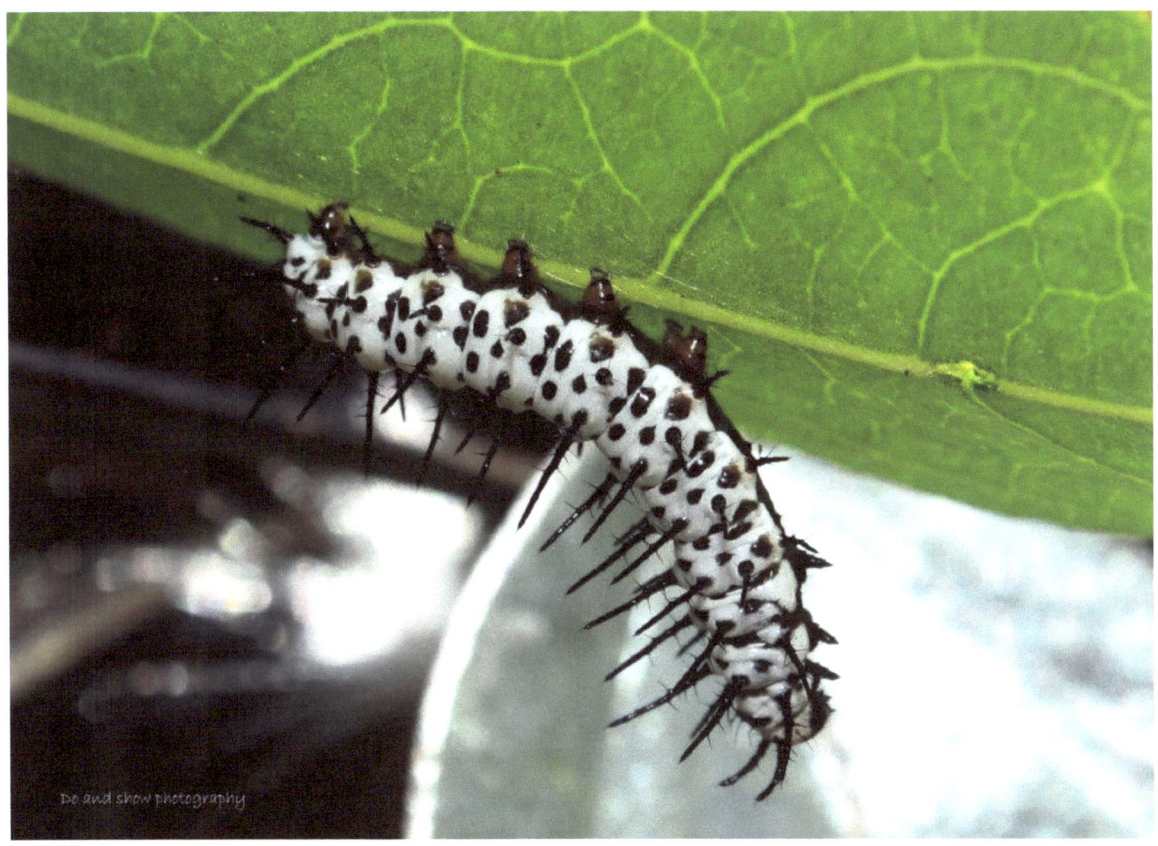

I am so thankful for the caterpillars despite my slight fear and aversion towards the insect world. Isn't it incredible how much they change as they become beautiful butterflies? Right there, I feel and understand it on a deeper level how it's possible for me also to go through great changes despite what anyone would assume whether I could or not. The universe is showing me that I could, it's possible. It's a very curious transition. The caterpillars bring some of their traits and qualities into their butterfly-hood, just maybe altered or modified. I feel so much gratitude to follow the butterflies with my eyes fluttering around, … as if the wind has picked up some flower petals and make them dance in the air.

Gratitude-enhancing ideas: if you are into science, get a butterfly growing kit. See it with your own eyes! It's different on pictures or videos. It's fantastic for your children as well to capture all the stages with their sponge-like minds. Then cut out butterfly-shaped papers. Prepare some paint and paintbrushes on the table that is covered with a protective plastic or paper. The paint will work better for this project if it's thick and has body. Paint only one side of the butterfly adding different colors in patches or planned design. Make the paint coating thick. Then carefully, fold up and lay the blank side of the wing on the top of the painted one. Using a cloth or paper towel piece, smooth it out. Open it up and be pleasantly shocked!

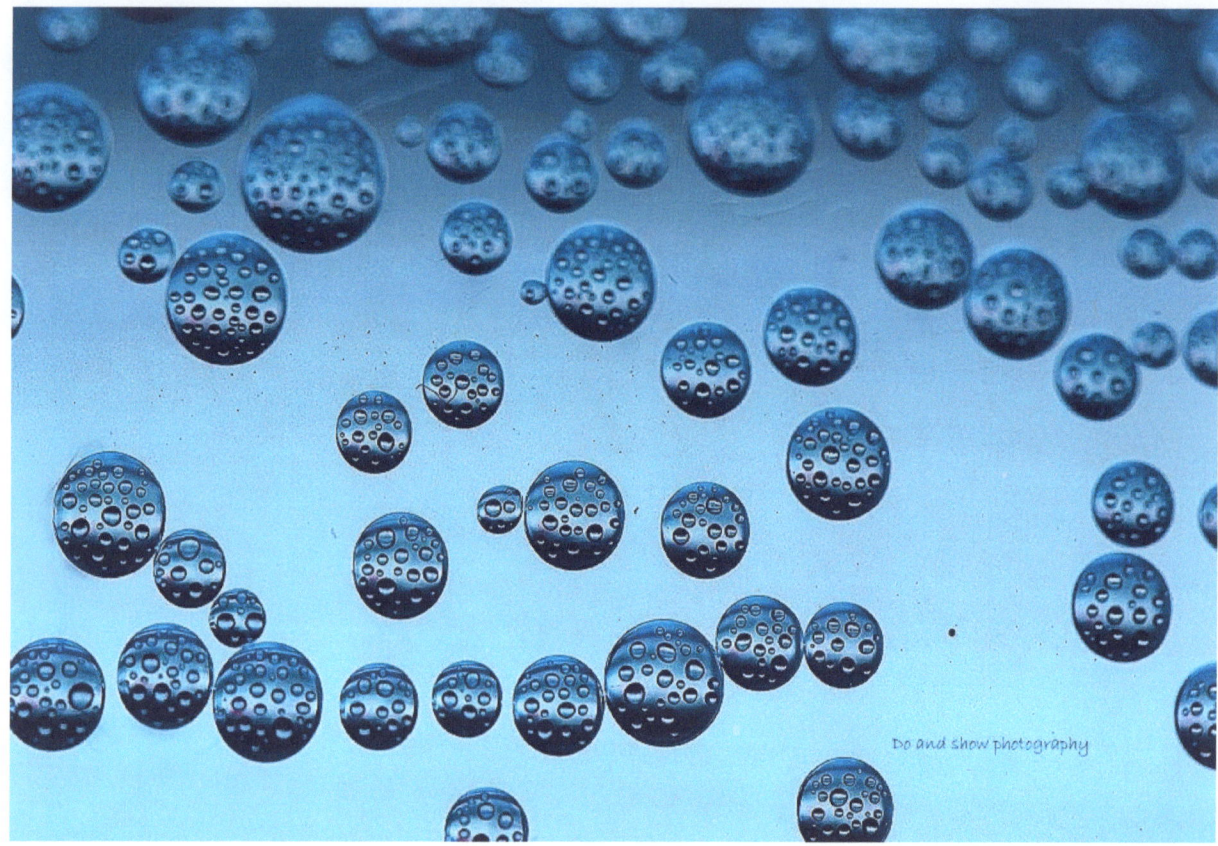

I am extremely blessed for having plenty clean and safe water for my family and myself. I am also very grateful for having cold and hot water in my home, conveniently flowing out of faucets and we don't have to wait for any tank to fill up when others have used it up. I am aware of how many people in the world can't say the same. This awareness motivates me constantly to watch my water usage and be the part of the solution instead of the part of the problem regarding clean water shortage on the planet. I feel gratitude for becoming aware like this because it's extremely important for me to help solve problems as opposed to create more. According to CDC, about 1.8 billion people have no access to safe drinking water. And I don't belong in that group! Neither do you. That's something profound to chew on and appreciate!

Gratitude-enhancing ideas: collect rain water to water plants, and wash off car and other items. Start utilizing a household filter to filter your water for drinking and cooking to lessen the plastic waste on earth and inside your body. Take shorter showers. Listen to water sounds for meditation, such as running water, or falling rain, or stream rushing through rocks. Feel the cleansing power of water.

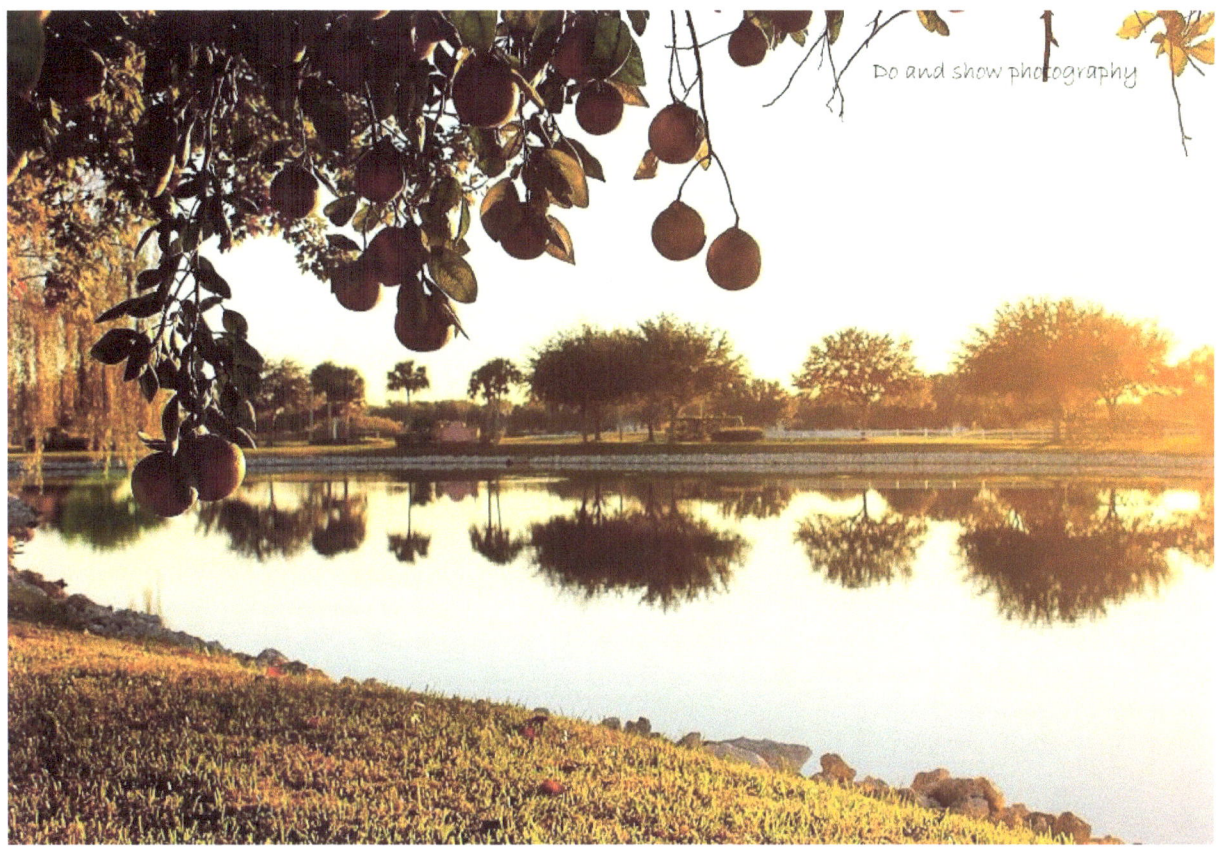

I feel very grateful for the fruits that grow on trees providing us juicy, refreshing and cooling fruits in summer days. With their vitamins and antioxidants, I can keep my body healthier. They look so lovely around my home and near lakes. The colorful fruits in various sizes and shapes are such eye-pleasing sights. They also attract beautiful birds and insects from around to admire.

Gratitude-enhancing ideas: find different ways to eat fruits that are health-supporting. Fruits, when they are cooked, they don't provide as much nutrients as when they are eaten raw. Besides eating them in their natural forms, chop them up to prepare fruit salads; or add them to homemade juices and smoothies; put some on the top of your salad or ice cream. For your children, offer them every single day a variety of fruit pieces on a tray. Let them pick and choose. If they aren't eating enough fruits nowadays, eventually with this method they usually become more open to try. Instead of forcing them, encourage them with a few kind words and set a great example for them daily. They copy more what we do than what we say.

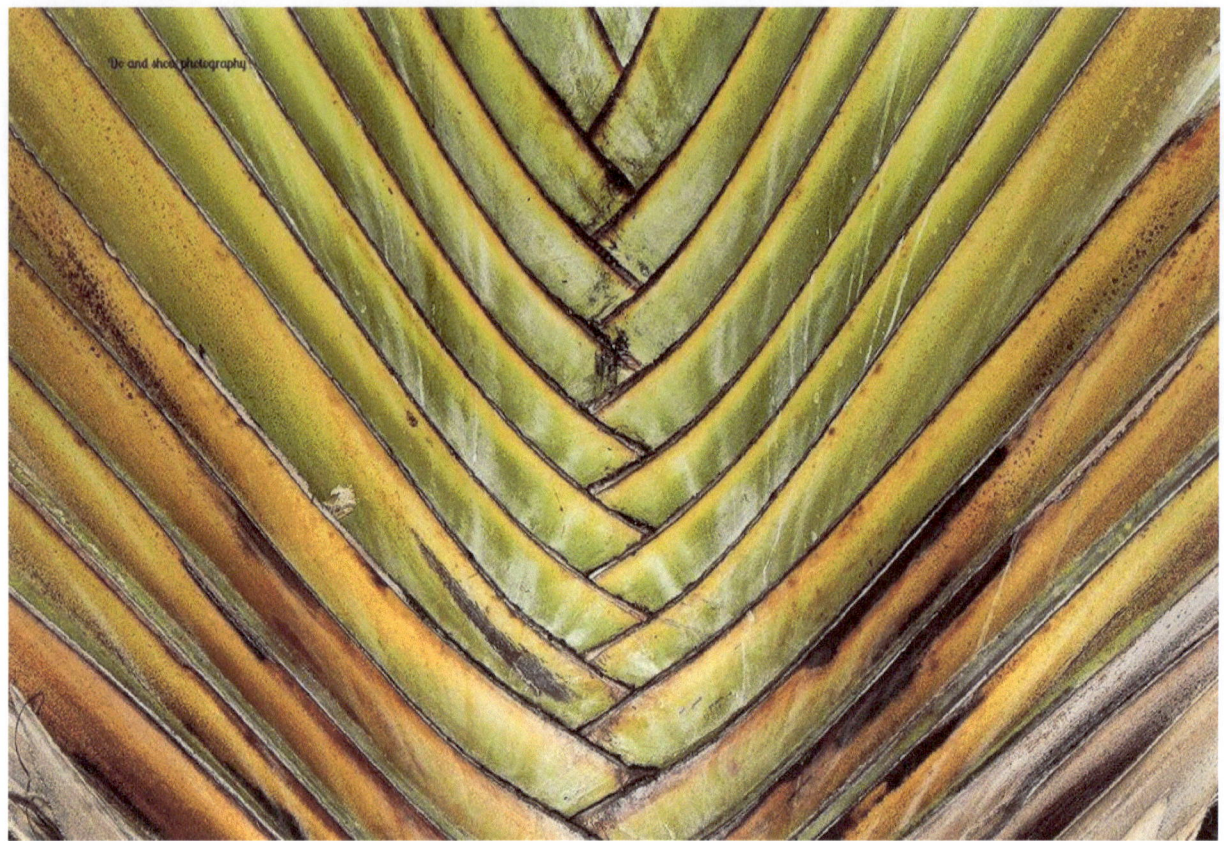

I am so thankful and excited to notice nature's gorgeous patterns around me. Isn't it amazing how many kinds of interesting patterns you can spot as you go about your day? Our eyes and minds are being entertained on a daily basis when we start becoming more conscious and appreciative. These designs are so clever and pleasant to look at. They are also wonderful to provide us with inspiration in order to create in the areas of art projects, business and everyday life.

Gratitude-enhancing ideas: as a child I recall being a great fan of printing, using pieces of playdough and pressing them onto various uneven and patterned surfaces. Imagine using polymer clay which then can be baked to ensure that it would hold its shape for good. Such pieces then can be used as mosaic pieces on a vase or lamp base, table top, clay pot, or they can become beads for jewelry, and so many more ideas. Brainstorm. They can also be framed in a shadow box or thicker picture frame, or simply just remove the glass. Involving your children in activities like this is a good way to bring out artistic talents. You can create patterns on half-cut potatoes, as well, using small items as cookie cutters and a marker cap to press into the potato. Then remove the excess potato flesh with a knife. Paint the surface of the potato where the shape or pattern is created and print onto paper or T-shirt, or a tote bag.

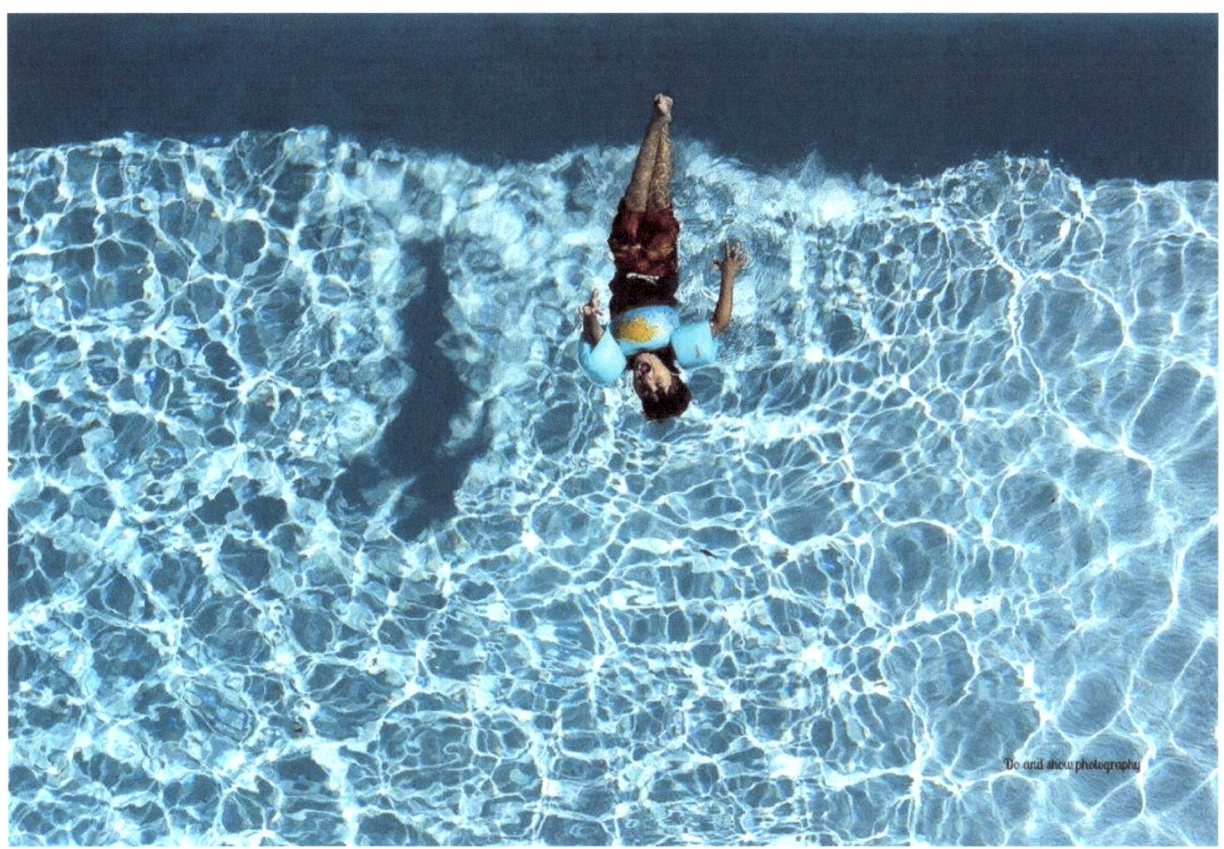

I feel so much gratitude for swimming pools and all the comfort and fun they can bring into my family's life. Ahhh, that cool, crystal clear water hugging my body when it's been heated up by the sun! It's so delicious and relaxing. It's very heartwarming to watch my children enjoying diving, jumping, swimming and rolling around in the water. The constant laughter and giggles showing me their joy, and that's priceless.

Gratitude-enhancing ideas: in summer nights or indoor pools, think glow sticks and glow balls! The same can be done for bathtub experience. Maybe you'd like to throw glow parties, sometimes. If you live in an area where autumn and winter are pretty cold, focus on the bathtub to create memorable experiences for yourself and your loved ones. For yourself, sprinkle flower petals in the water, and lit several scented candles around the bathtub. Listen to relaxing music or/and eat a nice soup while you are bathing. Have some romantic fun with your partner. For your children, besides glow sticks, use bubble bath and bath bombs sometimes. The snorkeling mask could be fun even in the tub. The key is to actually make these happen. Your child, most likely, would spark some more interesting ideas. Be open to consider them.

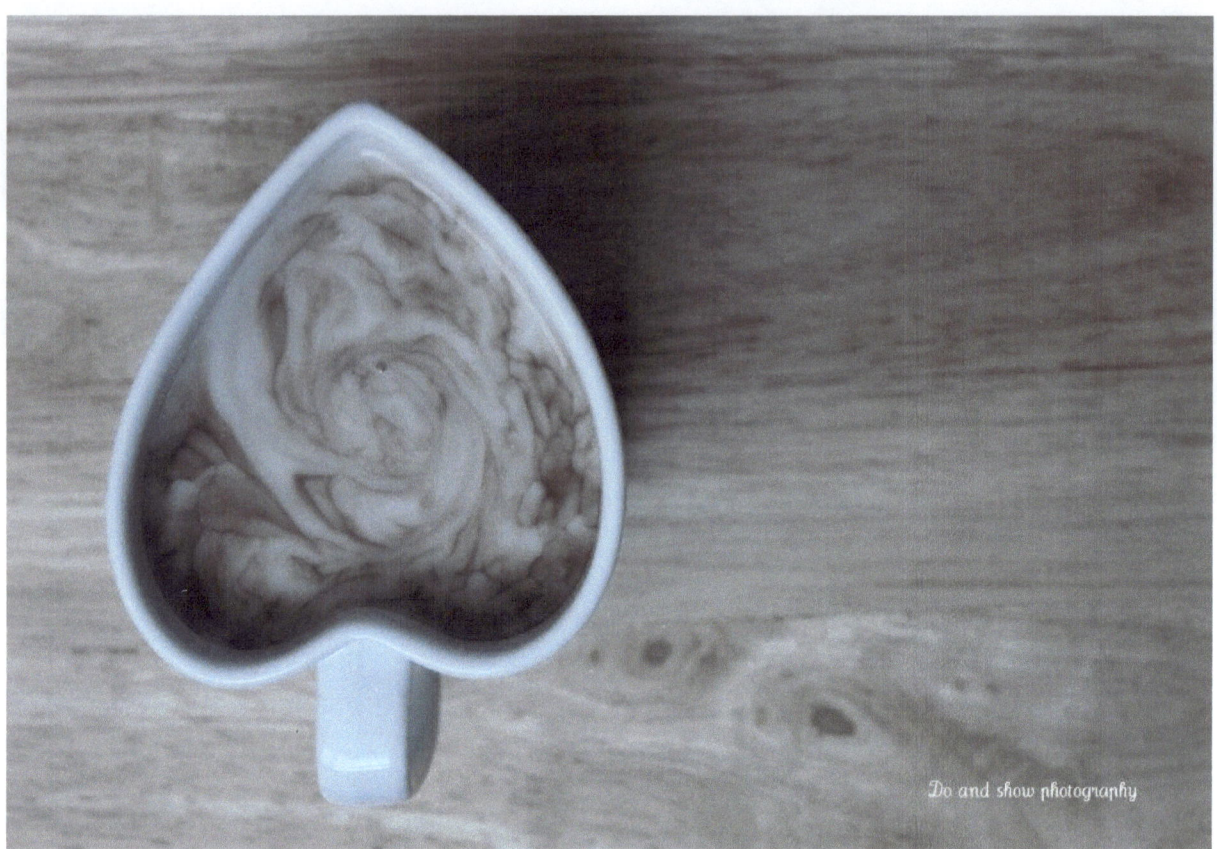

I feel so thankful for a hot chocolate on colder evenings or after a windy day. If you enjoy daily coffee, stop for a second and contemplate how restless you may be without it. The flavor, the aroma, the steam rising up, the warmth of the mug as you are holding it, and for last but not least the company and great conversations while you are having this beverage. What a lovely experience.

Gratitude-enhancing ideas: how open are you to try different flavors for your coffee or hot chocolate? How does sprinkling a little cinnamon or nutmeg on top sound? What about adding a few drops of coconut oil or cookie crumbs, mint chocolate chips or vanilla extract? Yes, there are those popular ice coffee flavors, but I am talking about creating your own signature drink. Explore. Have fun with it. Extend things to other food recipes maybe. And again, involve your family. Make coffee/tea/hot chocolate drinking time a special time with loved ones. Enjoy it together on the balcony, or in a hot tub, on a picnic at sunrise on the beach or at a lake, in a tent whether it's in your living room or under the starry sky, or in your car while watching the sunset.

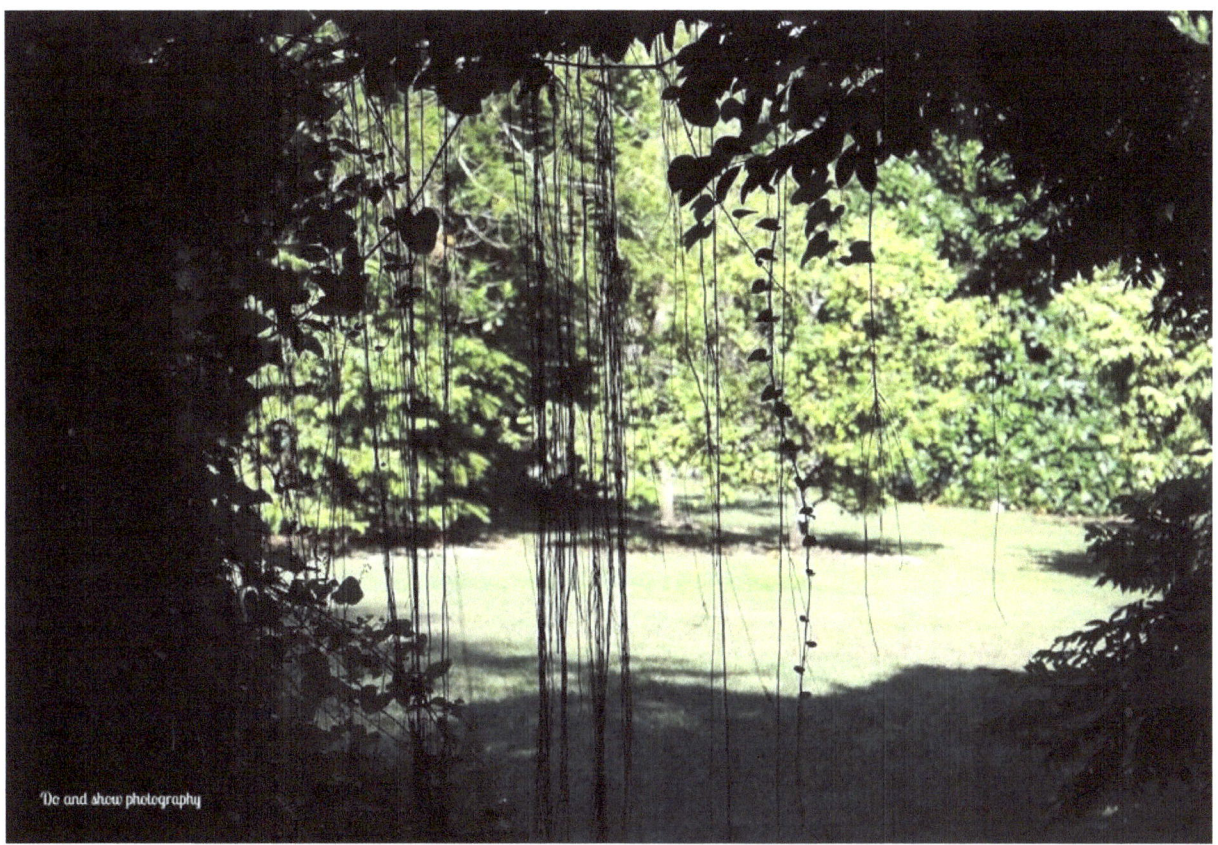

I'm extremely grateful for the number of hues and shapes I can see in green plants and leaves. Isn't it so ingenious how green leaves produce oxygen for us and animals? We pollute the air and breathe out carbon dioxide, and the plants around us everywhere keep the air cleaner. How wonderful that we can even bring many types inside in flowerpots! That green color is excellent for other things too, like to relax our minds and calm down when we feel agitated or angry.

Gratitude-enhancing ideas: if you are up to a room makeover, try a pleasant hue of the green for the walls, curtain, or furniture. See how it feels. Make time to go outside with your children and spouse, take off your shoes, walk and jump around in the grass. Be there in the moment and really give yourself over to the sensations. Use all your senses to feel the silky and soft grass under your feet and body, smell it. Lie down in it and watch little creatures with a magnifying glass acting all busy, become part of their world for a few minutes. Experiment with various leafy vegetables to prepare salads, soups, add them onto sandwiches and side dishes. Oh, I almost forgot the nutritious smoothies! Wrap ground meat with veggies into lettuce leaves or kale. For a crafting idea, try painting firm, thicker leaves or punch different shaped holes into them using hole punchers.

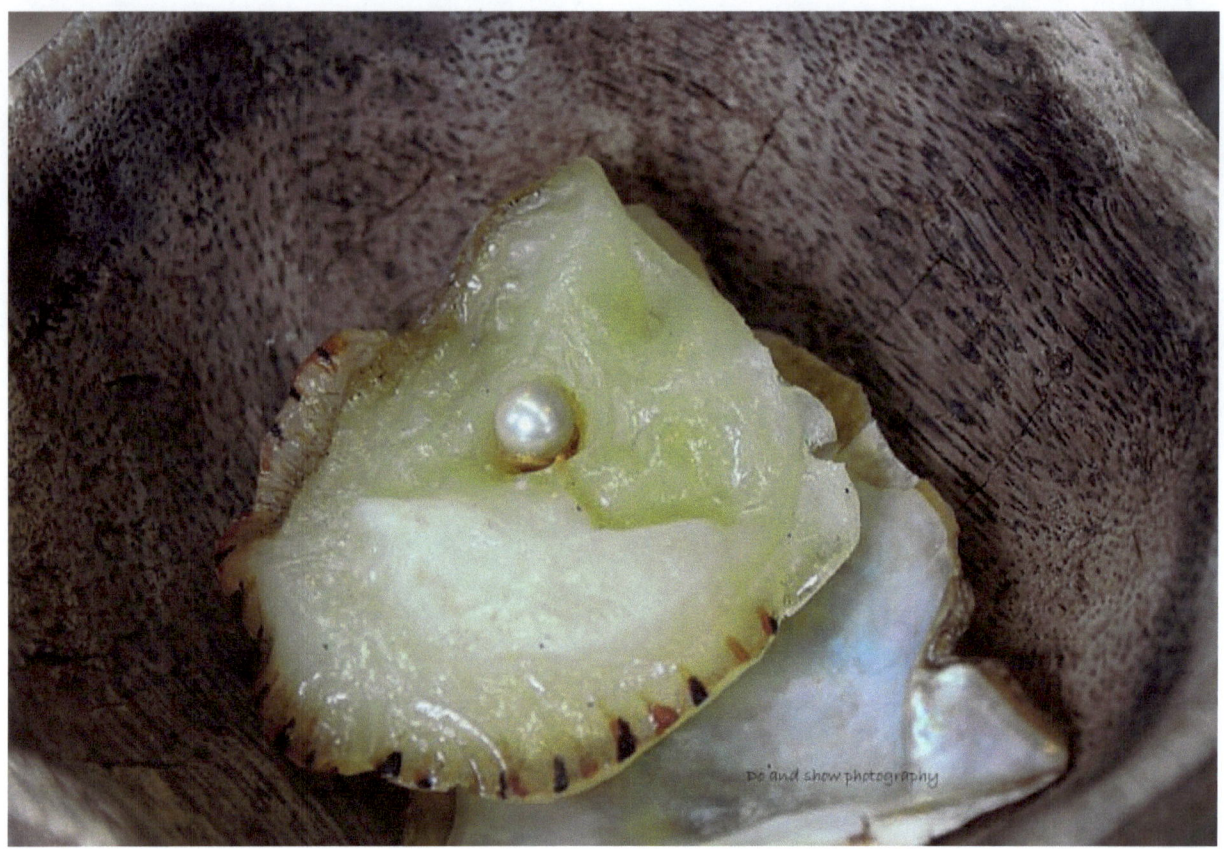

I'd like to express my gratitude for pearls and gemstones nature has been providing us for millions of years. Isn't it absolutely captivating how animals like oysters and freshwater mussels make pearls as part of their self-defense system against invaders? Then humans string these pearls up into necklaces, bracelets and other beautiful jewelry.

Gratitude-enhancing ideas: pearls are coated with conchiolin, that's what makes them shiny. You can purchase pearl colored paint and decorate items with it. Think wooden boxes, picture frames, wooden spoons, and much more. If you like wearing jewelry, try making some of your own. In craft stores, you can find endless variety of beads. Imagine a few afternoons spent like that with your daughter. If not for yourself, why not to make them for someone else as a gift?

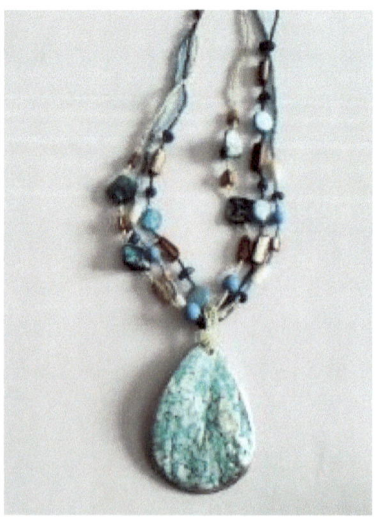

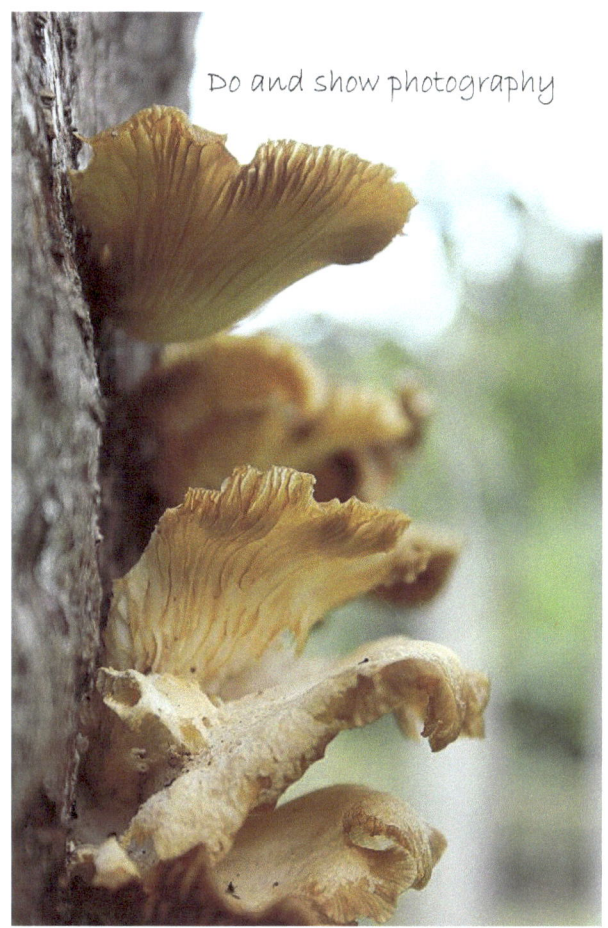
Do and show photography

I feel so thankful for the mushrooms of all kinds. Many of the species not only are delicious ingredients in dishes, but they're the prefect cleaners of earth. They break up and eat bacteria and things that are considered waste. They are essential key to save the planet according to scientific resources, like crclr.org or discovermagazine.com.

Gratitude-enhancing ideas: try different types of mushrooms in your food, and when you eat meat, have it with mushrooms because it helps to break down the meat more easily. There are also medicinal mushrooms that can be added to smoothies and other liquids in powder forms, like chaga or maitake mushroom, for instance. According to medicalmushrooms.net, these powerful mushrooms can greatly benefit one's health. I highly recommend to learn more and teach to your children about the fascinating communication among mushrooms and plants through the mycelium that are tiny threads running underground connecting to roots of plants.

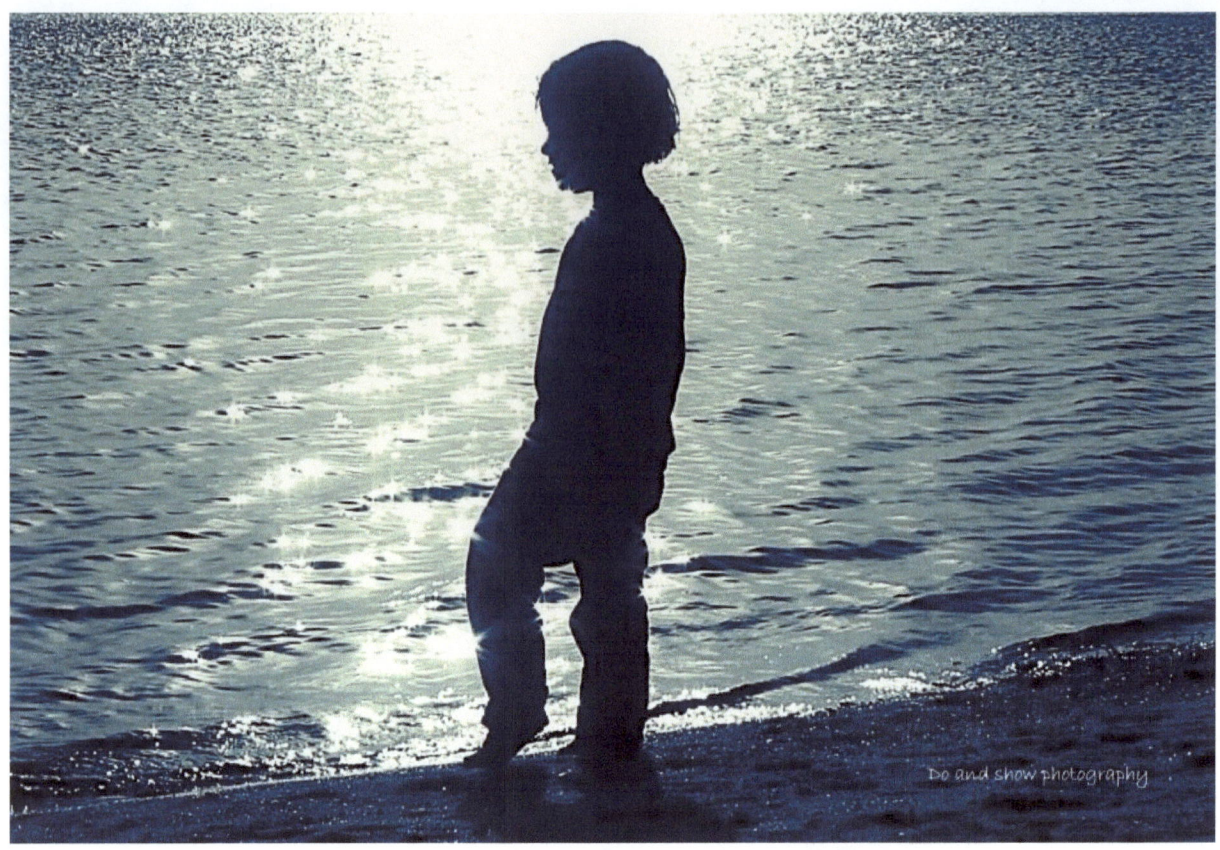

I am very grateful for being able to spend quality time with my children and take them to wonderful places. I realize sometimes that I take things for granted but the more aware and grateful I become, the less likely I will take anything for granted. I feel absolutely honored by the power and responsibility to be a role model for other individuals. I am also very thankful for the opportunities I've been presented daily to learn about inexpensive and easier ways to teach my kids about the world, and have fun together with them.

Gratitude-enhancing ideas: no matter how busy you are, it's crucial to devote at least a few minutes a day to fully be present for your child, each one of them, listen to their stories, and play with them. Just try if you haven't been doing so to spend a little quality time with them daily. It could impact their behavior and grades positively on a long run, not to mention their self-esteem and sense of belonging. It doesn't always have to be a literal game. Sometimes, it can be just cooking together, or folding the laundry while discussing what happened at school. Take Ralphie out for a walk while you sing songs or talk about the upcoming family trip. Let them take photos of family events and organize them into albums, story books or wall décor. One of my favorite activities is to create memory card games from our own photos. My children and my clients' children reportedly have had tons of fun by watching and reading homemade books about their trips and events that meant a lot to them. To go one step further, you can add questions that they can answer regarding these moments in their lives. It's an excellent way to enhance emerging writing skills.

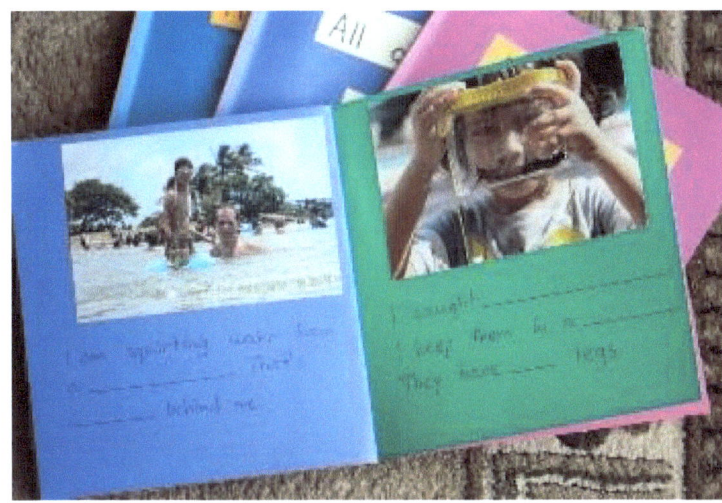

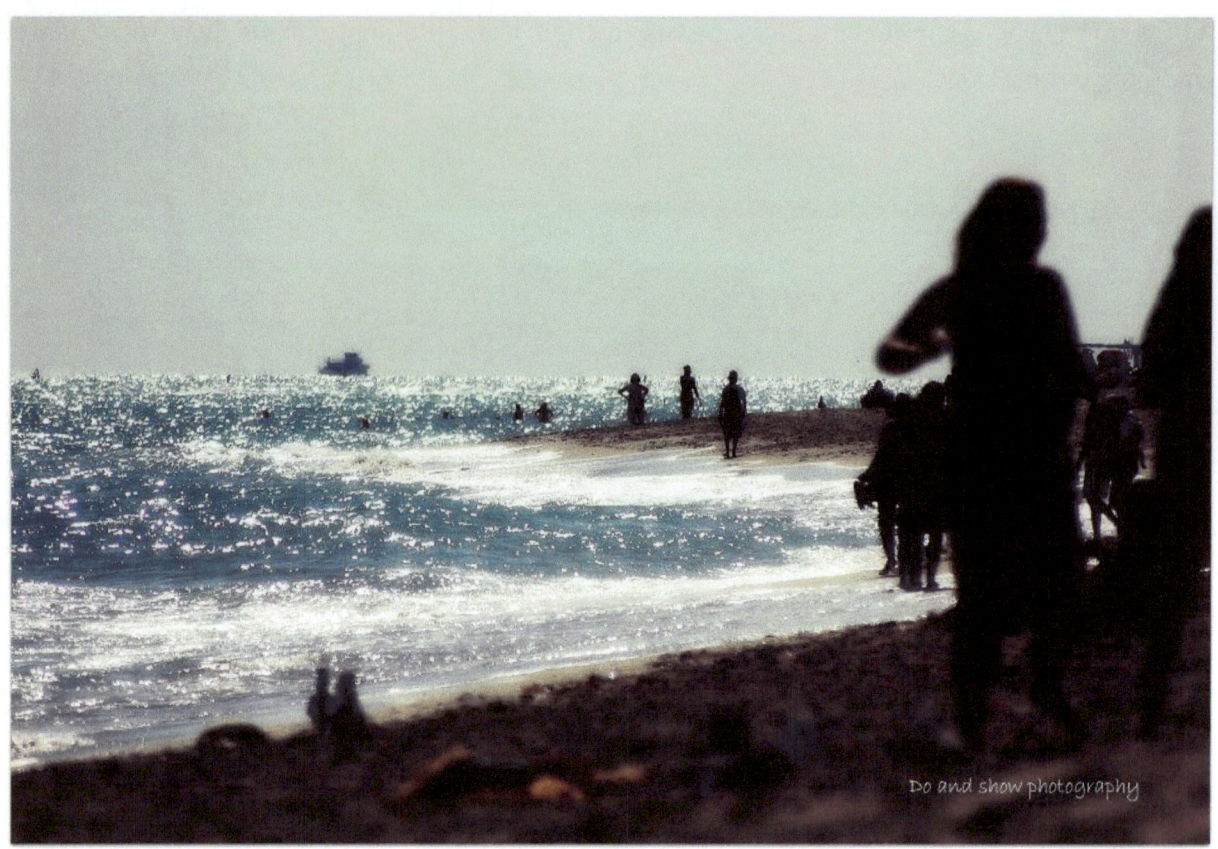

I have to write about my gratitude regarding the glistening effect of the sun on the water. It's been captivating my attention since my childhood. How mesmerizing it is, right? I catch myself admiring it and taking pictures of it again and again and again.

Gratitude-enhancing ideas: well, for one, allow yourself to be in the moment to admire it when you witness it. Point it out to your children too. This is the perfect opportunity to create gorgeous photographs with a telephoto or superzoom lens which helps you to see far. Look at the photo above and notice the cozy and enchanting mood it generates. It takes you away. We all need moments like that when challenges in our lives don't burden us for a few minutes. Give your brain a little break. It deserves it. You deserve it!

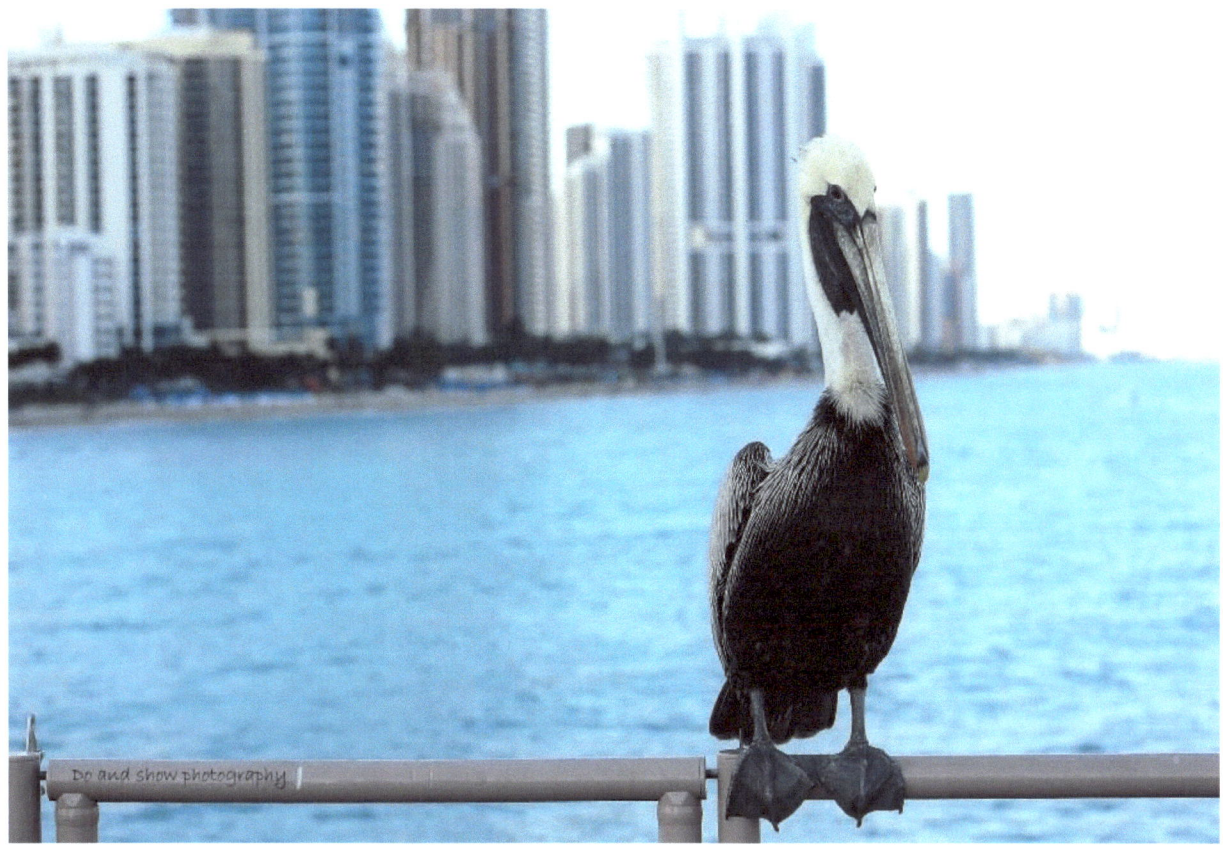

I am so thankful for wild animals that trust me enough to come near me, so I can observe them and admire them more closely. I think it's not only exciting to study nature but it's our obligation because nature and all living beings can teach us tons of valuable information on how to live a healthier and more balanced life.

Gratitude-enhancing ideas: commit to devote more time a week to connect with nature and animals. Watch them, study and photograph them, paint or draw about them, or even compose stories and poems. Encourage your children to do the same. Let the curiosity take over regarding these animals' magnificent survival skills and intelligence in some areas. How amazing is that they all have evolved to be perfect at what they do and what they are! Yet these qualities and abilities are often totally different which begs to admit that there are many types of perfection then.

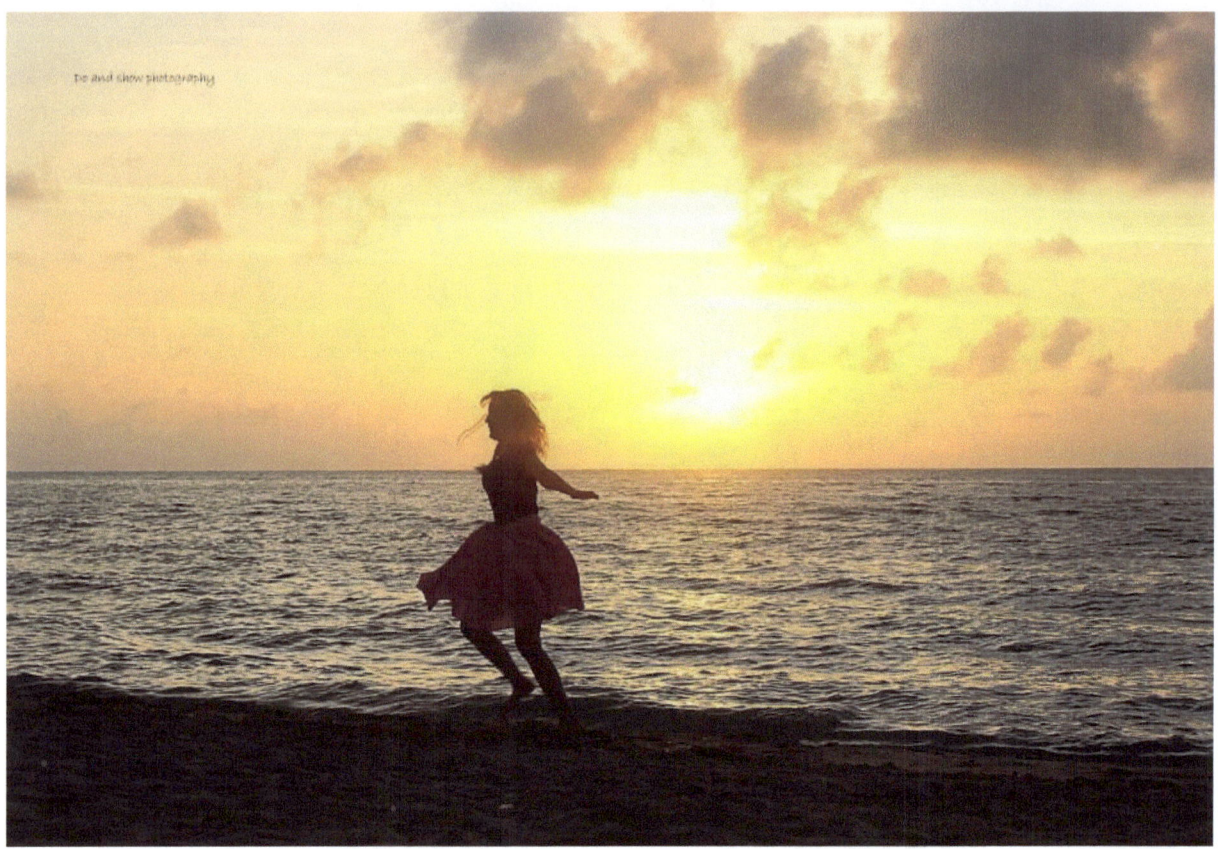

I feel an overwhelming gratitude for my well-working limbs, for my ability to walk, run, jump, dance or move around the way I desire. I must add that I am very thankful for the mobility of my loved ones as well, even if a few of them have it somewhat limited. Isn't it so great to be able to just get up and dance to our favorite tune or play tag with our kids? How about climbing a ladder to change a lightbulb or simply go for a walk hand in hand with our spouses?

Gratitude-enhancing ideas: I am sure you know what I'd like to suggest to you. Yes, get going more frequently! Get out of your chair more often, even if just for a 3-minute stretch, or to just get a glass of water. Skip sleeping in once in a while and go for a walk in the city or on the beach to see how the sun is rising. Put on your favorite song and dance like no one is watching you! Enjoy the moment! Grab your children's hands and get moving together. You know what else? Become increasingly aware how all this movement makes you feel; how alive you become with rushing endorphins and how instantly it elevates your mood.

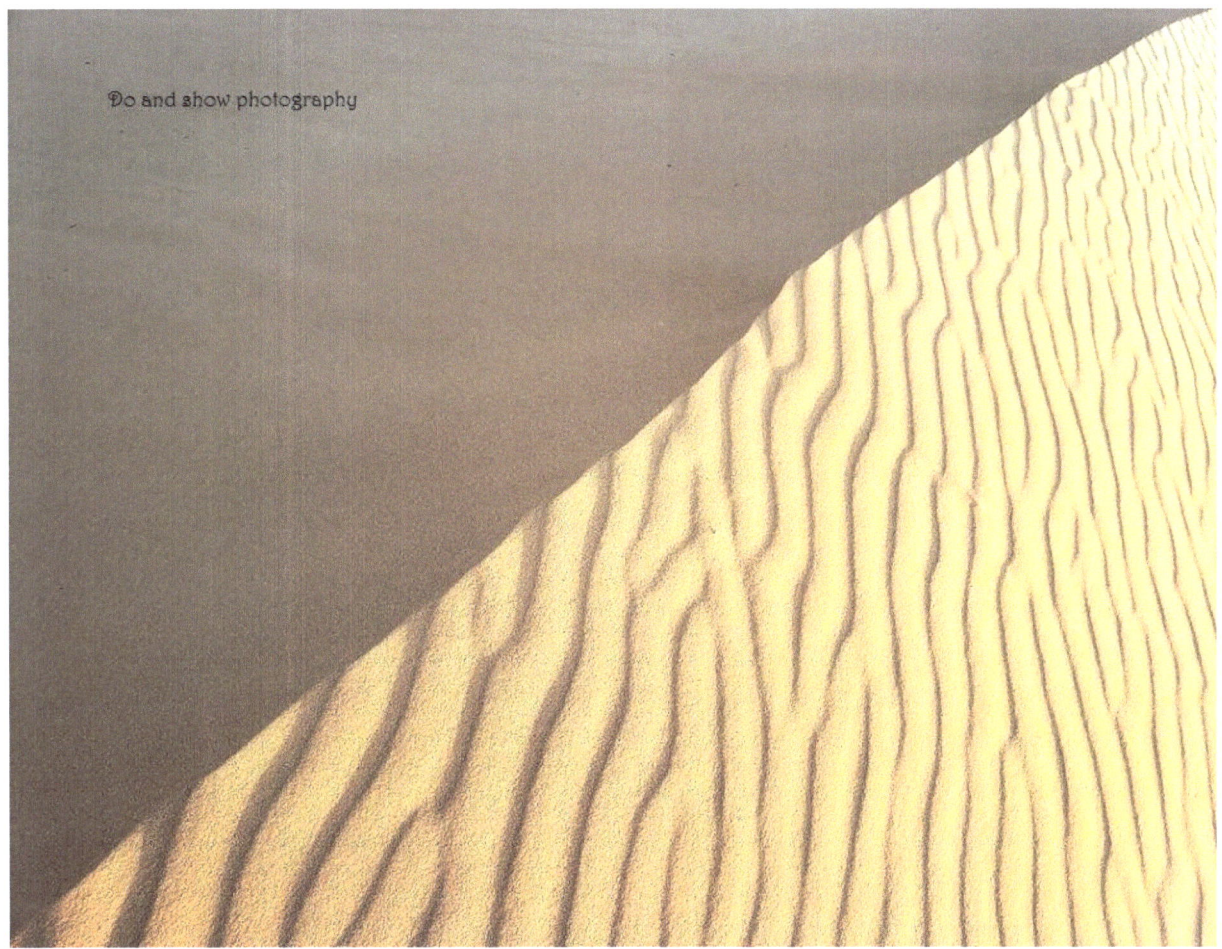

Despite their bleak and harsh environment and atmosphere, I am giving lots of thanks for the deserts of all kinds, and for the opportunities I've had to visit them and photograph them. I am looking forward to spend more time in these unique places. While sand can become an annoyance sometimes, what a wonderful feeling it can also be under our feet as we walk on the beach or in a desert barefoot! What an excellent material to entertain our kids with! Oh, and what a breathtaking experience to see when there are no footprints on the ripples of sand! Just imagine, no one walked there before you for a while! Like you can see on the above photo. I took it in Utah, in the Coral Pink Sand Dunes Desert, at sunset.

Gratitude-enhancing ideas: take off your shoes when you walk on sand. Try different types of sand. Which one feels nicer under your feet: the wet or dry sand, the fine or coarse? As you walk on sand (or dirt, grass, in water, as a matter of fact), you are connecting your body with earth's energy, hence, detoxing from electrical pollution. It's called earthing or grounding. What a self-loving gift you can give yourself! When you take a trip to a desert (do take!), truly enjoy the scenery and realize the uniqueness of the situation: you, being in a place where just very few living beings can stay alive for a longer period of time. Wow! Maybe, you'd also like to create a mini desert at home with your child in a large bin. Use real sand, some toy desert animals and palm trees. Make an oasis! Experiment with water and how much time it takes for the sand to absorb it. Allow your child become a scientist more often and also wear a lab coat. Encourage them to jot down their observations and plans to solve challenges.

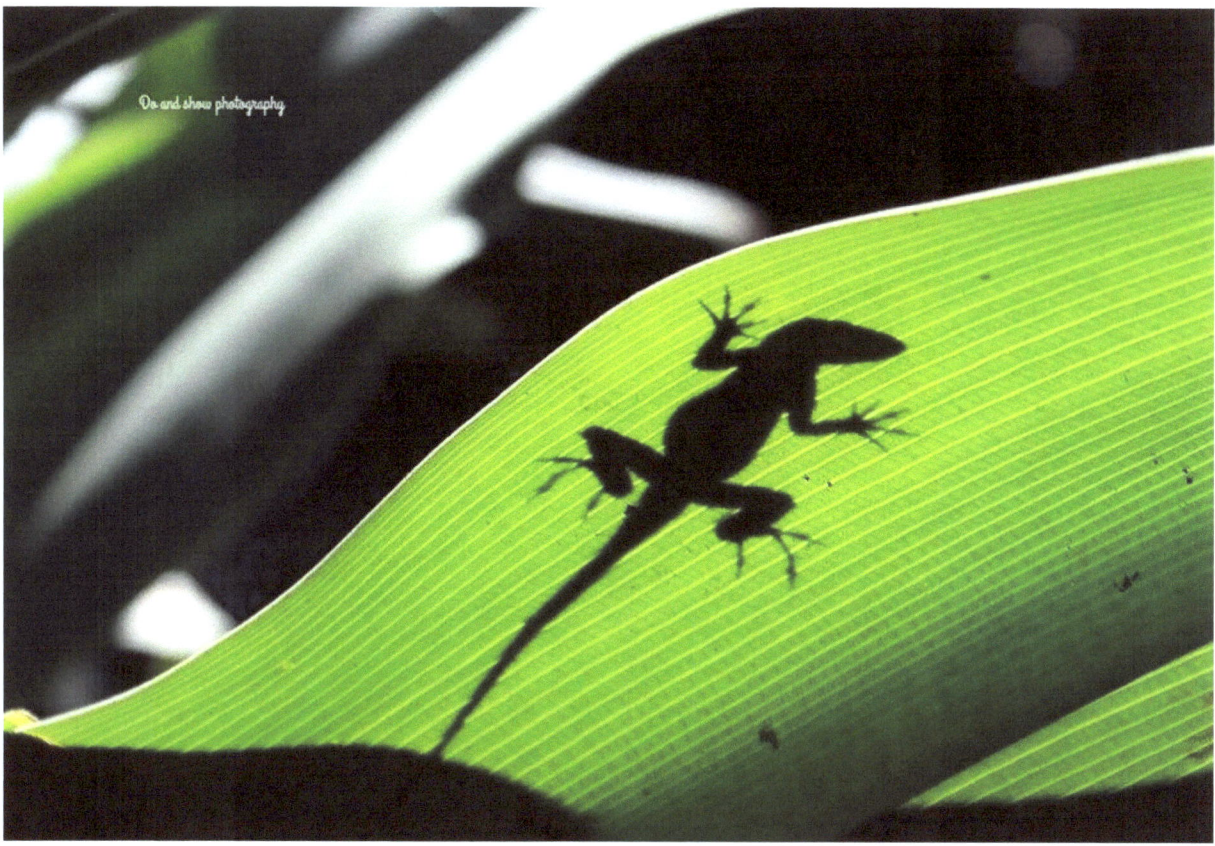

I have to express my gratitude for the engrossing shadow-play our sun can entertain us with. Silhouettes are equally beautiful. As a passionate photographer, I often become captivated by shadows and silhouettes of various objects. Isn't it incredible that utilizing the shadows and our knowledge about it we can tell the approximate time of the day?

Gratitude-enhancing ideas: engage in shadow puppet play with your younger children. You can use your hands to turn them into animals, or make simple paper-shapes or pipe cleaner figures that move around with the help of your hand. Have your little ones stand or make a statue on the concrete, and draw the outline of their shadows with a chalk. Let some time pass. Tell them to try to fit into the same outline and guide them to realize how it's changed and why. On an open area, make a human sundial using your own body's shadow. Besides all these, keep your eyes peeled for interesting shadows as you go about your day.

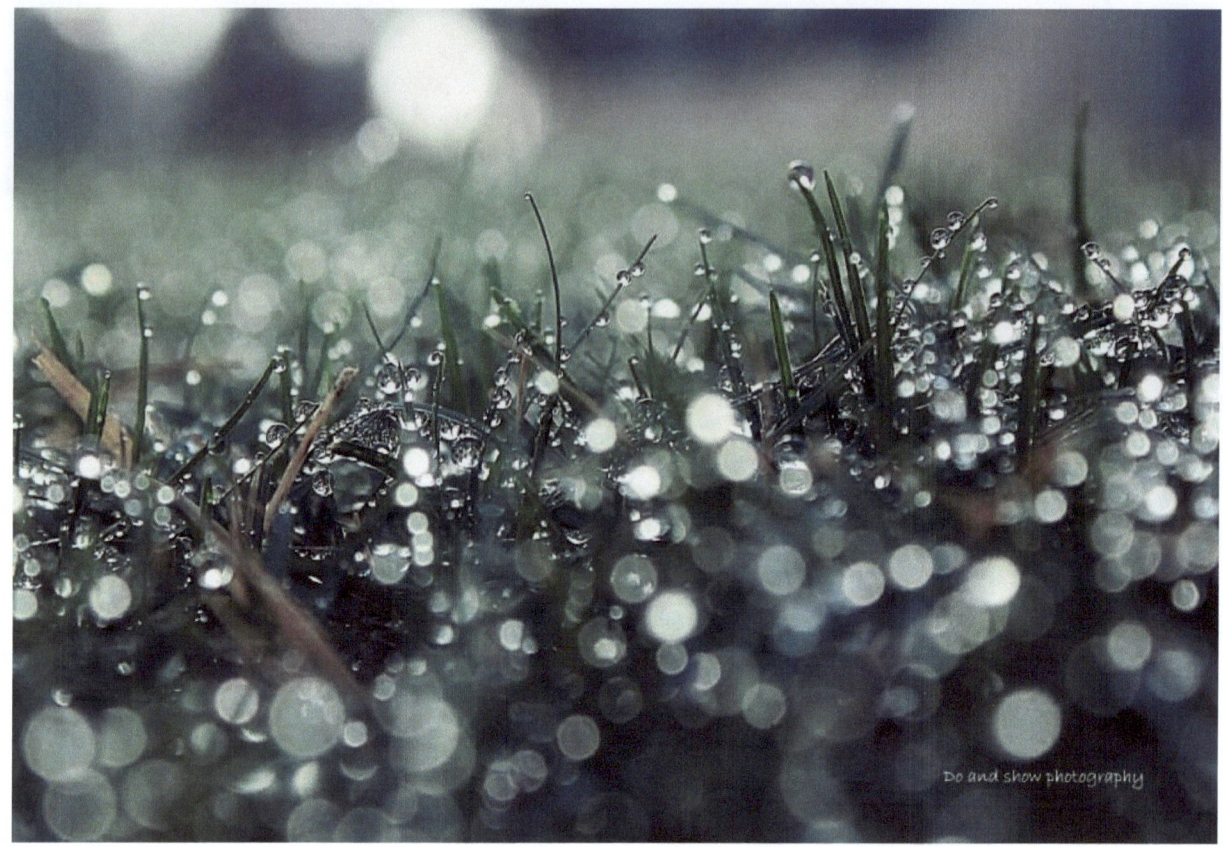

I am so very grateful for the morning dew drops on the grass and flowers, oh, and the spider's webs. It's nature's help to provide water for tiny creatures. On the other hand, what a mesmerizing image the camera can capture with all those clear-cut and fading circles: bokeh photography. Another intriguing side of these droplets is when they are on small insects and leaves, they magnify those sections of the animals and plants.

Gratitude-enhancing ideas: take photos of dew drop-covered flowers, insects and fruits. I'd also love to recommend finding images online or in books that are done with high quality macro lens. Be prepared to drop your chin! Fun activities with children: Using different food colors, droppers, and wax paper, let your little one suck up tiny droplets of various colors and squeeze them onto the wax paper creating patterns, shapes, art work. On paper towel, the colors will be absorbed and blend, while on wax paper, they stay separate and in bubble form. Here's a cool and practical idea for tiny water droplets. Did you know that catnip tea is quite powerful against roaches? Boil the water, add catnip then pour the cooled liquid into a spray bottle. Spray the tea into corners, behind furniture, sink, stove, etc.

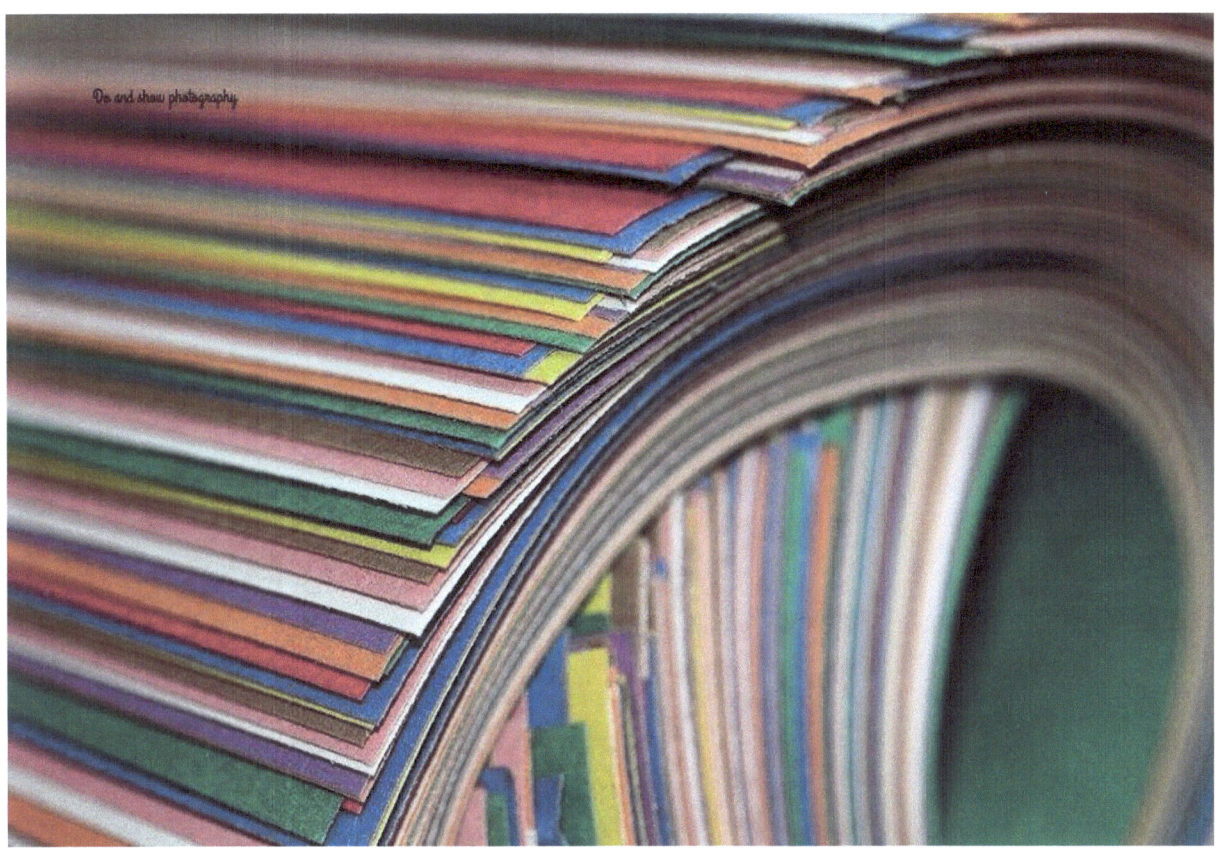

I feel so thankful for the invention of paper which happened around 100 BC, in China. There are countless ways we get to use paper, and how many colors and textures there are! Did you know that the human eye can see about 7 million colors!? Incredible! Imagine, we get to choose the color of our clothes, accessories, home décor, personal items and so much more! We also get to enjoy the comfort of a soft tissue paper when we have to blow our noses, and the absorbent paper towel when we have to wipe up spills, or the eye-catching patterned wrapping paper to cover gifts, and I could go on and on.

Gratitude-enhancing ideas: we must talk about going paperless as much as possible, in order to ensure future for our children and theirs. While we should use paper for numerous activities, we must do so wisely and without wasting. We also have to educate our children about this. Use the backside of the papers with print on them to write reminders, or calculate something, to write your gratitude daily, etc. so blank paper space won't go wasted. On the other hand, spend quality time with your children creating beautiful paper crafts, bookmarks, handmade cards, even books that are priceless family treasures. Recycle old materials. Encourage handwriting and do it yourself as well because it's going out of fashion. When you write down things, like your weekly and daily goals, your appreciation for things, your brain remembers it better. Encourage creating this habit with the whole family! Writing down by hand simply activates more centers of the brain than if you were only thinking about something. Brainstorm ideas what ways paper can be reused or recycled. Start or continue implementing them. Use scrap paper, for instance, to write daily loving notes to your family members and hide them in their pockets or lunchboxes. Save magazines and color prints for later projects. Kids love cutting out pictures, and they can come handy for homework assignments, and other interesting arts and crafts. Staple or sew pages together to make simple children's books. Add their photos and drawings.

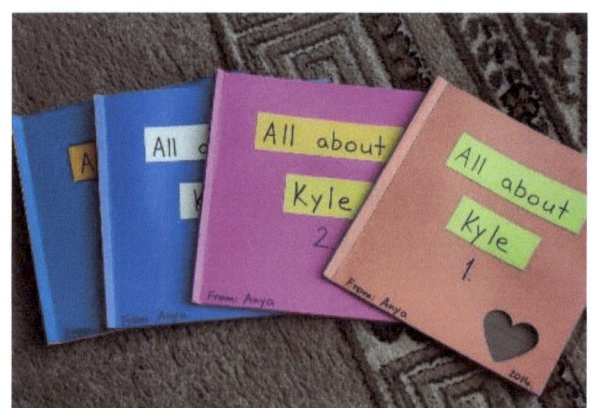

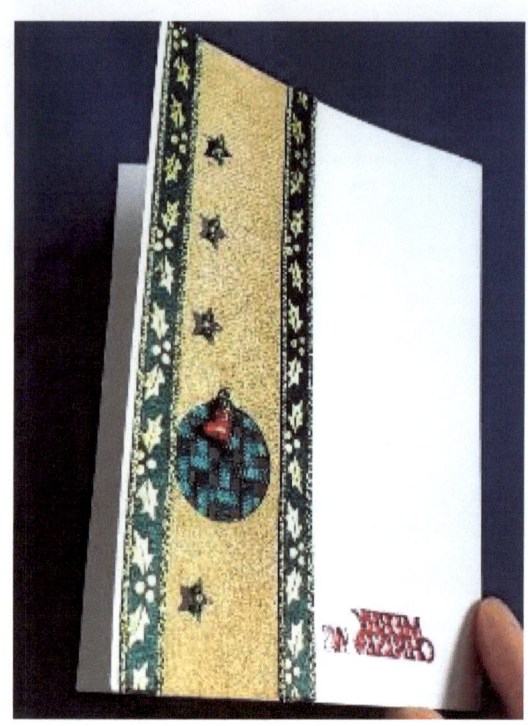

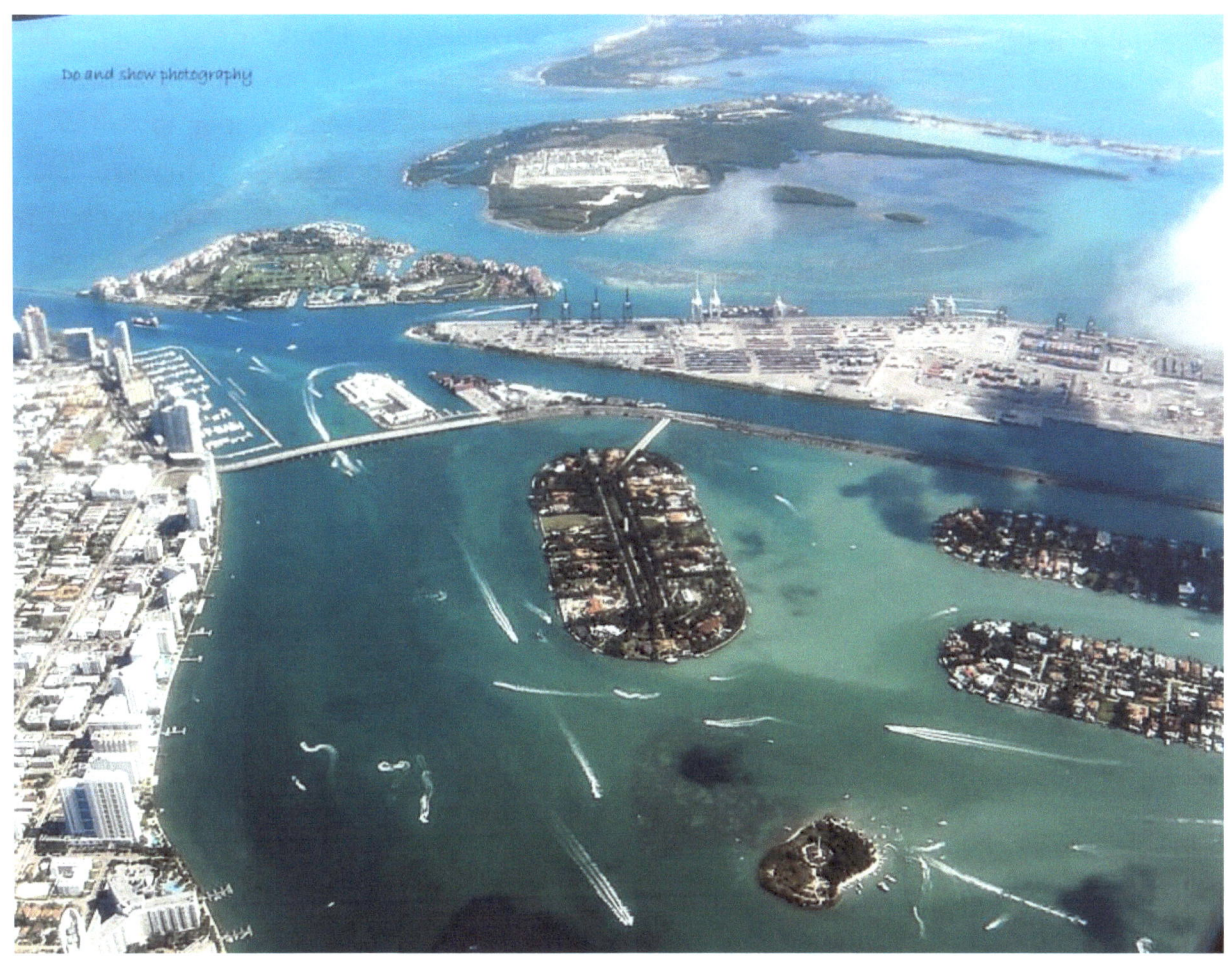

I am grateful for the air travel. What an incredible invention! It's not only making our travel time much shorter and more comfortable than hundreds and thousands of years before, but we can see with a bird's view. When I look down from the airplane's window, and I see the beauty of our planet, the magnificence of our cities and infrastructure, I realize how tiny we all are in the grand schemes of things, yet so very powerful when it comes to our decisions. I would also like to add how thankful I am for the fact that my loved ones and I had arrived safely to all destinations so far.

Gratitude-enhancing ideas: when you are taking the plane, do it with a great focus. Observe the details, notice things and allow yourself to be taken by the experience. Try to locate buildings and streets, and other landmarks. Point them out to your children. In case you have aviophobia, fear of flying, here are a few tips to make your next flight more enjoyable. Make sure, first of all, you are traveling comfortably physically: your clothes, shoes, luggage, level of hunger, thirst, energy, you aren't in a rush or forgetting something. Keep your mind focused on your destination and the reason why you're flying there. Get excited about it! Talk or daydream about it, look at pictures, read about it. Use deep breathing techniques and positive self-talk (I'd like to bring my other photo book into your attention that is about positive self-talk: From my beautiful mind to your beautiful mind, available on Amazon). One excellent calming breathing technique is consciously slowing down your breathing while closing your eyes and counting to five or six slowly. At the same time, your shallow breathing turns into deeper breathing. When you inhaled, hold it for another 5-6 counts, then exhale while you're counting again 5-6, then hold your breath for another 5-6 counts. If you find these number too high for this breathing exercise, count to four. The act of counting itself will deter your focus from your anxiety and regulate your breathing. Make sure you are sitting in a comfortable position with a fairly straight back. Besides all this, clarify what your fear or anxiety has been rooted in. It could be fear of tight places, claustrophobia, or fear of crowds or anxiety over getting sick more easily, or other aspects of flying. Just breathe and visualize lovely scenes. Bon voyage!

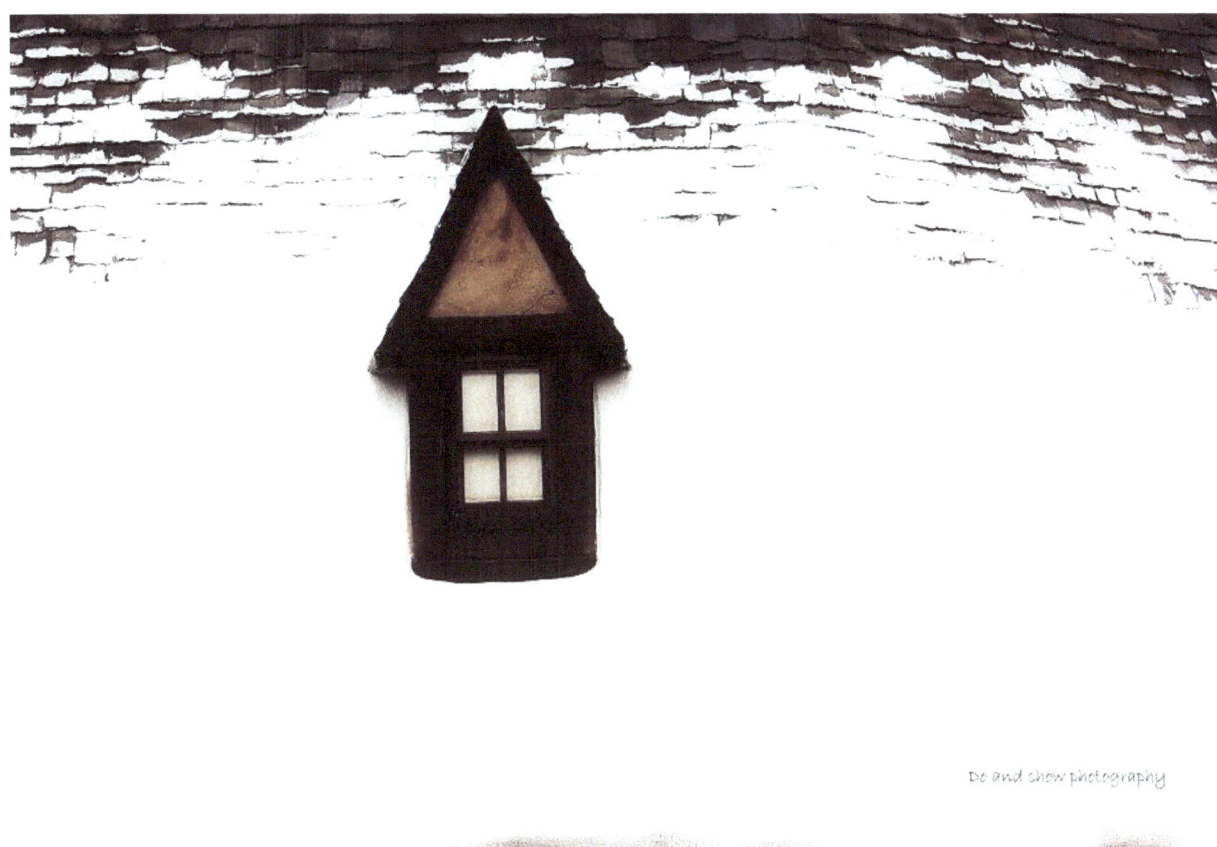

Do and show photography

I am expressing my gratitude for snow that is so fluffy and clean to enjoy and have fun with it. Oh, I recall wonderful memories from my childhood when I was sitting at the window, looking at the snowfall, as everything was covered with snow, and I saw the footprints that were left by people walking their dogs or rushing home under the yellow street lights. It was so peaceful. Snow clouds … like giant white pillows floating in the sky… When I focus on the beauty of it instead of how cold it is and how it may make me shiver, it generates warm feelings inside me instead of unpleasant ones.

Gratitude-enhancing ideas: let your inner child be happy again and play in the snow with your child or without. Walk in the snowfall with an open mouth looking up and catch those snowflakes with your tongue. Create a snow globe. You can use mason jars or empty globes that are made for this purpose. Choose small figurines, or print out photos of your loved ones, then laminate them to make them sturdy and waterproof. Using glue gun and glue sticks attach them onto the bottom of the jar or the lid, whichever way you would like to do it. Let it dry. Add distilled water and some baby oil or glycerin, also glitter or snowflake shaped sequins. The glycerin and baby oil will make them float more slowly. One-of-a-kind gifts are so wonderful for both the giver and receiver.

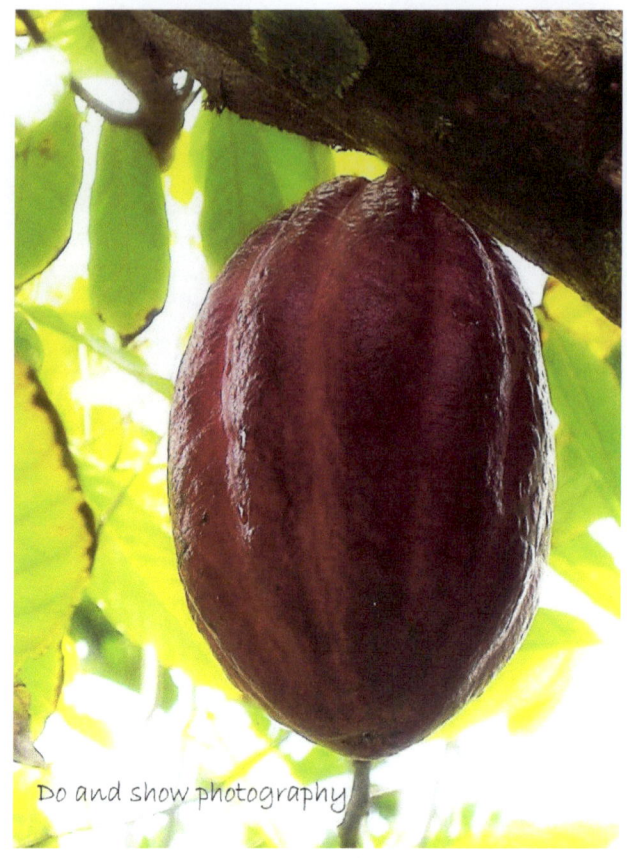

I feel so very thankful for the cacao tree and its fruit. The cacao beans are the basic ingredients of the chocolate. That mouthwatering flavor of melting chocolate on my tongue or the hot chocolate drink with some marshmallows! Delicious! Just think about how many kinds of chocolate you have tried already. How did they make you usually feel? What type of chocolate is your favorite if any?

Gratitude-enhancing ideas: have you ever tried to make your own chocolate? It can be easier than you think. The fewer ingredients you add, the healthier it is usually. I use coconut oil, melted in a glass bowl that is placed into hot water. I add raw, unrefined sugar, honey or agave nectar and bitter cacao powder. Mix it well. Then if you wish, you can mix in peppermint or almond oil extract, etc. To make it more interesting, put in dried fruit pieces, nuts or coconut flakes. Think of more ideas. Pour the mix into chocolate candy molds or silicon ice cube molds, then place it into the freezer for half hour, and voila. This is more of a dark chocolate though. You make it as sweet as you would like. What about dipping fruit pieces, dry fruit pieces, cookies, waffle chunks and more into melted chocolate? Get excited about broadening your ways of enjoying chocolate. Maybe you also wish to bring it into your marriage life.

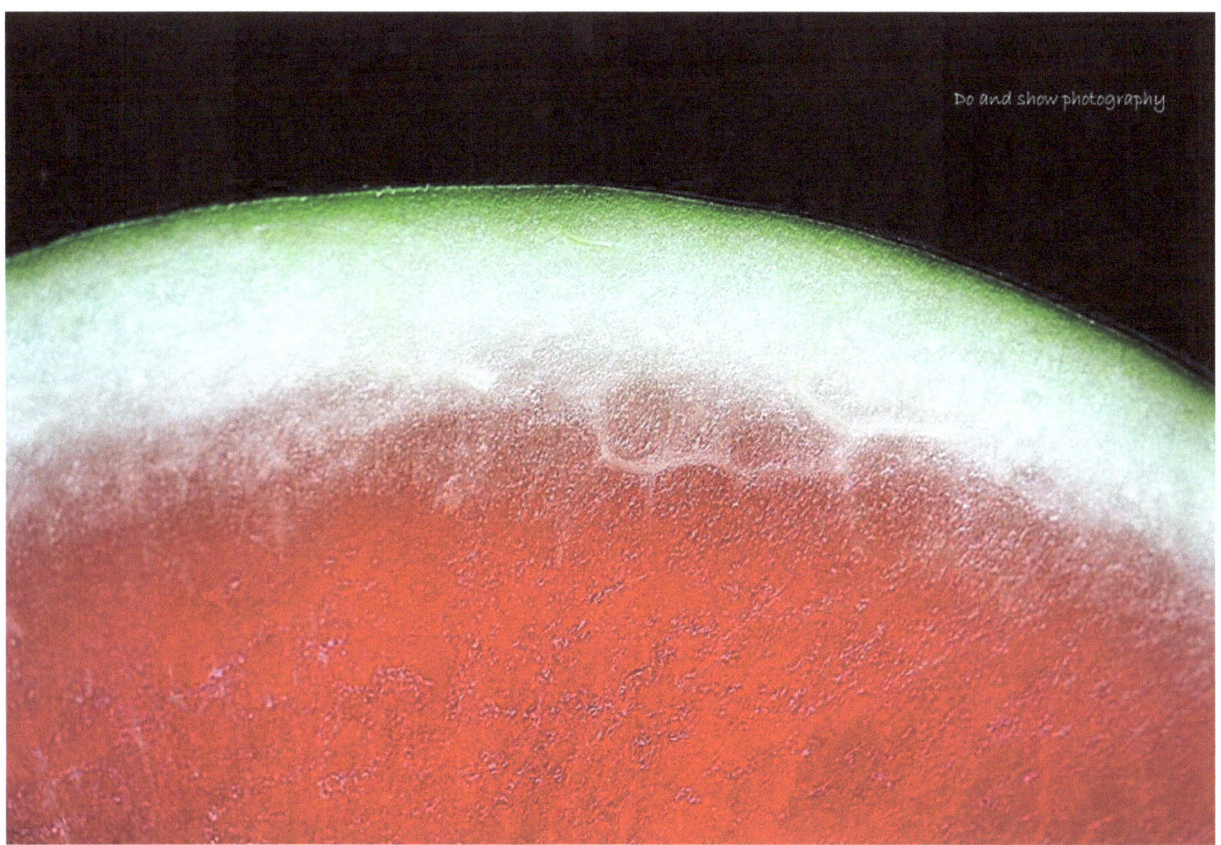

I am very grateful for the juicy fruits that I can enjoy every single day, different kinds and in different forms. How fascinating that we are provided with various types of fruits in each season! Spring fruits are helpful in detox after winter, while summer fruits are more cooling. What a heavenly way to hydrate and satisfy our sweet tooth at the same time!

Gratitude-enhancing ideas: fruits are the best-serving for your health when you eat them fresh, raw, organic and ripe. When cooked or baked, they usually become acidic and less useful due to the destructive effect of heat on nutrients. If you aren't having fruits every day, I strongly recommend starting it for your own sake. Don't just eat your apple or mandarin in a rush or while you are driving. Enjoying it means paying attention to what you are doing. Engage your five senses. Take a few minutes to eat, only eat without distraction so your digestive tract can metabolize it better. Oh, yes! Chew it well too. That's like pre-digestion. I've tested it numerous times. Raw, crunchy fruits and vegetables become mushy (predigested) in the mouth after being chewed about 50-70 times each bite! Now observe how many times you chew a bite of an apple or lettuce. Surprise, surprise! When you swallow food in a rush, while it's still chunky, your stomach juices – obviously – need to work harder and longer to digest it. This might result in excess bloating, indigestion, wasting of nutrients, etc.

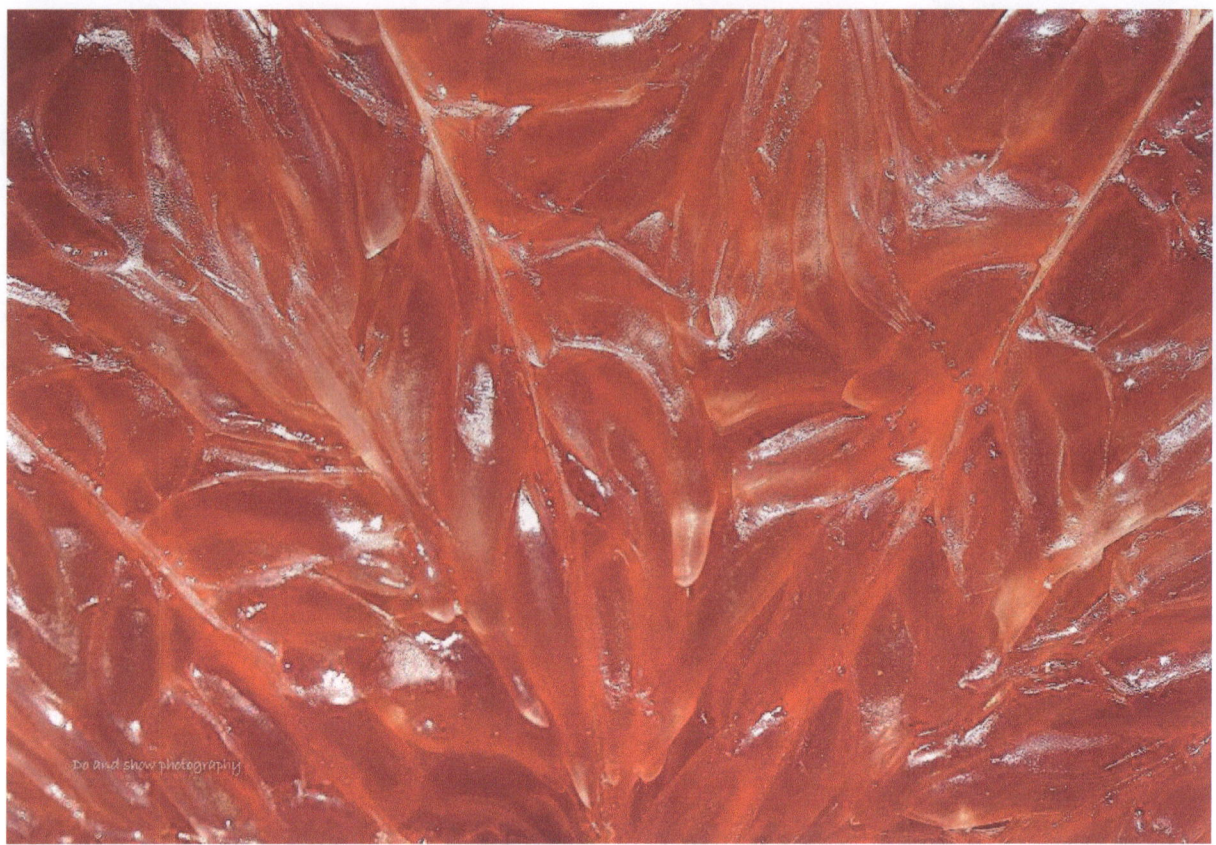

Wow! Right? I am astonished by the intricate details of fruits and vegetables. In various colors and textures, they create such distinguished flavors to enjoy. I often photograph them using a macro lens. It fascinates me to look at them up lose. My gratitude has been growing constantly because of the usage of my camera, these wonderful plants, and my eyes and mind to appreciate them.

Gratitude-enhancing ideas: get your magnifying glass out, or a microscope, or at least your camera and zoom in! Observe the thin fibers, and tiny seeds, the grainy surface or other details inside fruits. I highly recommend checking out a wonderful artist who paints very large pictures of fruit slices with a dramatic lighting, and amazing details. His name is Dennis Wojtkiewicz. You'll be absolutely impressed, surely.

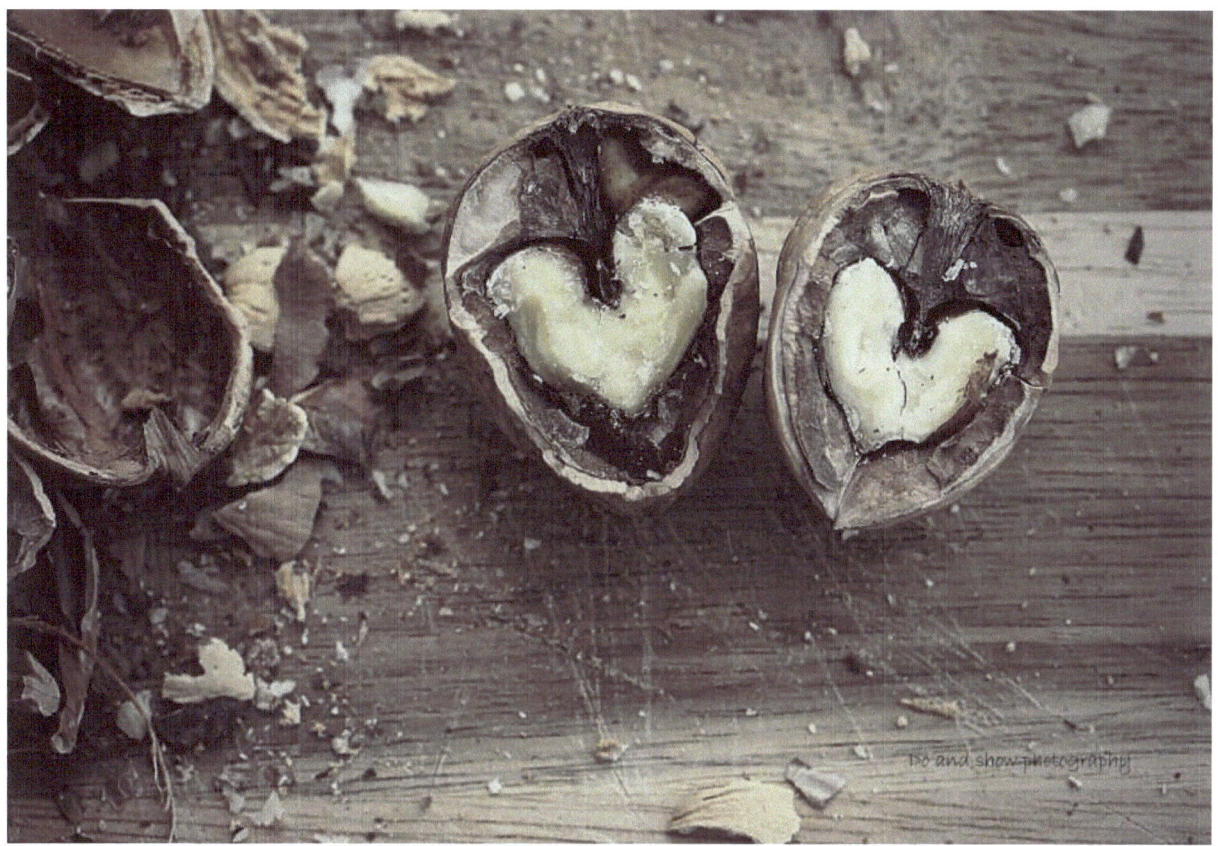

I feel so very thankful for nuts that get my body ready for the cold winter with their nutritious fatty content. The same is true for the animals that eat them or hoard them. Isn't it fascinating that nature takes care of us this way too? Just take a look at this photo. Do you see the heart shape? Very interestingly, walnuts are excellent heart-healthy foods. When you crack the shells and carefully remove the nut from it, you'll also notice that they look like a brain. Guess what! They are wonderful foods for your brain as well!

Gratitude-enhancing ideas: instead of shelled nuts, get them in their shells, and you remove their protective shells that can give you more reassurance that no fungus has been growing on them. Another important health tip is to soak nuts in filtered water for 1-2 days, in the fridge. This makes them better digestible and more nutritious. Add them to your salads, smoothies, on the top of puddings and cremes, bake with them and eat them just as they are. Explore the different types of nuts out there: Brazil nuts, hazelnuts, walnuts, pecans, pistachios, cashew nuts, pine nuts, almonds, macadamia, chestnuts, and coconut.

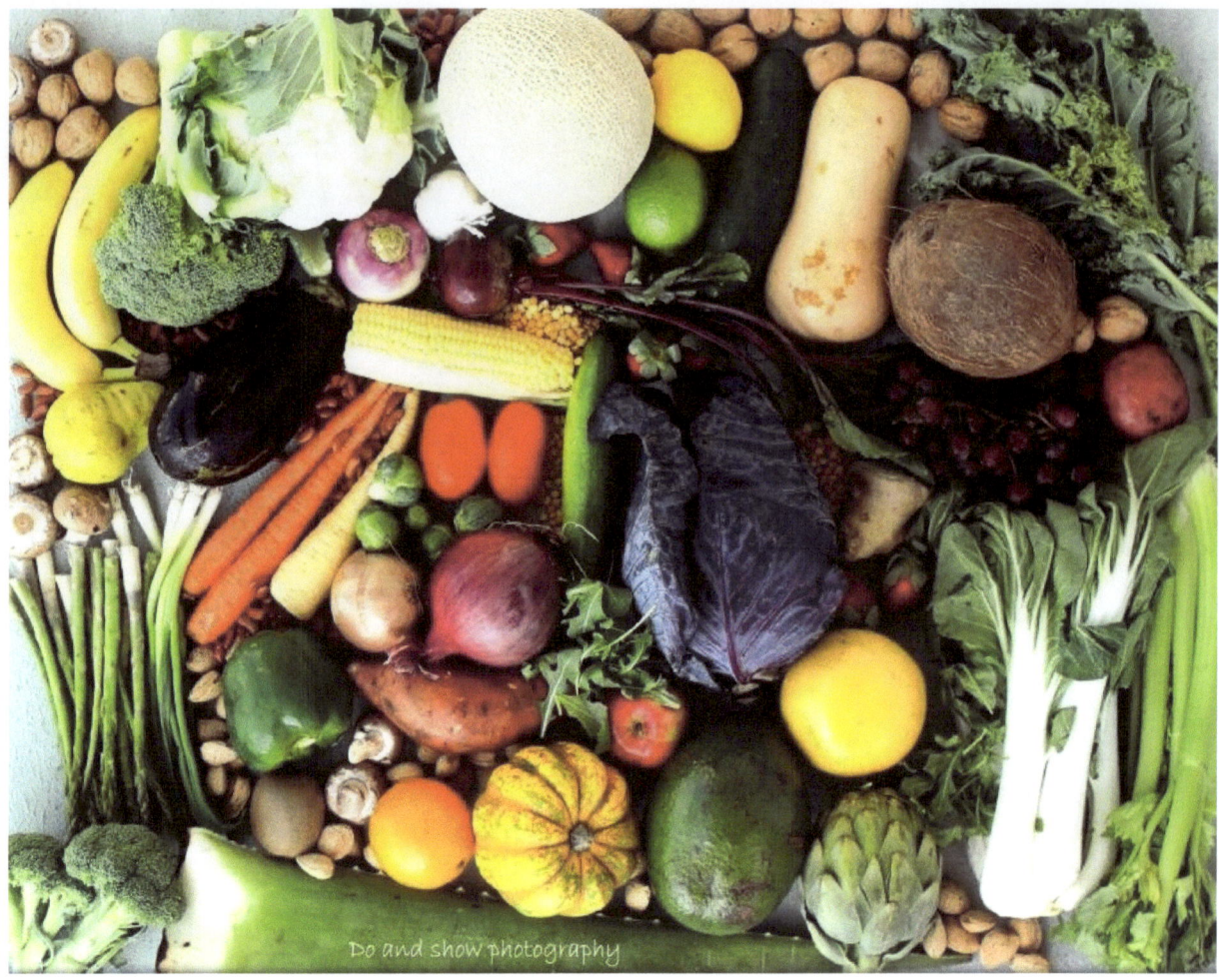

I feel so blessed having food on my table every single day, for myself and my loved ones. Every time I eat these delicious gifts of nature's garden, I feel gratitude. I admire their shapes, colors, flavors, textures and how they behave in different cooking situations. According to foodaidfoundation.org, there are about 795 million people in the world don't have enough food to live a healthy life. This translates to 1 in 7 people are hungry! And I am not one of them! That's absolutely huge! Do you have enough food for your family daily? Now that's one very big reason to be grateful for every single day.

Gratitude-enhancing ideas: while eating out is fun and convenient, overdoing it won't make you any good. When you cook at home, you know what you put into your food. You mostly know the quality of the ingredients; you picked them in the supermarket or your garden. You are more able to cook for health, not just for the taste buds and the sight. Cooking from scratch is easier than you might think. I've been doing it for …, well, all my life. And I am a super busy mom and wife, author, coach, photographer, traveler, crafter, and more. It's a matter of shifting mentality. It's for your health and longevity. Remind yourself often that every other thing in life relies on your health and longevity. Start cooking more at home, follow simple recipes and make up your own, and engage your kids, so they can get used to it and spend quality time with you, also, learn by doing and observing. If you've been afraid of cooking, face your fear. You know by now that you can't outrun your fears, you must stand up to them and transform them. Use curiosity and positive self-talk as your best allies. Chop up veggies to make different salads. Add soaked nuts and seeds, olive oil and lemon juice or balsamic vinegar. Make a soup by mixing preferably organic vegetables into water or vegetable/bone broth. They don't need much time to cook. Add spices and Himalayan salt for extra nutrients and flavors. Drop an egg in it! Put some noodles too. Bake vegetables in skin in the oven. Nothing else really needed there. They take about an hour at least. The skin helps keeping the nutrients inside while when you boil them, they get away. Slices of meat can be marinated for a few hours in salt, spices and sauces, like mustard, soy sauce, etc. Then just sauté them or broil them. Bon Appetit!

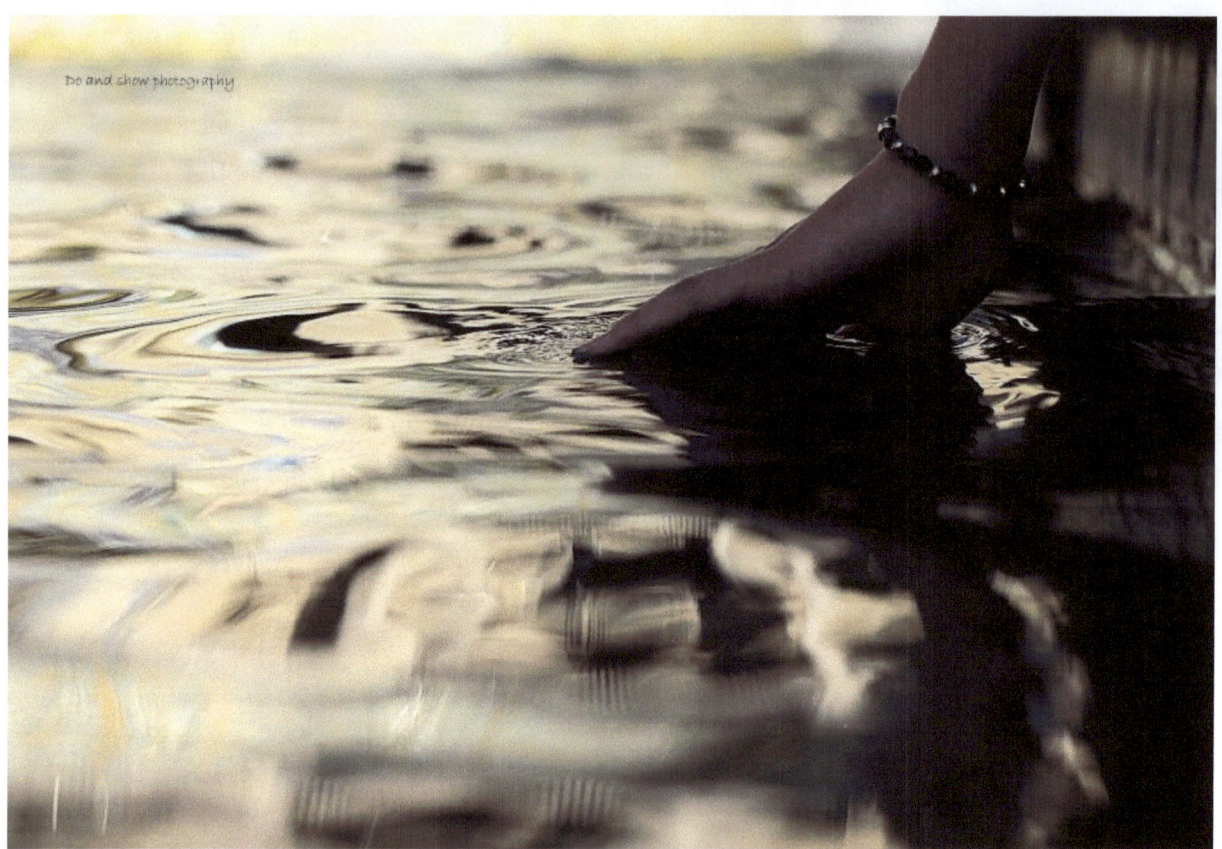

I am very thankful for my skin and the nerves in my skin so I can touch and feel so many qualities of the things around me. I know all my senses, including touch helps me to stay safe and enjoy life more. With the tip of my fingers I can feel if something is hot or cold, if wet or dry, if soft or hard, bumpy or smooth. It feels really nice to touch the surface of cool water on a warm day, and feel the ripples my hand creates.

Gratitude-enhancing ideas: how often do you actually pay attention how items and surfaces feel to your touch? How conscious are you about them? Becoming more aware of these sensations can be a life-saver, or at least a health-supporter, but besides that, it's once again about living in the moment instead of worrying about the future which doesn't exist, or instead of being stuck in the pain and guilt of the past which had already been done and gone. So, consciously make an effort to bring your focus back to the moment, what you are feeling with your skin. When you walk through a clothing or home décor department store, touch various fabrics and surfaces. Even close your eyes for a second and just be there. Give this gift to your fingers from time to time.

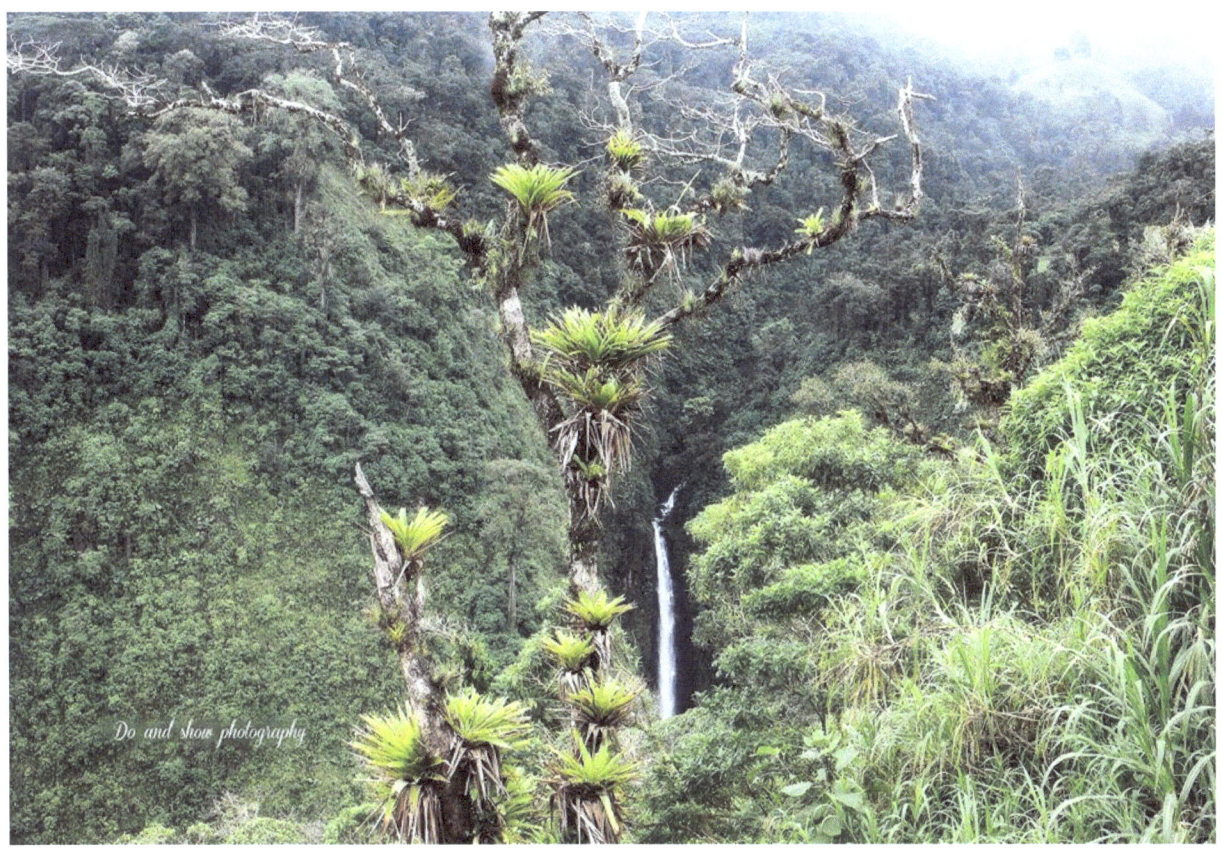

As I walk in the rainforest and listen to the waterfall, the howling monkeys and the singing birds, I always realize how blessed I am to be able to travel to these places. How beautiful! There, where I am surrounded by very high trees, and all kinds of living creatures that may even mean danger to my safety, I feel exceptionally fortunate and thrilled.

Gratitude-enhancing ideas: when you are on a trip, check into taking excursions into the wilderness to connect with nature. Of course, always let others know where you are heading and when, and hire guides. Discover the area and its animals beforehand. Learn about its plants. When you visit the place, try to find all what you have read about. Pay attention to details and behaviors. Become increasingly aware of your own feelings and thoughts. Realize the great opportunity to detox from the city's pollutions of many kinds. Record sounds and images. Make videos. Talk about your ideas, feelings and thoughts in that moment on the video so later you can relive it. While some animals look adorable and safe, it's better to observe them from a good distance. Here's a unique idea if you are up to working with your photos and researching a little. This can serve well to educate the whole family or a class of students about your adventures. Make a PowerPoint presentation out of your trip. Yes, it takes work but there are people who literally enjoy doing this type of work. I am one of them. Relive your memories and share them.

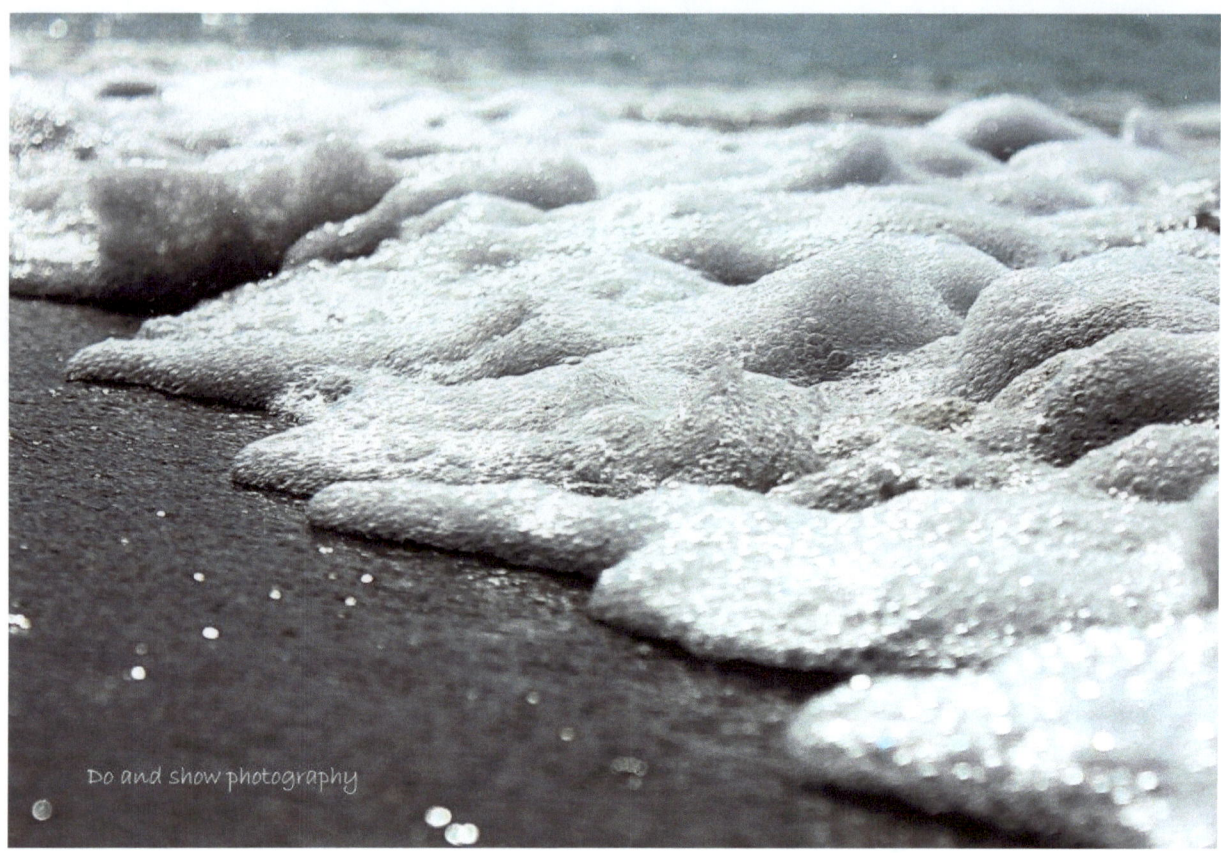

Ahh, what a lovely and exciting feeling when I walk in sea water or run my fingers through the waves. I feel so thankful for all those bubbles, the caressing of the water and the scent of the salty air.

Gratitude-enhancing ideas: put a little soapy water in a cup. Through a straw, preferably stainless steel or glass to reduce plastic pollution for our planet, start blowing air into it. You can even experiment with pasta straw. I've seen numerous children having a blast with this activity, but who says we, adults can't have this kind of fun? Have it together with your youngsters. Make it even more interesting by adding food coloring. Have you ever taken underwater pictures or videos of bubbles, like in a hot tub or as the waves that are crashing on the shore? Try it! Another great memory of my childhood has to do with clear glue, plastic strips cut from plastic folders, a projector and darkness. With my brother, we used to pretend being doctors by viewing fake "veins" via projector. We glued two plastic strips together cut in the size of our projector films. We had to watch it while the glue was still fresh and moving around in form of bubbles. They looked like living cells flowing in the vein. Maybe this will spark an idea for you too, even if it doesn't involve the old-fashioned projector.

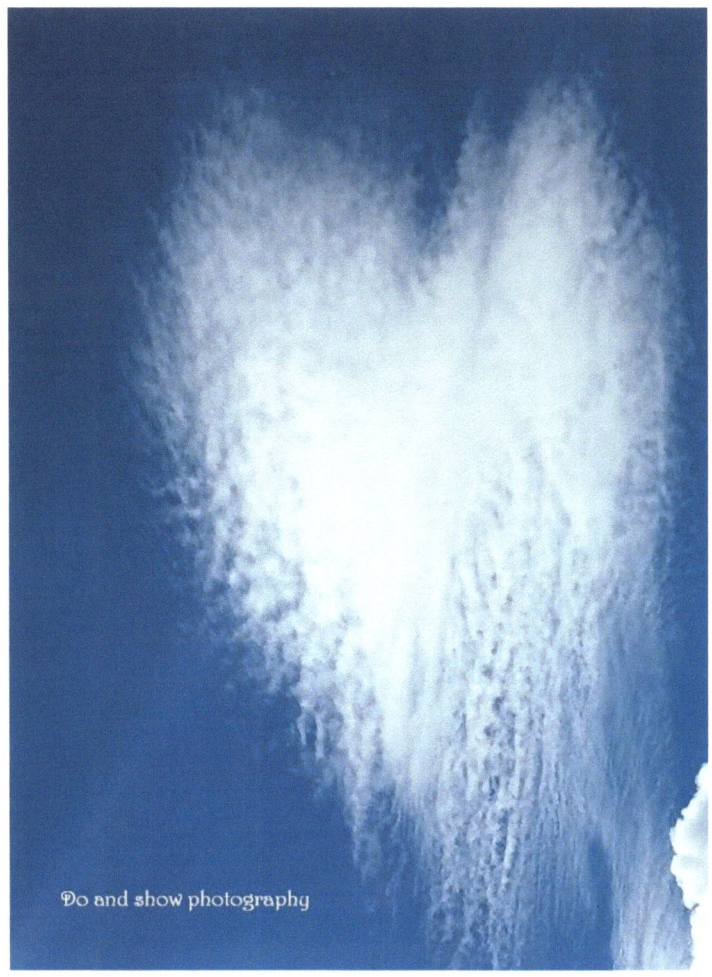

I am extremely grateful for the blue sky and the ever-changing clouds. When I take a little time, even while waiting at the red light in my car, I tend to discover enthralling cloud shapes, like this heart too. Even though, I had to turn it around. It helps me see things from another angle.

Gratitude-enhancing ideas: during driving, as you come to a stop for a couple of minutes, glance at the sky and the clouds. See if you can recognize animal or plant shapes, buildings and more. Another childhood memory, actually, a dream that has just popped to my mind. I dreamed once traveling on a fluffy pillow way above the cities, and I still recall the feeling of peace in my heart, and endless comfort and calmness. Close your eyes sometimes (not while driving!), and instruct your child to do the same. Have a guided meditation when you are talking about floating on clouds, using a soft voice. Guided meditations, as such can be a great tool when you or your loved ones are experiencing upset or anger. You can simply talk about how you start floating with the clouds, how that makes you feel, what you are seeing, and how it's making you calmer and more relaxed.

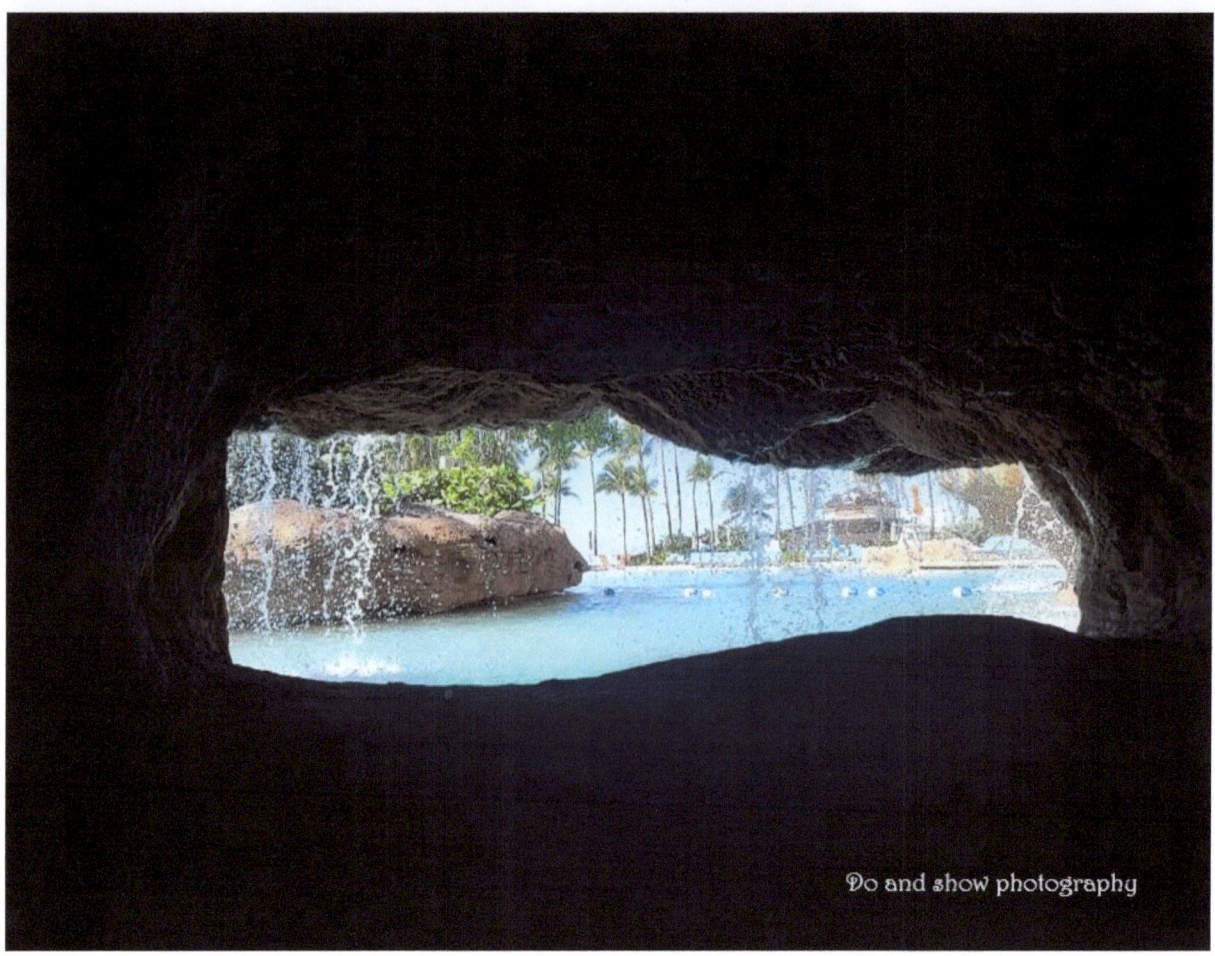

I feel absolutely thankful for my trips to tropical places. I love every aspect of it. It's the ultimate image for a perfect vacation. Azure blue waters, palm trees swaying in the wind, waterfalls, coconut drink, and kind locals making our time memorable.

Gratitude-enhancing ideas: what else can you do to enhance your sense of gratitude besides committing to being in the moment as much as possible? There are the obvious smart ways to make sure your experience will be more pleasant, and less stressful. I have mentioned some before. Be on time, plan ahead, pack smart, learn about the place, foods, and also its dangers. Try a massage when you can really focus your ears and other sensing organs toward what's going on around you in the moment. Try some local foods and drinks. Listen to their music and dance to it. Talk to people who live there. Have a vacation as it's supposed to be enjoyed. Let your not important calls go to voicemail.

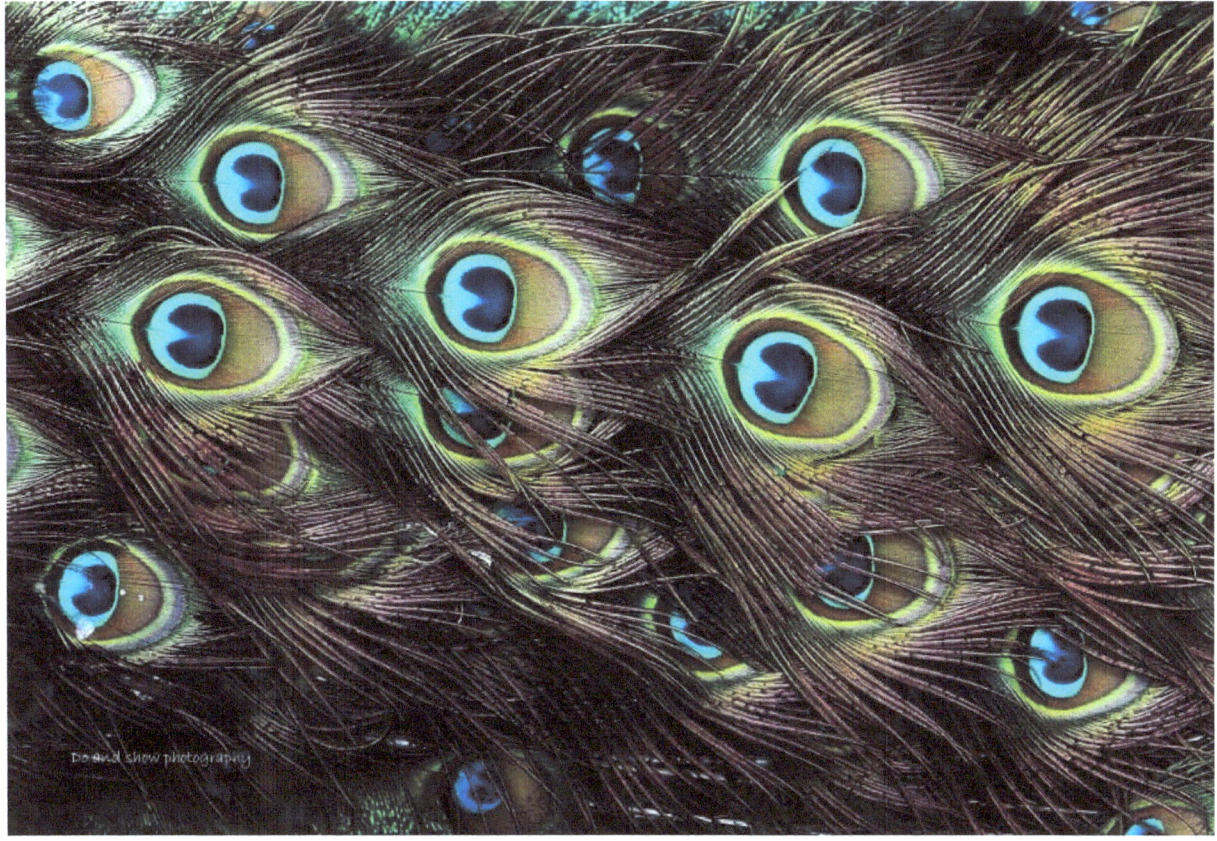

I am very thankful for the gorgeous feathers that cover the bodies of birds. It's not only that these feathers protect them and make them look so pretty, but they inspire various industries to create feather-like designs. This photo I have taken of the tail of a peacock as he was walking around. These spots look like eyes. Just mesmerizing.

Gratitude-enhancing ideas: I believe we vote with our wallets. Whatever you keep buying, you are voicing your preferences, hence, encouraging the industries to continue with certain practices like killing birds or plucking them alive. Grow your awareness of these cruel practices. Instead of feathers and items that have used feathers, choose other items. To respect nature and its living beings, and I mean all of them, it is not just our choice, it's our obligation. We are part of nature. Yes, let it inspire you! Paint it, draw it on paper or canvas, sculpt it, decorate your clothes and home décor items with stitches that resemble feathers, and let the birds live their lives as it was intended. Spread this message to your children. It's especially their future that is at stake.

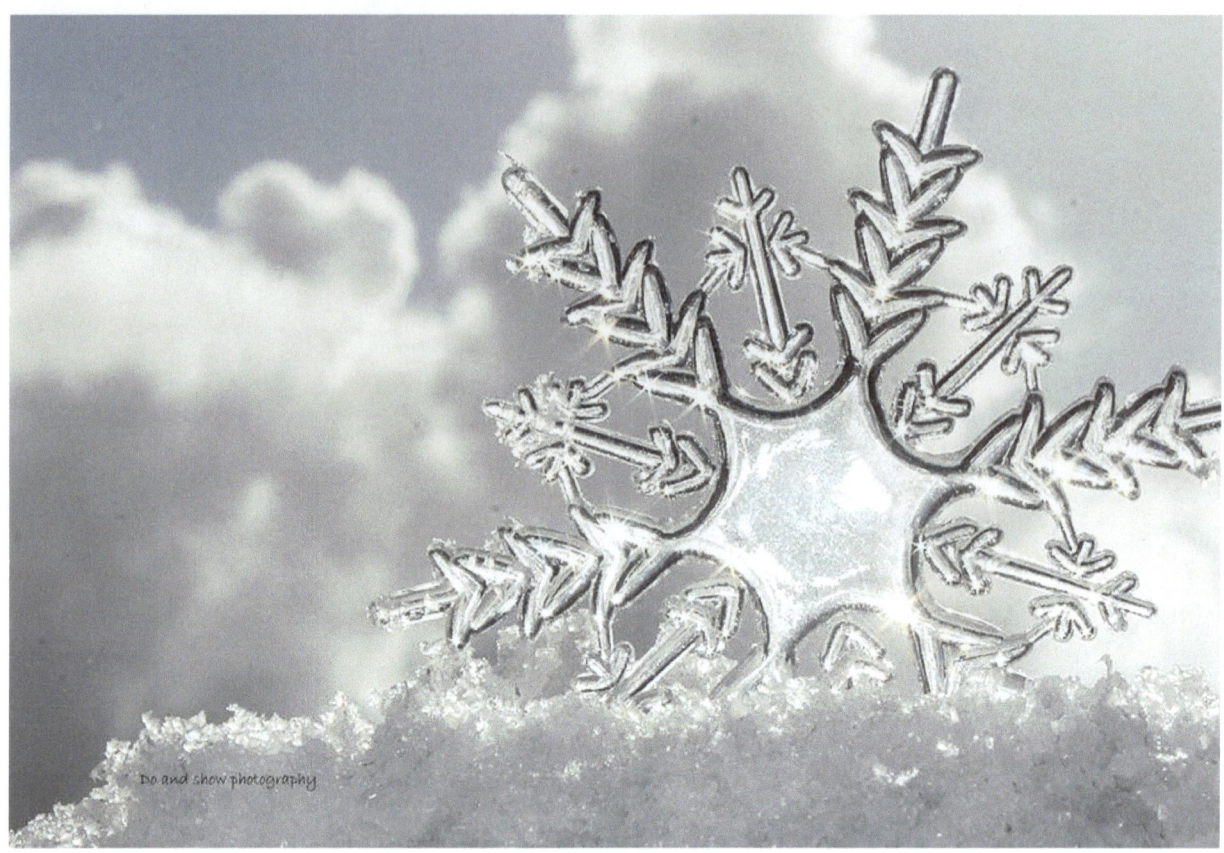

I have mentioned my gratitude for the snow. Here, I want to narrow it down to the mesmerizing shapes of the snowflakes. They say we can't find two of the exact same snowflakes. I've also read recently, scientists talked about this not being so. Either way, I think we can agree that snowflakes, when they are enlarged, capture our attention. It's fascinating how the physical laws make it happen that they form those usually symmetrical ice crystals. Just stunning!

Gratitude-enhancing ideas: the first thing that comes to my mind is cutting paper snowflakes. This has been another favorite activity of mine from childhood. And I have been still cutting them, laminating them, and a few years ago, I started naming them too! Through years of practice, they have become more and more intricate. There are very easy tutorials to help you out in this. I recommend you try it and involve your children as well. They will be amazed when you open the snowflake. It's a great opportunity for them to learn or practice some math skills. Naming art work is such a creative fun. You just ask what it makes you feel like or think of. Is it like a busy intersection, or stormy waves at the sea, or excited about the holidays, or reuniting with a loved one?

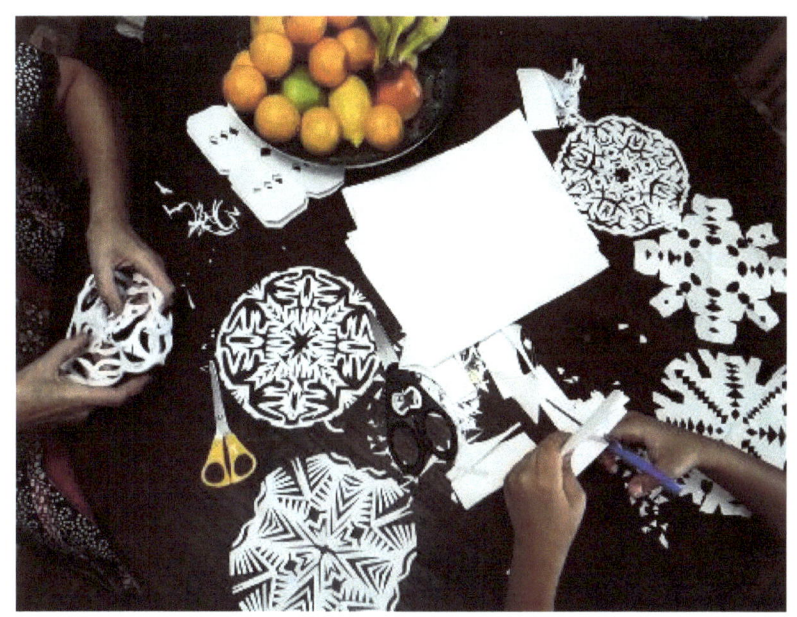

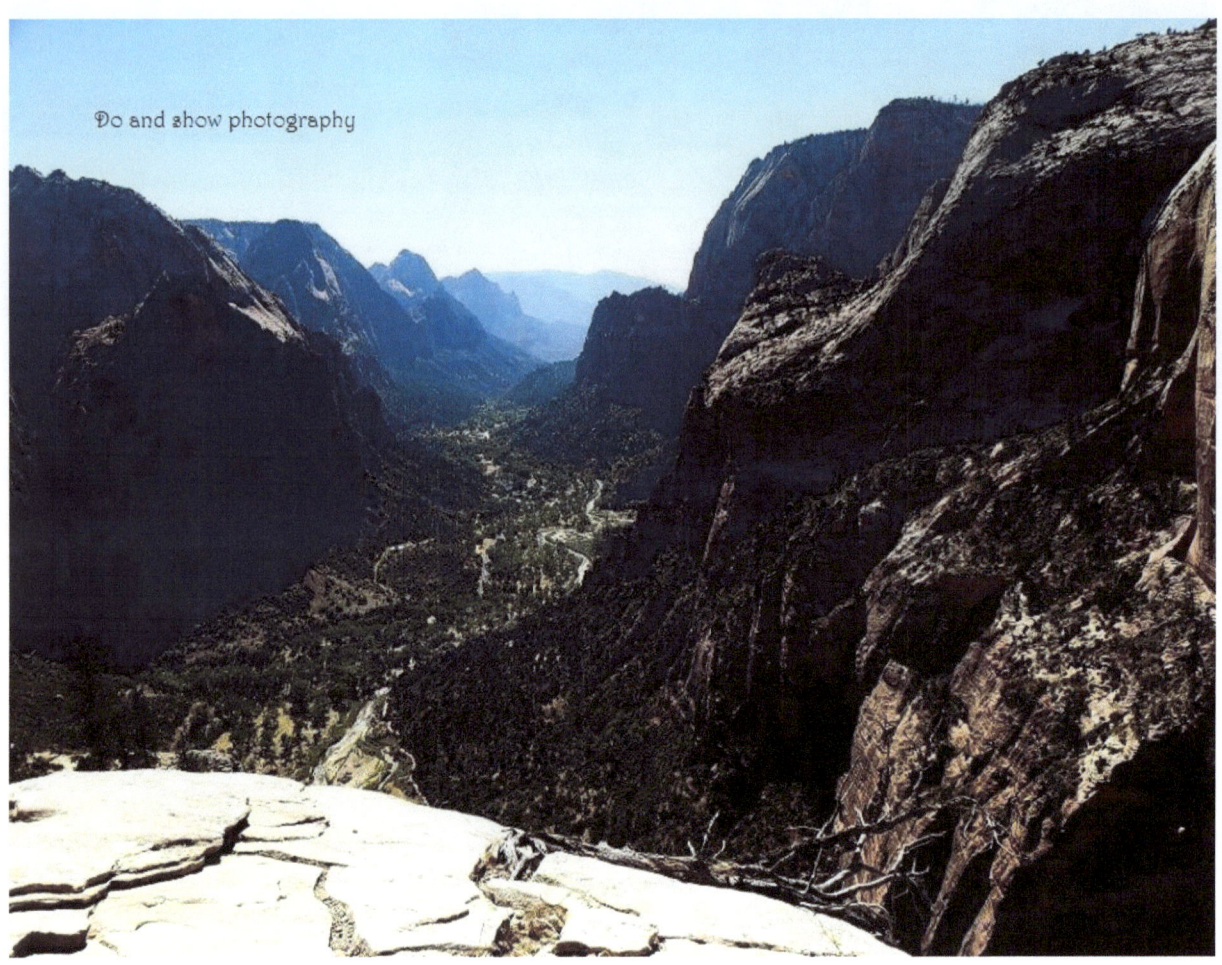

I am so very grateful for the strength and ability to go on long hikes, whether it's about going uphill or downhill. And it's not only that! I'm also enjoying it fully with all its challenges and discomfort. I feel so strong and capable when I am hiking a difficult path, like this one above, the Angels' Landing hike at Zion Park, Utah. It's absolutely empowering to complete it and get to the top. Oh, and the breathtaking view that I get as a reward... So thankful for all. During some of these hikes, I get to face fears, and overcome my obstacles. I feel like a winner!

Gratitude-enhancing ideas: not a hiker? How many times have you tried? On what locations? I wasn't always a passionate hiker either. Keep on giving it a try. It's about so much more than just walking for hours and seeing pretty landscapes. It's about disconnecting a little from the crazy-busy daily life, and reconnecting with nature. It's about inhaling fresh, clean air. It's about Getting inspired to paint, write or photograph. It's about having fun with a great company of people. It's about feeling increasingly empowered. It's about sunbathing. It's about doing lots of things for your overall health. While hiking, become very aware of all this and enjoy!

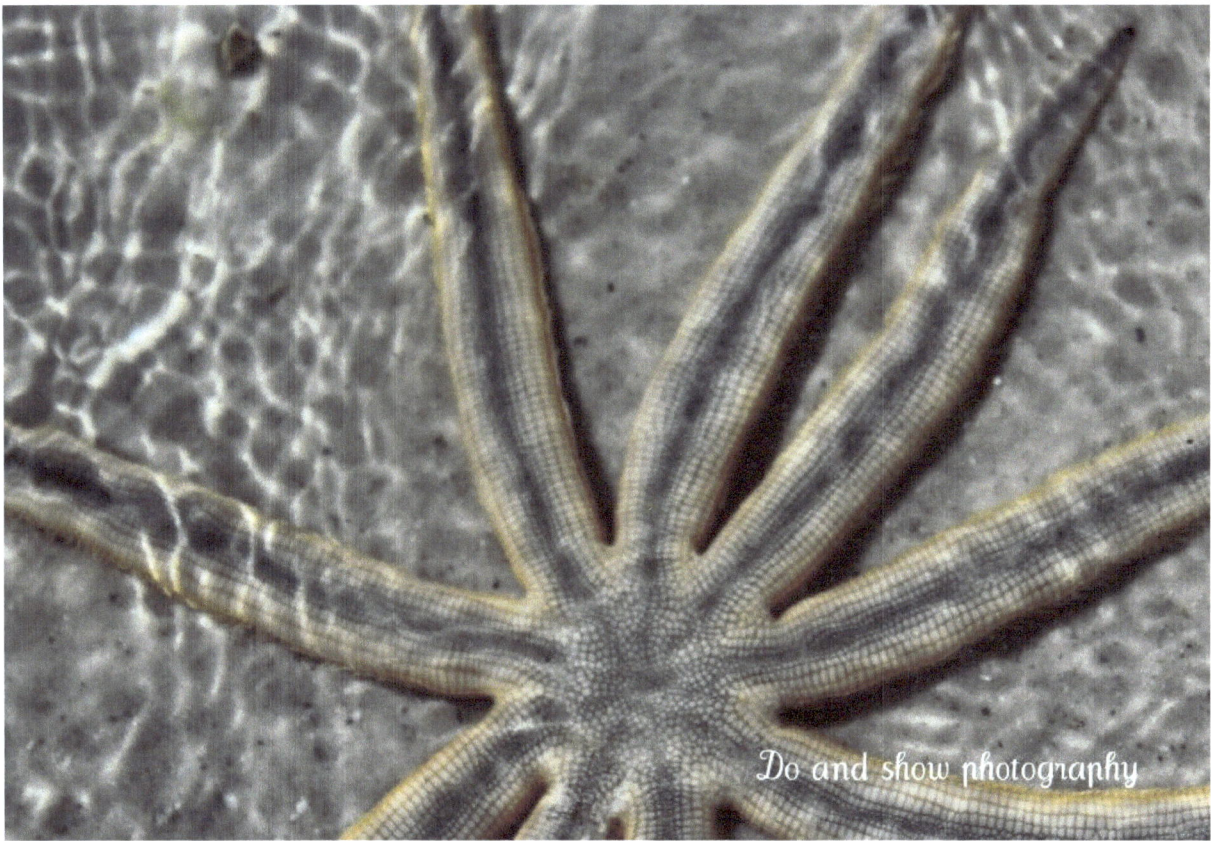

While humans have tried to separate themselves from the animal kingdom, I feel very blessed and glad knowing and experiencing that I get to see animals flourishing in their own habitats. I love that excitement when that happens, and it does, every day. I notice them, even in my city, because I am looking for them. I believe observing animals and their behaviors can teach us a ton about how to live life fully and in a healthier way.

Gratitude-enhancing ideas: of course, the number one thing will be is to become more conscious and start looking for them. Realize the value in sharing space with wild creatures. How often do we get to learn about them while watching them in live? How often do you get to point out interesting behaviors or qualities/features of animals to your child? Get excited, and they will get excited too. Bring them back to the real, busy, curious, valuable childhood, the way a childhood should be lived instead of becoming overly sedentary in front of technology screens. Above all, talk a lot about living in harmony with nature, respecting and protecting it. Again, their future also depends on it. Encourage drawing what they have seen, read further about them. Create animals from different materials. Photograph them. Learn about how to stay safe around them.

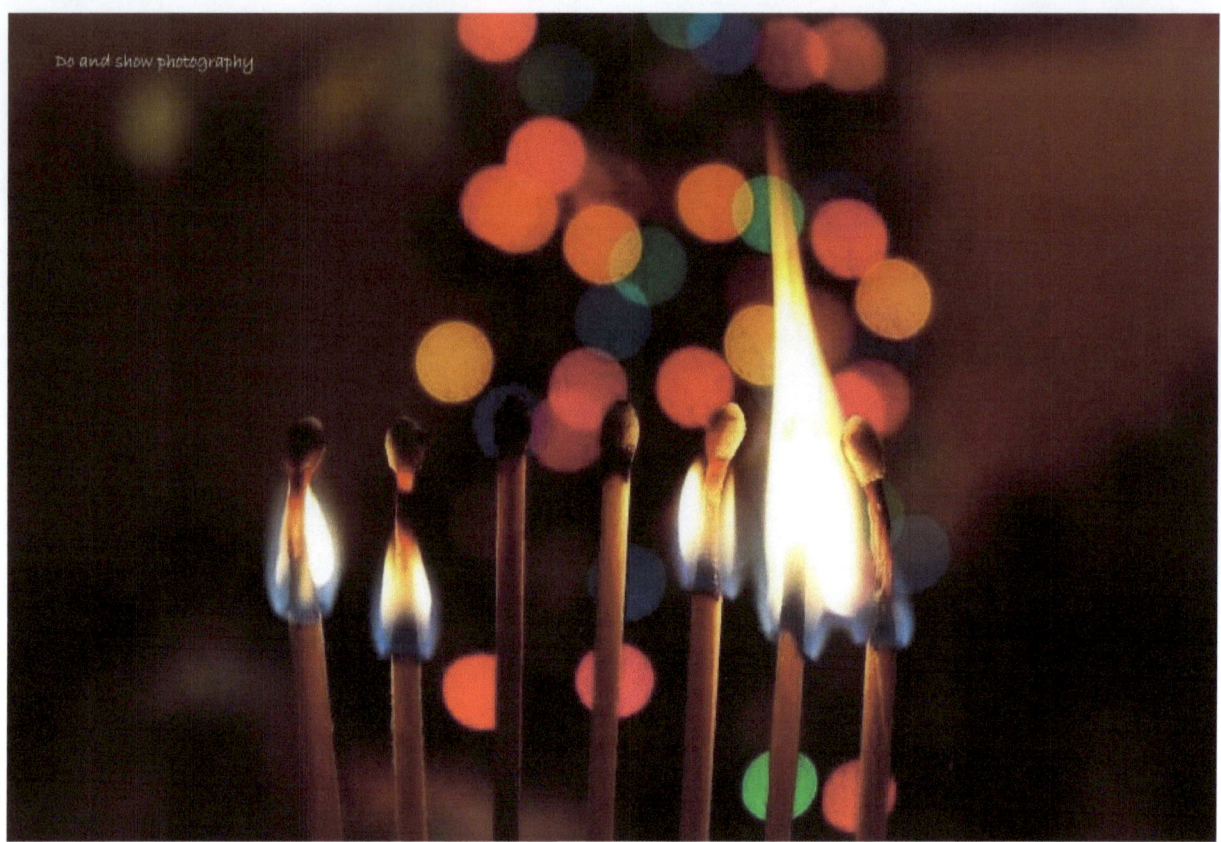

We, humans, have discovered fire a very long time ago, and I am absolutely grateful for that. I am grateful that fire helps me cook some of my food to make it more digestible and palatable. I am grateful that fire keeps me warm and provides more light to see. I am grateful that fire in the wilderness can keep dangerous animals away. I am grateful that fire can be part of amazing shows and events. I am grateful that fire can melt things to make them more malleable. At the same time, I am also aware of its potential dangers.

Gratitude-enhancing ideas: go camping with families and friends, and build a camp fire. Roast marshmallow and sing songs together. Sit in front of a roaring fire of a fireplace. Sip wine with your spouse. Exchange glances and kisses. Be in the moment. Feel the heat on your skin. Admire the movements of the flames. Let it take you where it may, down memory lane. As you are sitting at the campsite, talk about the history how long ago, people used to hunt and gather around fires. What a difficult lifestyle it must've been compared to ours now. In fact, it still exists in some remote places. Appreciate that you don't have to live that way anymore, only if you choose so. Once again, you can contemplate and feel grateful for having the comfort of your home, supermarkets, heater, and more. Today's young generation can use a guidance in realization how comfortable their lives are. Point it out to them.

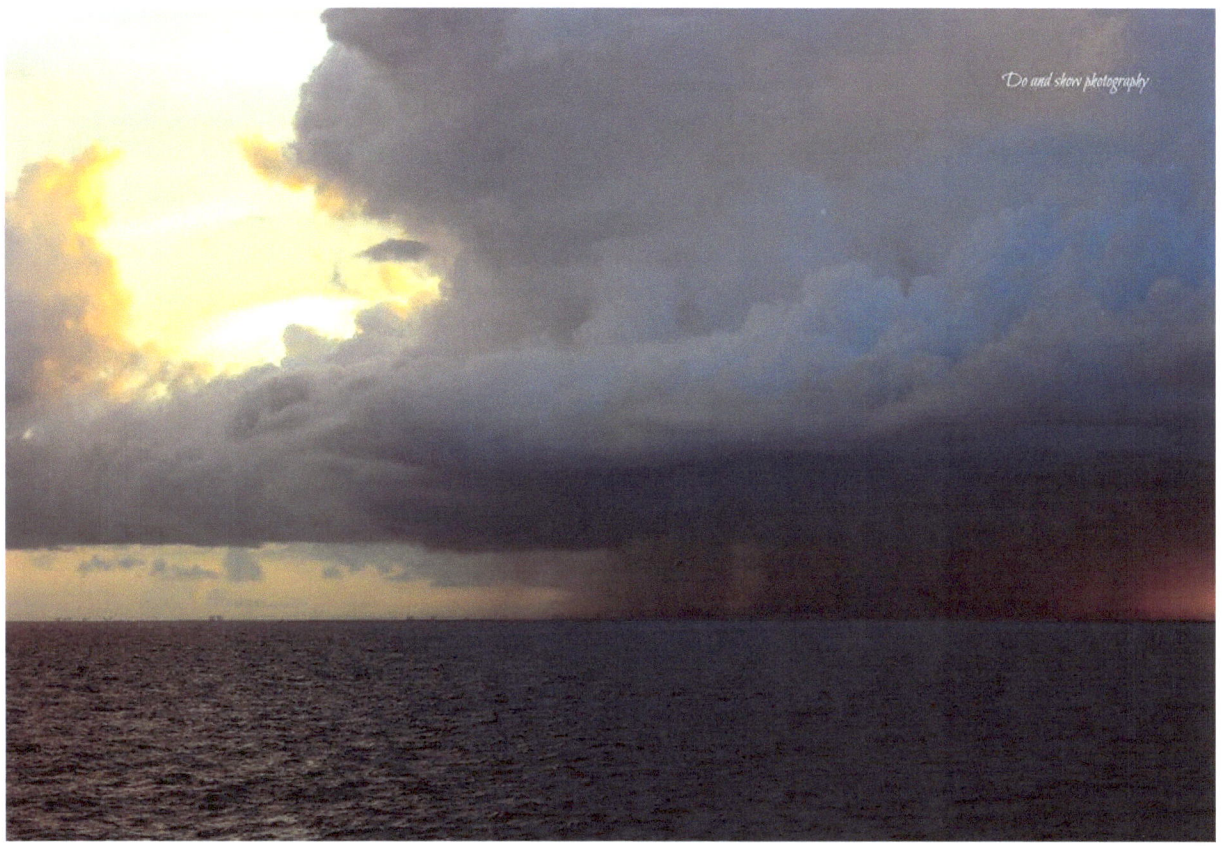

Wow! What a downpour over the ocean! While I rather have a rain-free day for most of the time, I feel thankful for the stormy days as well. They create such a dramatic scene no matter where they occur. It's very exciting for a passionate photographer and writer like me. My other part of me, the one that is all about creating a healthier planet is jumping from the pleasure also, because of knowing how the storm clears up things and brings in fresh water for the animals. I am extremely thankful for having to go through storms without getting injured or having my belonging destroyed.

Gratitude-enhancing ideas: don't always hide completely from the storms. Obviously, there are cases when that's the wise thing to do. Observe them for a few minutes from a safe distance, of course. Feel their power and cleansing effect on nature. Watch short videos or documentaries about them. Teach your children how to be safe during storms. Feel the gratitude for being able to stay safe or possibly even surviving powerful storms before. Unfortunately, many people have perished in big storms. Know about the common mistakes that can get people killed, even post storms. According to AccuWeather, after floods, for example, electrocutions are a common way to die. Carbon monoxide poisoning and misuse of candles are other reasons. Cardiovascular events due to stress and deadly falls are two big ones, too. Knowledge is important.

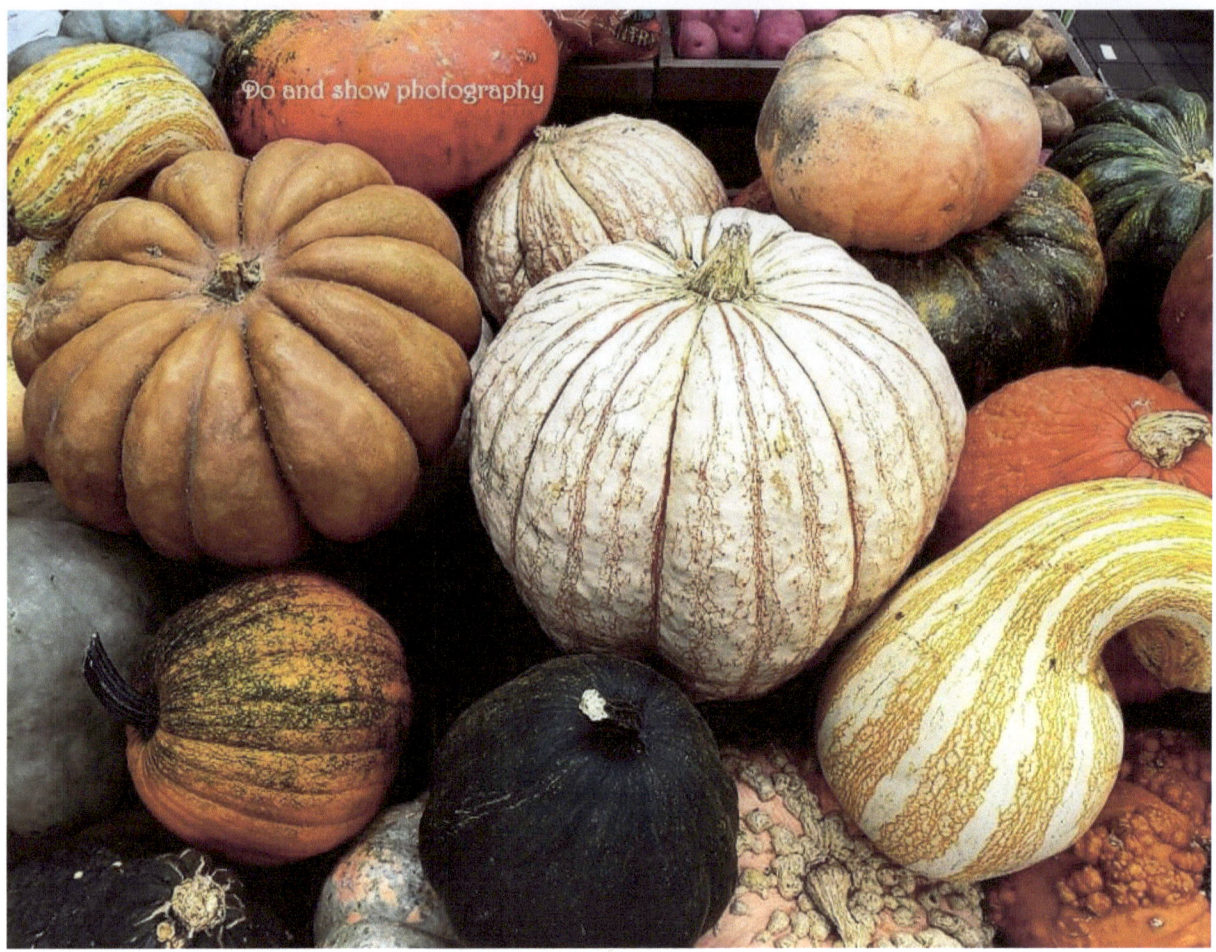

Every single year, around Thanksgiving, this or something similar is the sight I get to admire. I have so much appreciation for these colorful squashes and gourds. They are very delicious and nutritious as well. I love how creative people get with the ideas of using them for decoration and food recipes. Can you imagine the holidays without them? It'd be hard, right?

Gratitude-enhancing ideas: lay your eyes on the various shaped and colored squashes around the holidays. Try out new ones. You can simply bake them after cutting them into chunks and scooping out their seeds. You can also steam the pieces or add them to stews and soups. Cream them to make dips. I even make ice cream from baked or cooked squashes using my ice cream machine. Exercise open-mindedness and encourage your family to do so, too. Remember, you don't have to like them, but appreciate that you get to try them. For decorations, try some new techniques. It doesn't have to be always the traditional jack-o-lantern. Use pins and buttons, ribbons or beads. Paint patterns or shapes with non-traditional colors. Of course, provide your children with tools and supplies so they can exercise their creativity as well. Follow safety rules.

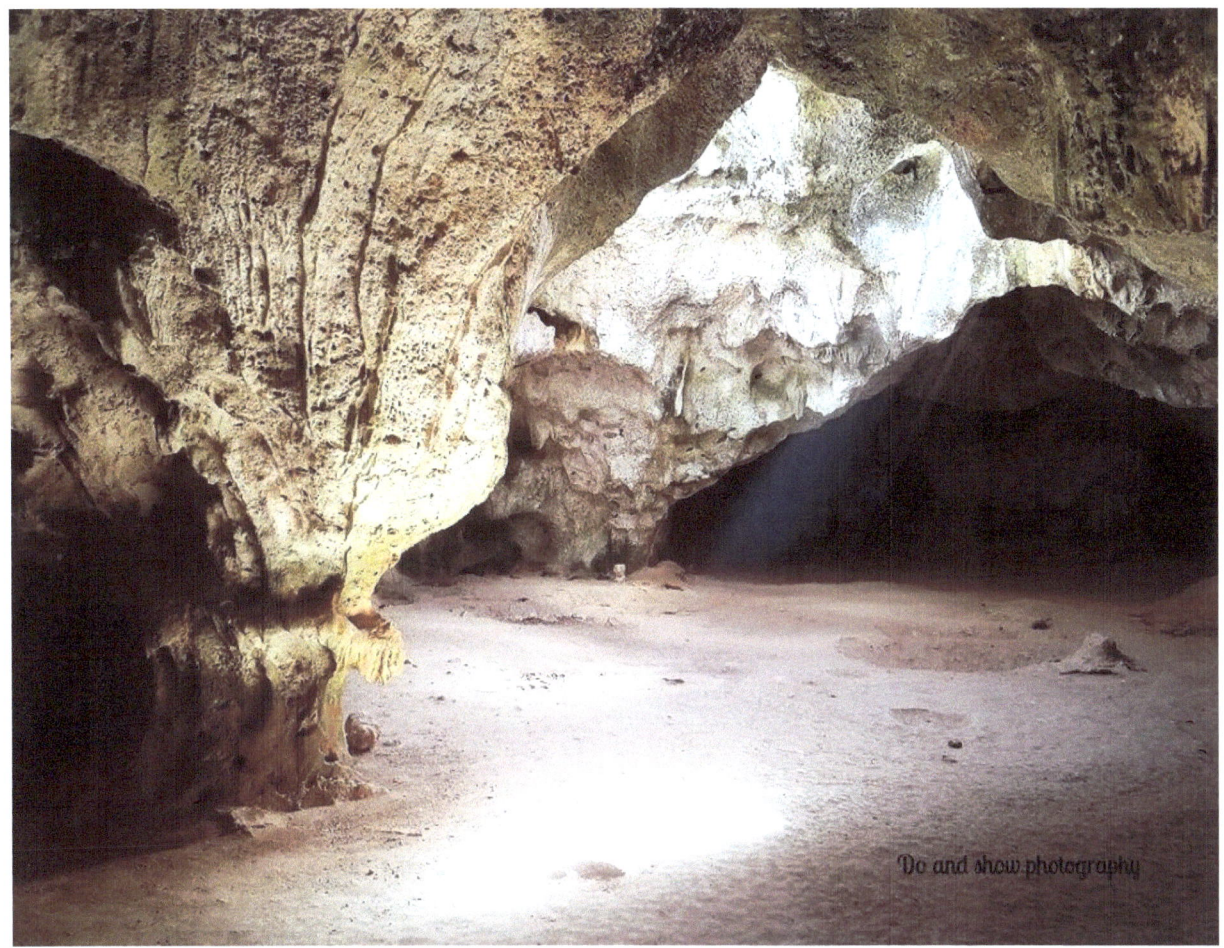

Our ancestors used to live in caves according to many excavations. Now, I really appreciate that I can visit caves, imagine how challenging it could've been to live there, observe cave animals, pictographs and even admire light rays breaking through holes.

Gratitude-enhancing ideas: go on cave tours with your family! To find them really amazing, it's a good idea to do some research and learn about when they were created, who/what lived and lives there and how differently their bodies have evolved (if it's an animal) to adapt to darkness. Animals living in caves are often blind or with a poor eyesight because they don't need to see. Their other senses are heightened because of this. Children often find this kind of information very surprising and exciting. Also, try to copy or make up pictographs with your kids. Dip your finger into finger paint and try it that way. Creating secret pictographs that correspond to letters and numbers can be actually quite a fun. It can be used among family members as secret codes. It can make communication and certain chores more interesting for young children. When they are happier, you are, too.

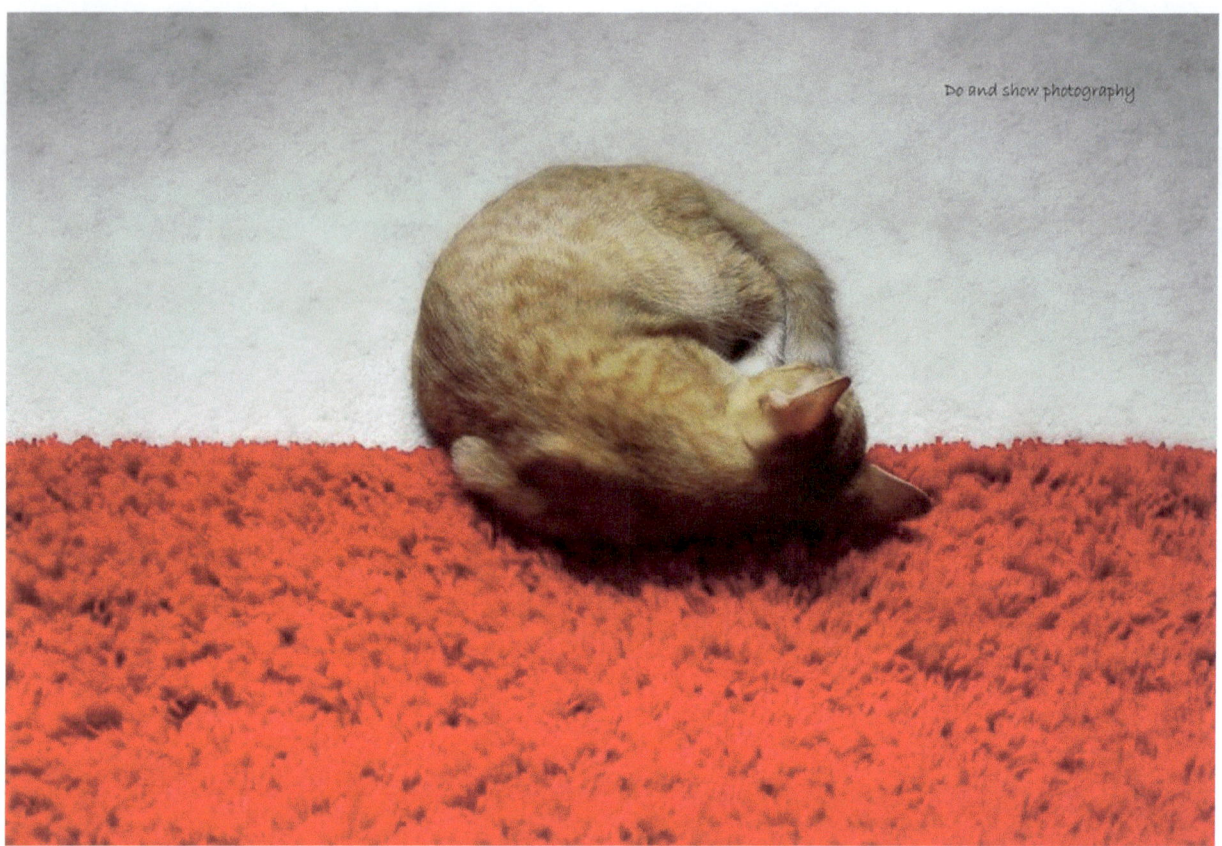

Do you have any pet? I've had several kinds. I currently have a cat and a python, and they bring me tremendous joy and stress relief. I could fill a small book with all my gratitude for my pets.

Gratitude-enhancing ideas: if you don't have a pet, consider getting one, even one that is quiet and doesn't need much of your attention, like a turtle or a fish. If you have children, it's even more amazing opportunity to teach them about living things and their needs. It feels exceptionally good when pets are saved by us, you build up trust towards them, they look up to you, need you and love you back. If you already have pets, but you don't connect with them too often because of different reasons, try to steal a few minutes from other activities in order to be there for them, and ultimately for yourself that way. When you start creating a deeper connection with them, it's like you enter another world. They help you slow down which is absolutely essential for your overall health. Watch them without interfering. Create a photo book about them. Talk to them, unload what bothers you or what makes you excited. Notice how they respond. Meanwhile, enjoy the benefits of getting things off your chest. There are excellent scientific "toys" in 3-D that can give you more insight regarding their internal organs and bone structure. It's truly fascinating. The more I learn about my pets, the more I admire, respect and love them.

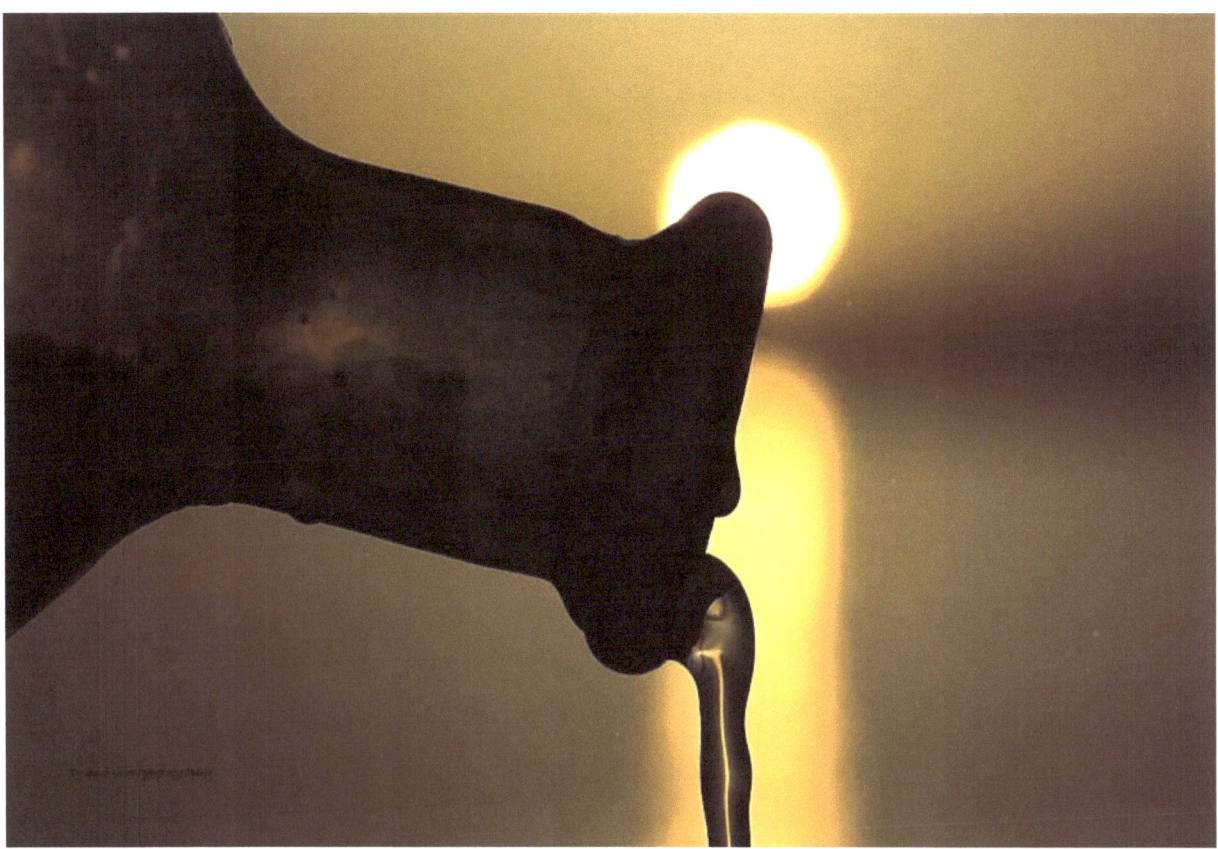

I am very thankful for the so-called golden bridge that is created by the sun on the surface of water at sunrise or sunset. What a marvelous sight! It almost makes me feel sometimes like I could walk on it. This time of the day has something magical in it.

Gratitude-enhancing ideas: when you take photos of the sunrise or sunset, try a different way. Zoom onto the golden ripples and waves. Omit the sun from your picture for this time. Also, observe the sand on the beach and its orange color. Remember that it's not safe to look into the sun (at all), or the glistening waves for too long either. Listen to your body's signs. Use sunglasses. Paint or draw this beautiful scene. Let it inspire you to write stories or compose poems and music about it. Allow the magical vibration and mood surround you, penetrate you and take you away a bit from your worries and sorrows.

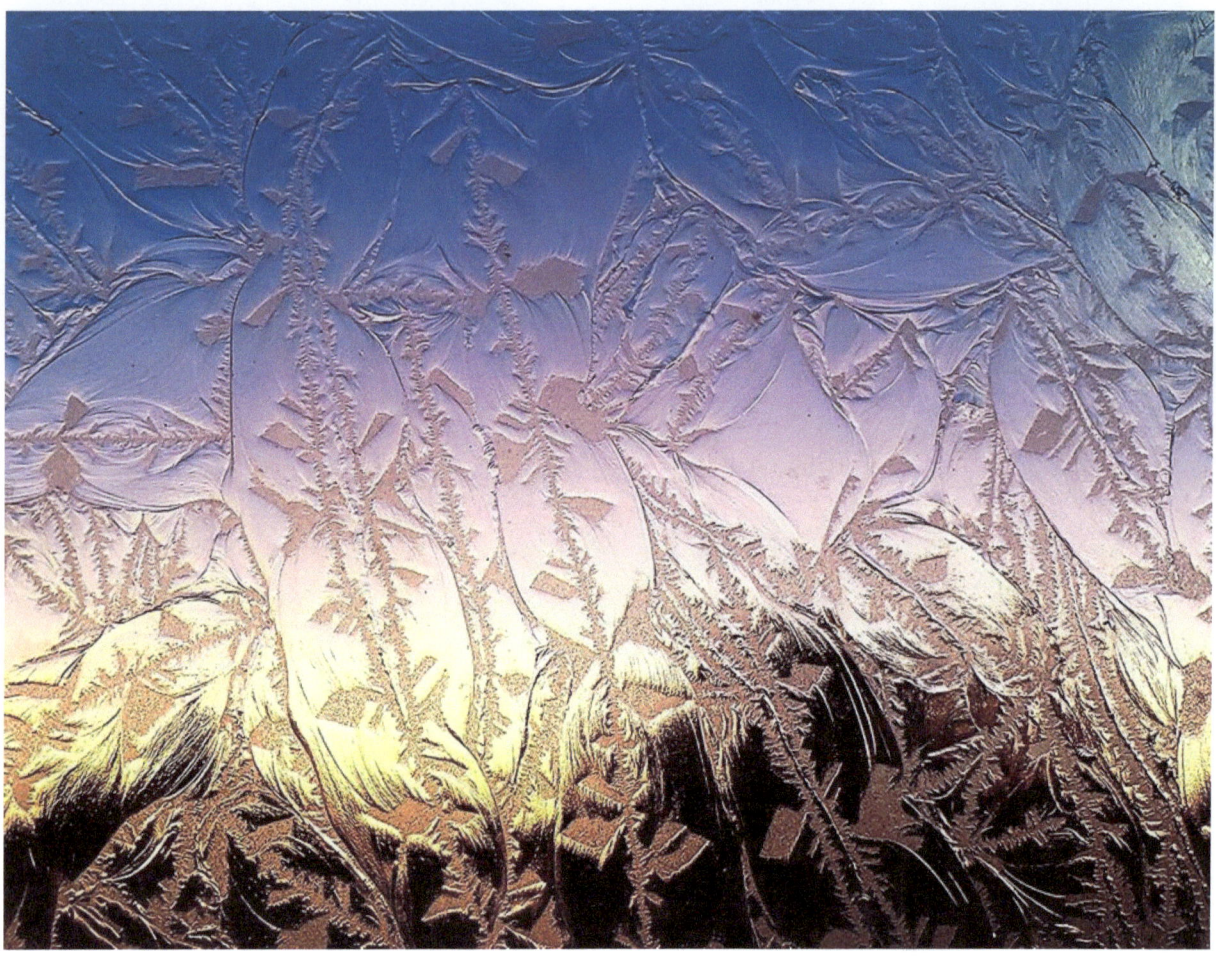

What an amazing trick nature brings to our attention on the winter! We have flowers blooming in the spring, summer and autumn. For winter, we get to admire the frost flowers on the window pane. Nature dresses up our windows!

Gratitude-enhancing ideas: paint frost flowers on your window in the winter using a special paint for glass, especially if you live in a warmer climate. Let your child join. Make different shapes, and different numbers of flower petals. You can also cut paper snowflakes or flowers and tape them to the window. I'm actually fond of the smaller sized paper snowflakes laminated and hung on my Christmas tree. They are very durable and beautiful. My other point is that they are one-of-a-kind! Snowflakes really look like frost flowers.

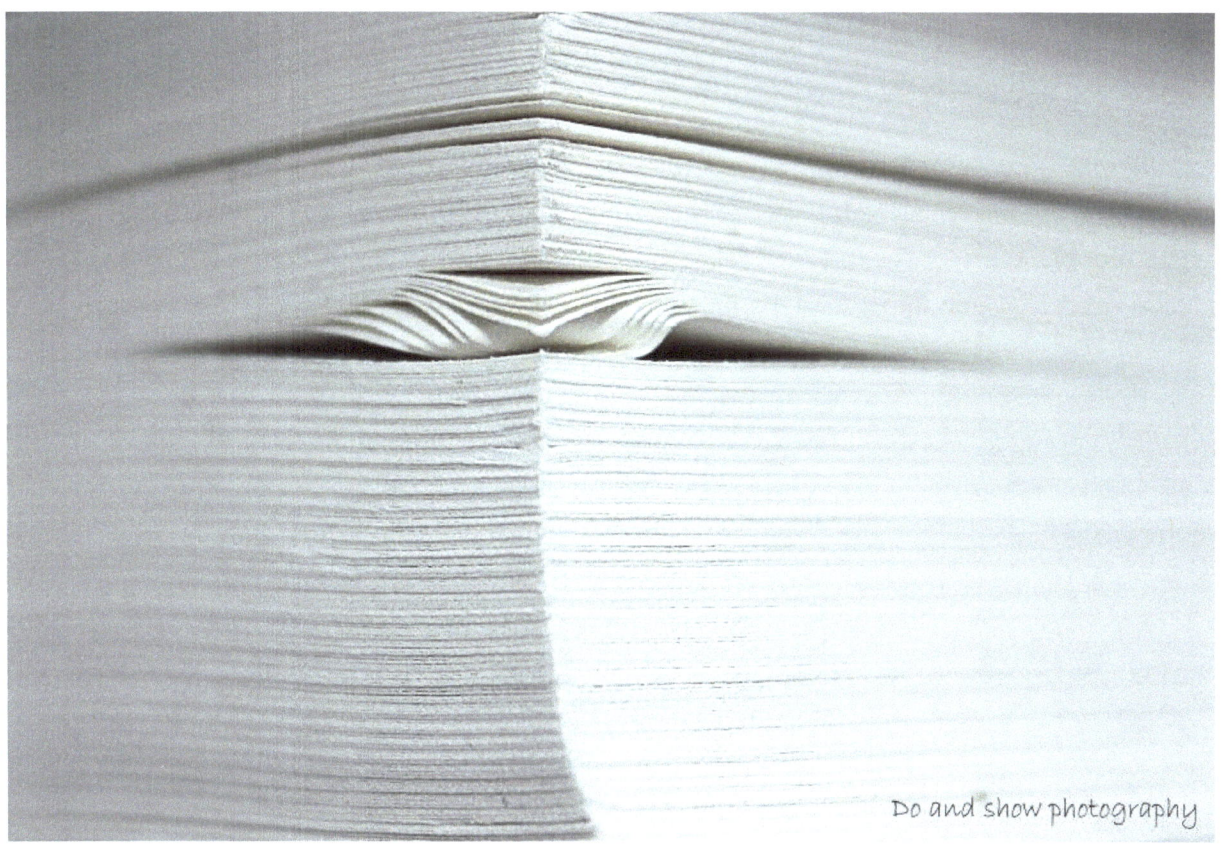

I feel absolutely grateful for all the books I've read in my life and all the books I have access to. I believe books are very wonderful treasures, and this is one of my main reasons why I write books too. The wealth of information and images that can be found is priceless. In my opinion, we are and we should be learning and growing every single day till our last day on this planet. One way is to read books, and another great way is to write books. Isn't it amazing that in our modern times, we can find books on almost any topic, and we can purchase or rent them fast? Now we have eBooks available to us which is great to reduce the demand for trees and paper. According to bustle.com, an average American adult reads 12 books a year, while an average CEO reads around 50-60 books a year. Another piece of interesting fact according to geediting.com, Asian countries, like India, Thailand, China and Philippines are top countries in terms of number of hours spent on reading per person per week. A few European nations, like Sweden, France, Hungary, Poland and Spain are near the top too. USA and Canada are around the place 20.

Gratitude-enhancing ideas: if you feel you aren't a bookworm, contemplate the statistics I mentioned above. Yes, there are several ways we can learn new materials, indeed, but books are and should be essential part of it. If you think you have no time to read, consider reading a page a day at least, or a page a week. Start somewhere. The important thing is to create a habit of reading. Once you get used to daily or weekly reading, you will start craving it, and your mind will find solutions to rearrange your schedule to make it happen. That's how the human brain works. Isn't it fascinating? The key is to get started! No more excuses. CEOs are extremely busy people but they are very aware of the benefits of reading so they make time for it. It's also a matter of self-discipline, but self-discipline has a lot to do with understanding and mindset. This is why it's crucial to grasp how powerful this habit is, and how detrimental the opposite could become. I'd like to propose the idea of writing a book as well. For me, the number one book that has changed my life the most profound way is my first book I have ever written, even though, it wasn't the same that was published first. Think of it this way. You write about your childhood, or your first love, or just make up a story for teenagers, or conduct interviews on a curious topic and then collect them in your book. Either way, your personal style, opinion, knowledge, emotions and beliefs will shine through. It will be something that is only one in the entire world. I hope I've sparked some excitement inside you.

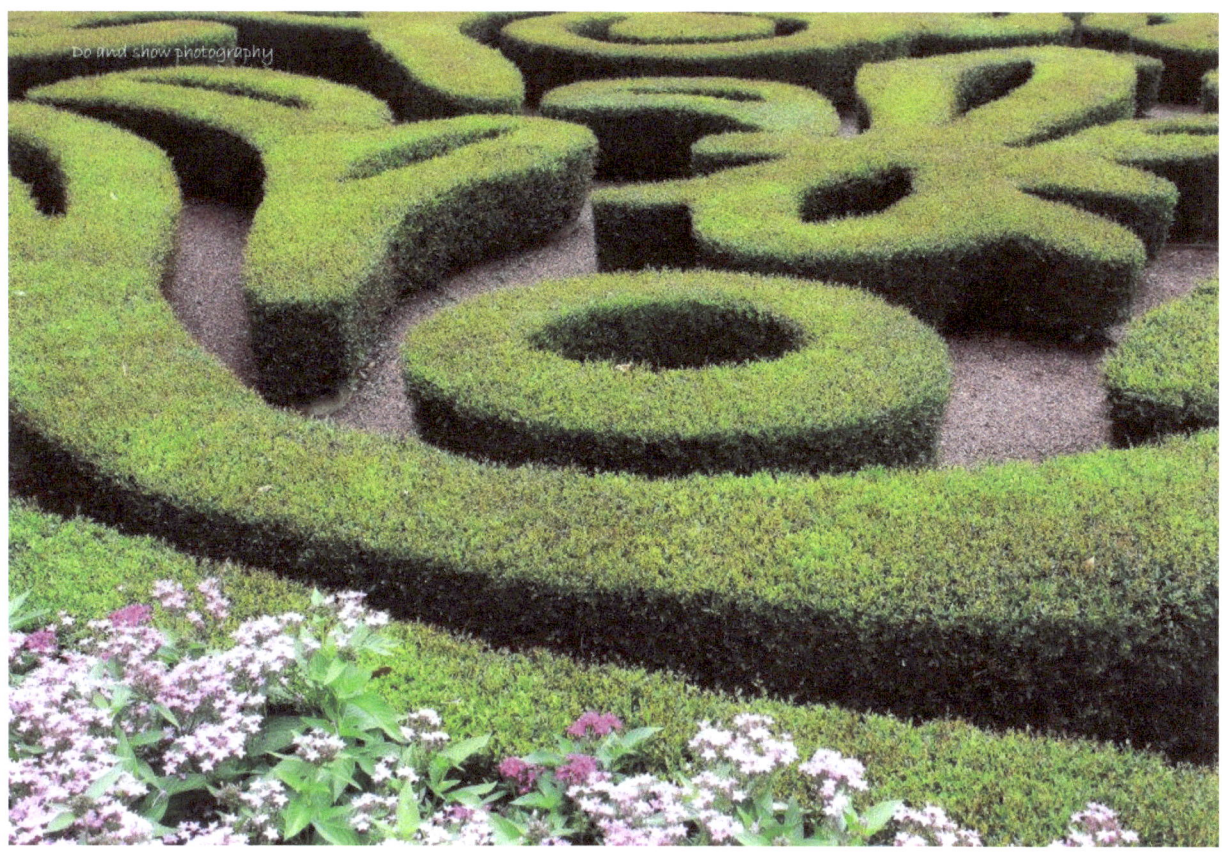

I love walking in gardens. I am so appreciative for their natural beauty and how they make me feel. There are endless ways they could be designed. That's another area for me to express my deep gratitude for, areas where I can exercise my creativity. It's just so very exciting!

Gratitude-enhancing ideas: if you live in an apartment, you can perhaps make a miniature garden in a wooden box or a glass bowl, using succulents, lithops, and other small plants. Lithops are a type of succulents but with even thicker, fleshier plant parts (leaves/stems). They almost look like colorful rocks. Design a maze with your child. Put it together from cardboard. If you have small pets like hamsters or turtles, they could go around in it. Hedge mazes are a lovely way to enhance the look of a garden. In a large garden in the back of your house, you can sow the seeds or plant seedlings in a shape of mazes. Gardening can certainly become a way to release stress and make your soul fly.

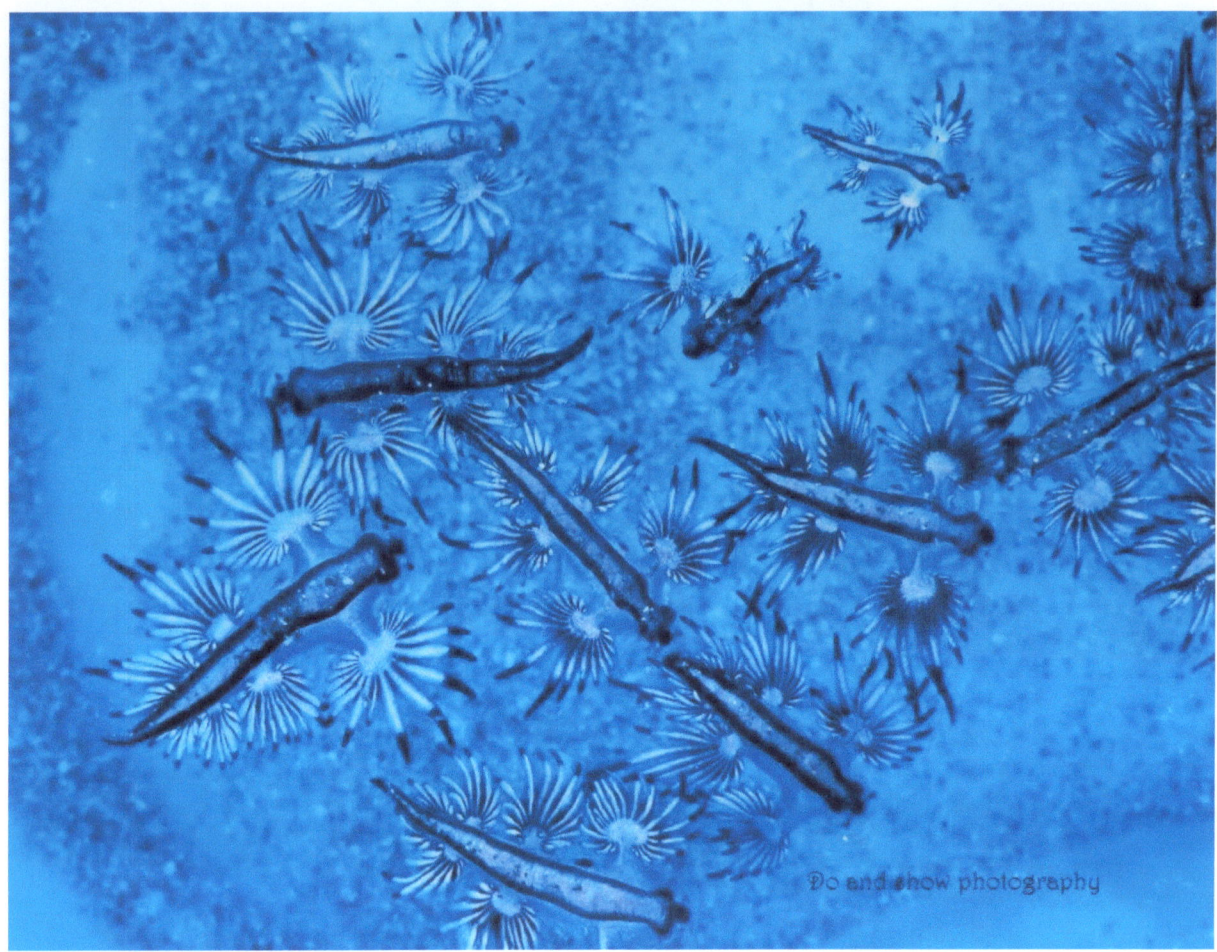

Ahhh, these are blue glaucus, or sea slugs in a blue pail. I am in aw, with so much gratitude towards exotic and unique creatures, and for having the fortune to be able to observe, touch and photograph them. Do you know what they feed on? Portuguese man o'war jellyfish and their stinging cells! How amazing is that! They store these stinging cells in their own tissues, which makes them a little dangerous to touch. The animal kingdom is so incredible, and when I have the honor to watch creatures like these, the first thing that comes out of my mouth is "wow".

Gratitude-enhancing ideas: share experiences as such with your children. You'll make their day. Recreate them through art. Another name for them is blue dragon. Try out various techniques to make blue dragons: painting or drawing them, sculpting them, sewing, mosaic, cutting and pasting paper pieces together, or even in the kitchen by preparing blue jelly. Here's another great gift idea, or to do it together with your kids. Picking photos from the net about exotic animals and plants, and by adding some details about them, you can create a photobook, completely designed by you, or your children. It's a great way to enrich your knowledge and theirs.

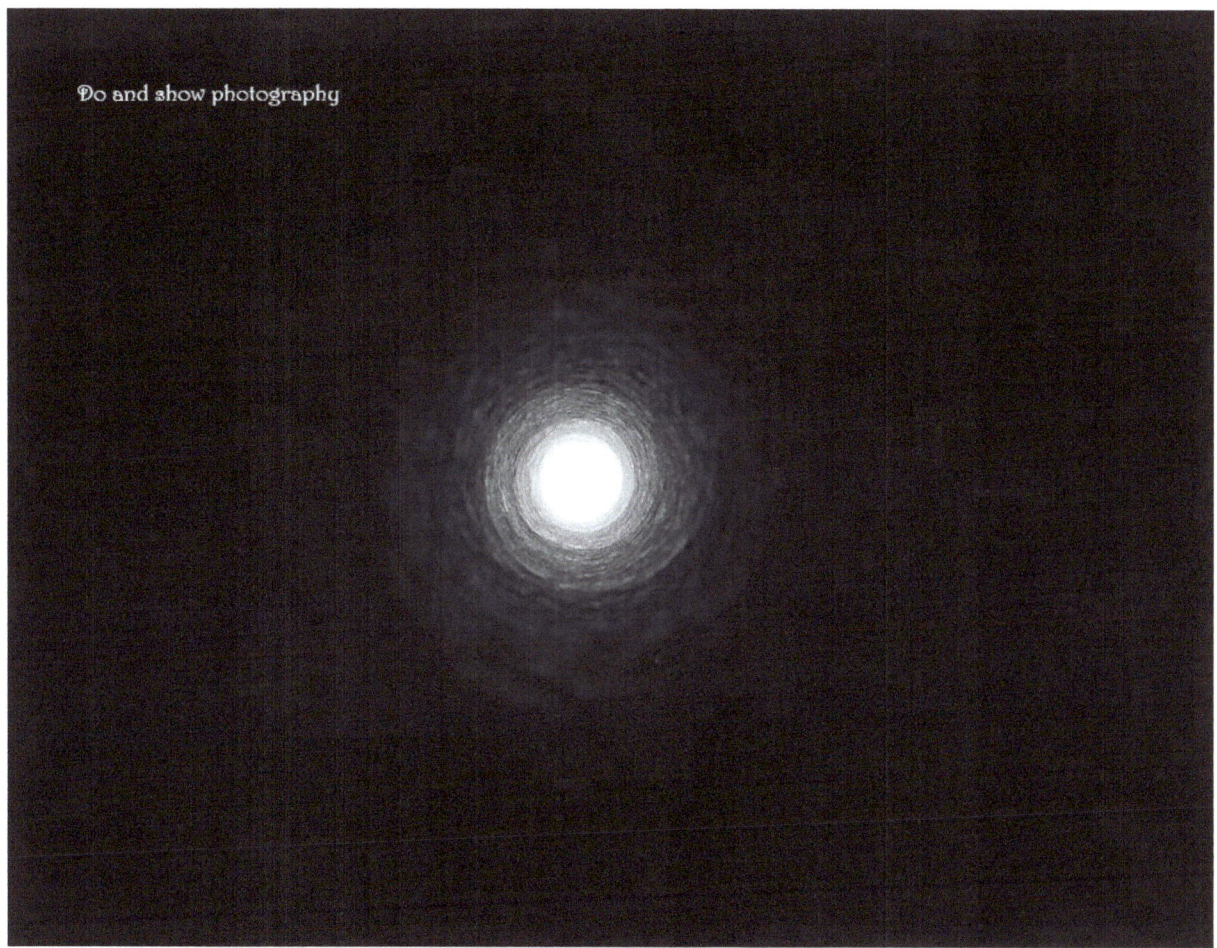

Can you guess what this is? Many people have found it captivating. It's actually a long paper tube inside. I am so thankful for having a photographic eye and feeling enraptured by everyday items when photographed in a particular angle or light. This reminds me of how things are in life too. When you look at something boring or not so great from another angle or under a different light, it can become a real beauty or mesmerizing sight.

Gratitude-enhancing ideas: sometimes just stop your mind getting way too busy with what needs to be done for the clients or what you will cook for dinner, and pull yourself back to reality that is right there. Look at common objects. Find something interesting about them. Look through the lens of your camera and see how they would look within frames from a certain angle. If you appreciate minimalism or abstract art, a light switch or curled up sheets of paper can become an elegant piece of framed wall art for your living room!

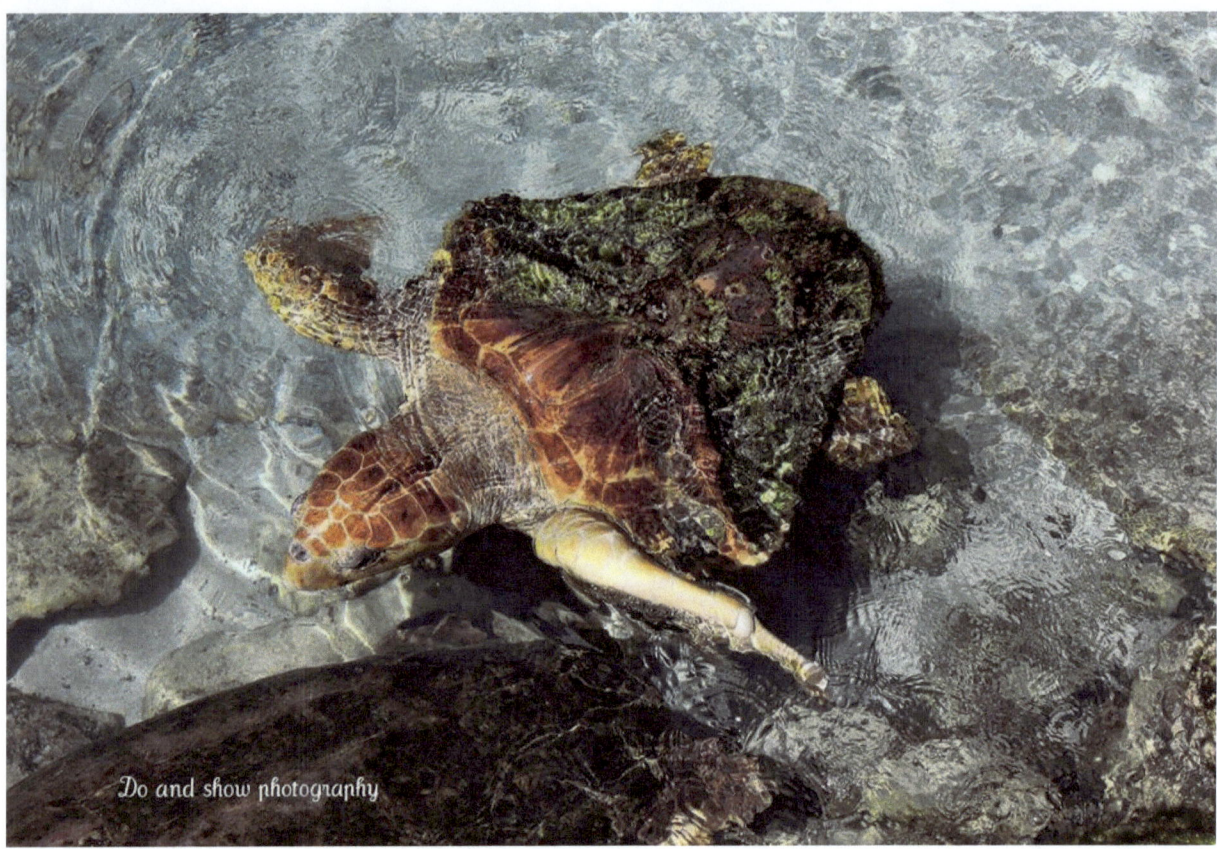

I feel very grateful for animal rescue workers who help injured animals to recover and live on. I am also thankful for my re-programmed mind that now I am right away focusing on the fact how people help instead of how they have caused the problem in the first place. This sea turtle was injured severely by the propeller of a speedboat in South Florida. As you can tell, a large part of his shell is gone. In the sea aquarium they nurtured him back to health.

Gratitude-enhancing ideas: while humans do contribute or directly cause a large number of accidents or harm to other living creatures, many people are also very resilient and determined to reverse the damage or save animals. You get to choose along with your family in which group you live your life. I believe that consciously learning, and I mean devoting time and effort to get familiar with the pressing challenges and issues of our only home, earth, should be every person's partial agenda. It's not our future anymore. It's really becoming our present more and more. Huge shifts in an alarming direction are happening already in front of our eyes. Make sure your children are up to date with information and encouraged often to take steps towards restoring the healthy circumstances for all living beings on this planet.

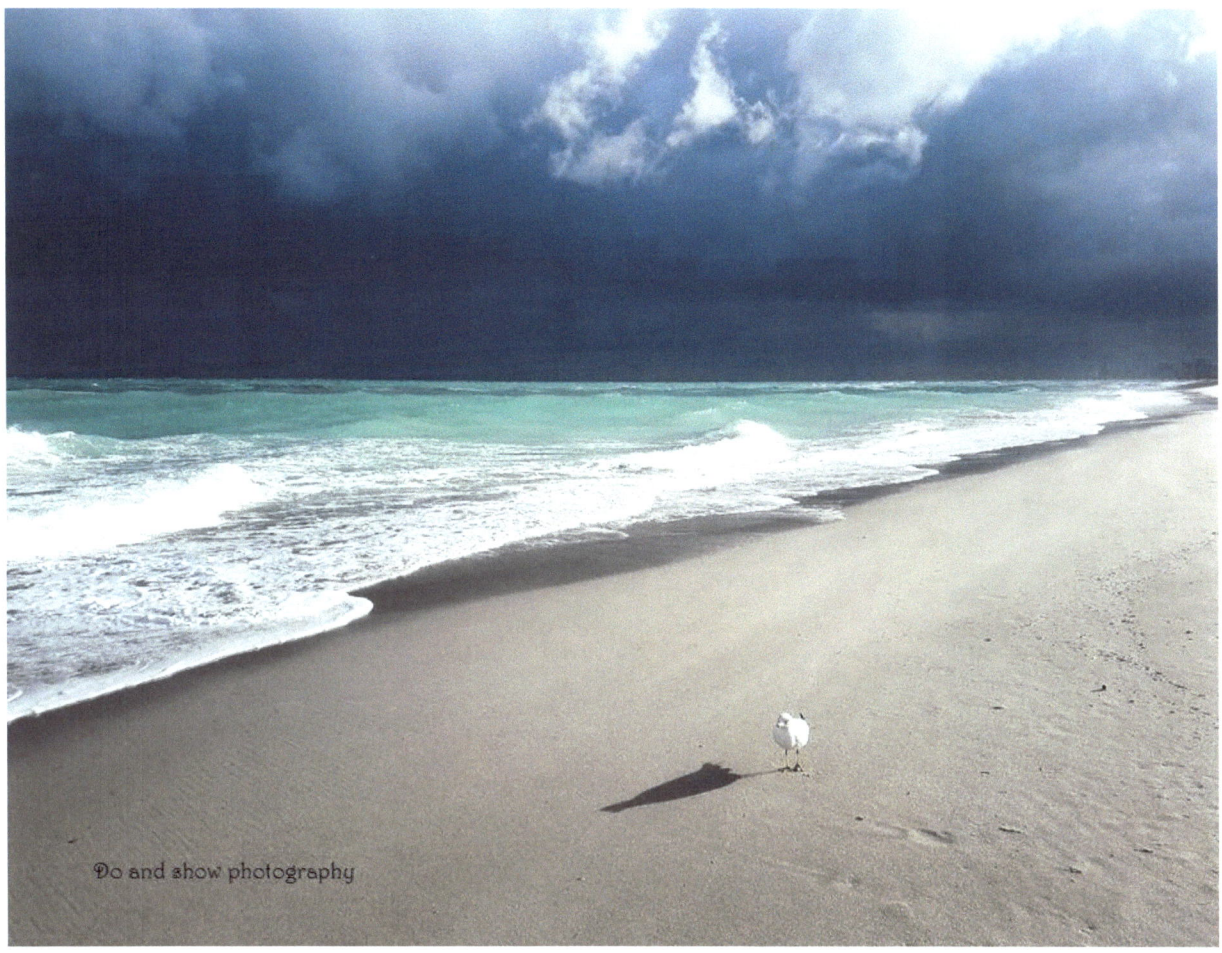

I know this picture looks like a painting with exaggerated colors, but it's an actual photograph of mine from the beach where I live. I have to express my huge gratitude for breathtaking moments like this one. The storm clouds were approaching from the ocean side, at the same time, the noon sun was shining very bright on the land side generating this picturesque seascape. I couldn't believe my eyes for a while, but it was real!

Gratitude-enhancing ideas: these kinds of moments don't come very frequently. If you'd like to catch them, you have to make a choice sometimes to drop everything and run out there to get close to it. That's what I do. Sometimes we must allow ourselves to deter from our planned route and schedules and enjoy spontaneity. The special moments are for those who don't wait and take time for capturing them.

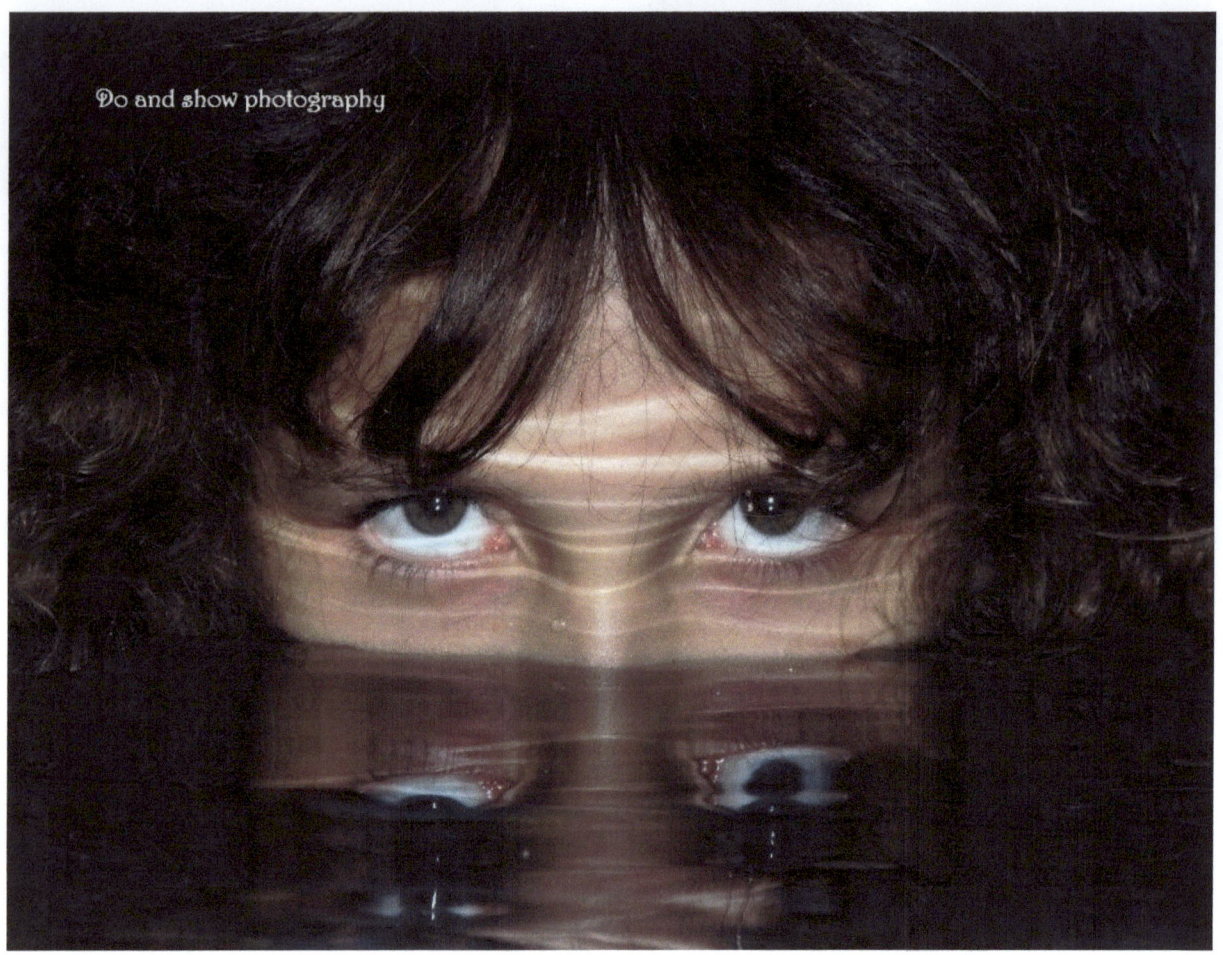

I am extremely captivated and thankful for my beautiful and powerful brain. It's been over 15 years that I've started studying the human mind. I've learned so much about it, and what is even more important that I've been implementing lots of it. Do you believe you – because of your mind – are absolutely powerful!? I totally believe it and have been witnessing the evidence of it on a daily basis. I understand now well that my decisions do matter and impact other living beings' lives. I realize the huge weight and responsibility in this, … also, the power itself.

Gratitude-enhancing ideas: besides learning about your brain regularly, keeping also up with the latest research and study results, I highly recommend doing some brain exercises. I do them daily because I want to have a sharp cognitive thinking, great memory, problem-solving skills and creativity into a very old age. Also, I think the key to living life more fulfilled and happily is to not only learn how our minds work, keep us safe, and sort of trick us into believing things, but we must begin implementing what we have learned. I've started following Jim Kwik, who is known worldwide about his abilities to read super-fast, calculate in his head incredibly well, and memorize and recall a large amount of data. He has excellent, few-minute long, daily exercises to enhance your brain's abilities. Definitely, daily meditation should be inserted into your schedule. Even if just for a few minutes a day. Whether you play tranquil music in the background, or you do it in silence, focus on your breathing which you consciously have slowed down, count slowly up or down, or focus on a serene scene, or a particular color, but get yourself into the habit of daily meditation. As an ongoing exercise, observe how your mind reacts or responds to certain events and triggers. Instead of beating yourself or mind up for it, admire and become curious what might be hidden behind all this. Use your mind to outsmart your mind! Sounds silly or paradoxical? Since you have conscious and subconscious minds, you can start utilizing your conscious mind to get your subconscious more under your control. I could write a whole book on this topic, but for now, I'd like you to understand that your mind does most of the things/decisions/reactions to keep you safe, first of all, and ensure your basic needs are met. All the decisions you make are based on your belief system. Your beliefs are what you have accumulated throughout the years and decades; they are basically thoughts that got confirmed over and over again. This, of course, doesn't make them necessarily true. What seemed to be true or worked for you ages ago, doesn't mean it stills stands true and serves you well. So, simply, allow yourself to become more aware of your own thinking habits and patterns. To close my lines for this subtopic, I'd like to bring it to your attention how often you hear that people have defeated the odds because of their will or determination to accomplish something. It's absolutely enchanting how the human mind is and what it's capable of. Remind yourself of this frequently.

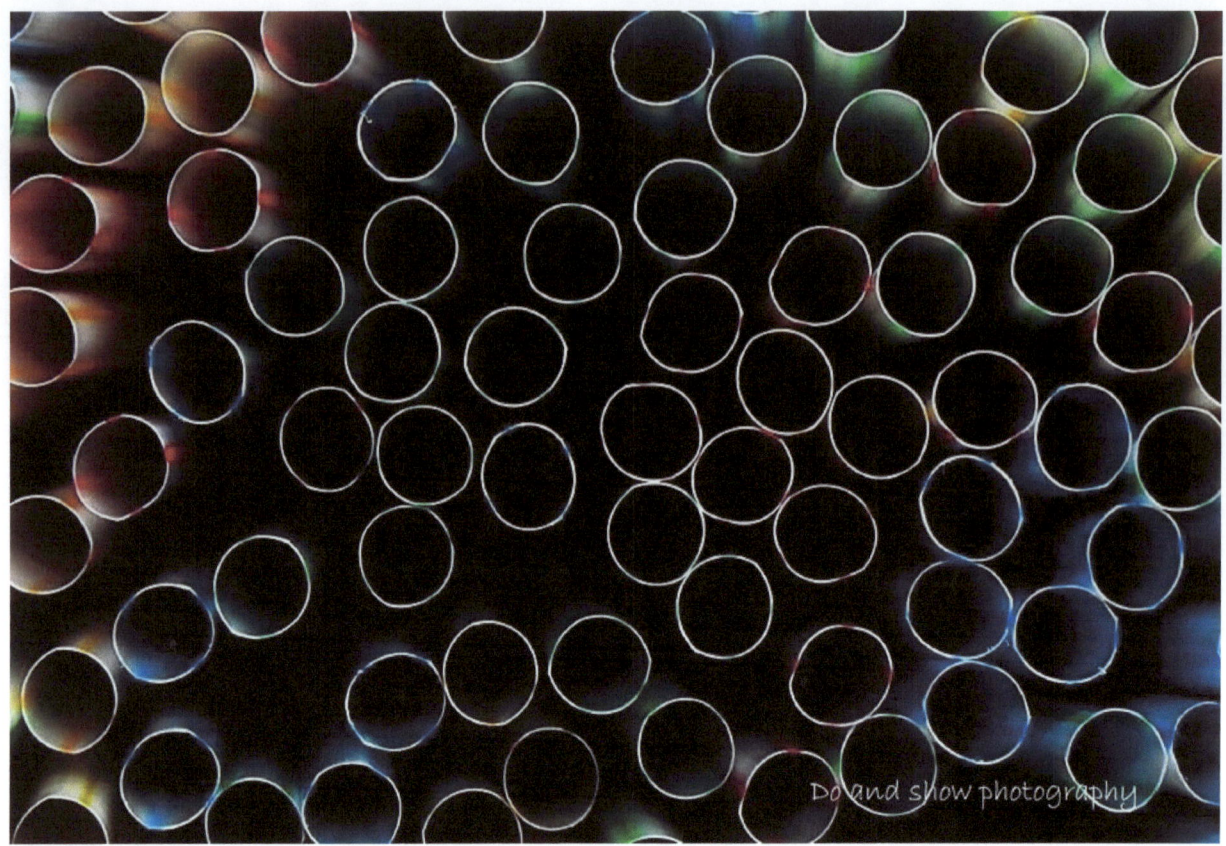

While plastic is a huge pollution concern for our planet, it did help humanity in countless ways, and I'd like to take the moment to express my gratitude for that. However, now I am much more focused on reducing plastic waste. In some occasions, plastic, like these plastic straws do make an interesting photo. I believe humans can come up with a number of solutions to decrease the amount of plastic manufactured and used in the variety of areas. It's a great challenge, and as such, it provides a big opportunity to grow.

Gratitude-enhancing ideas: I am sure you know what I am going to say here. Keep on finding ways to replace plastic with biodegradable materials. Teach your children about it too. Search actively for items that don't add to earth's toxicity. There are now utensils and plates that are biodegradable. Reuse shopping bags. Buy wooden toys instead of plastic ones whenever you can. Use glass or stainless-steel straws. Put food, drink and other items also into glass or paper containers instead of plastic ones. Your children need to follow in your steps with this kind of mentality. Support their curiosity by listening fully to their ideas and reasoning. Do your best to answer their questions. Keep them excited about solving problems. You never know when any teenager (it's happened before), or your teenage son or daughter would spark an amazing idea to solve this crisis.

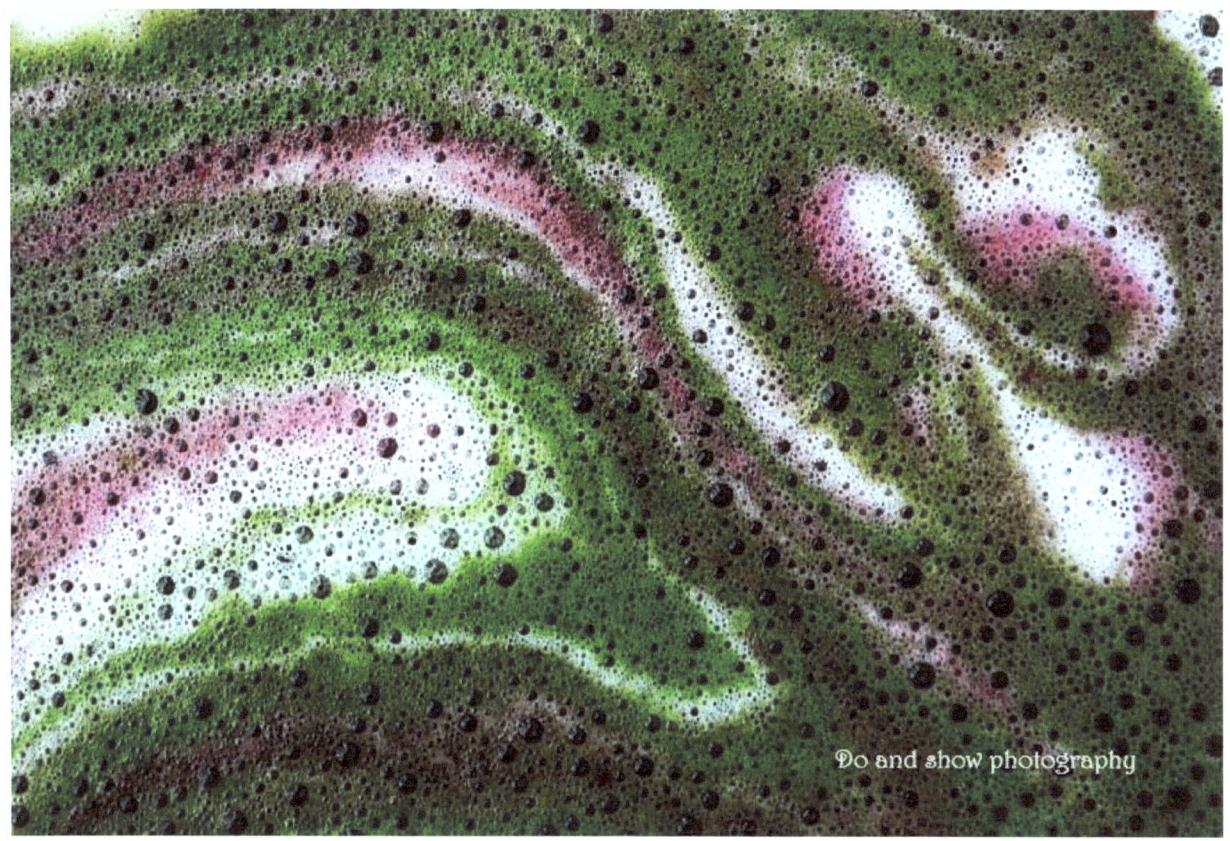

Wow! Look at that! Lovely swirls of colors and bubbles are in my freshly made juice. I am so thankful for my juicer and blender that help me prepare these delicious, nutritious and health-supportive smoothies and juices every morning. My gratitude is endless towards all the goodies from the gardens I can put into these machines, so I can support my body with care. They are truly wonderful stimuli for all my senses.

Gratitude-enhancing ideas: don't get nervous or uneasy around homemade juices and smoothies. They don't take a lot of time to prepare, and you'll know exactly what you put into them. Oh, and let's not forget the love energy you also add to these beverages. Everything is ultimately energy, so I believe your love towards those you make your liquid food for will transfer into it. Be patient with yourself. Explore a lot. Listen to your senses and taste buds. You don't have to rigidly follow anyone's recipe really. Remember, they, who created those recipes are people just like you. Don't let any unpleasant outcome discourage you. Just keep on adding, taking away, tweaking, etc. Use the recipes as guidelines. The most important point may be to keep your focus on why you juice, how it cleanses your cells, how it provides you with larger amount of nutrients and antioxidants and faster than if you'd want to eat all those ingredients instead.

Here are a few points to consider when you make juices and smoothies. Juicing requires a big amount of produce, and they should be cleaned and peeled. To clean a juicer also takes longer time than to clean a blender. However, one glass of juice will provide you with much more nutrients and antioxidants than the same amount of smoothie because smoothies have added water or milk. Juicing really means extracting the fruits' or vegetables' own juice. Both beverages have to be consumed soon after being made. Remember, it's a "live" food meaning unheated, minimally processed, unpreserved, chemical-free (especially if organic), therefore, it attracts bacteria and fungi. Those boogers know what to feed on, and that's not junk or processed foods. The various ingredients may separate in their sitting, so it's also more appealing when consumed fresh. For a juice, always add more vegetables than fruits because the juicer strips them of their fiber which would slow down the sugar absorption into the bloodstream. So, plain fruit juice has lots of natural sugar. It's still much better than refined white sugar products but it's sugar. Vegetables contain less sugar than fruits. A great base for both, juices and smoothies: cucumber, celery stalk, greens, lettuce, bok choy, jicama root. Choose high water-content produce, and preferably organic and fresh. For smoothies, you can slip in soaked seeds and nuts, avocado, banana and even dry fruits if you wish because you will pour in some liquid. Don't add too much though because it still should be a thick liquid consistency and not like a dip. Again, explore to find your preference in terms of pulp amount. I also love making smoothies with fresh aloe gel, turmeric and ginger roots, black pepper to unlock the turmeric's immune-system supporting compounds, and even bee pollen which seems to be the most complete food on earth. These ingredients should be used in small amounts, of course, and you won't taste them in your drink. A mount of evidence suggest that they act as powerful foods when it comes to creating a better health. (according to Mercola's website, or Livestrong, just to mention a couple).

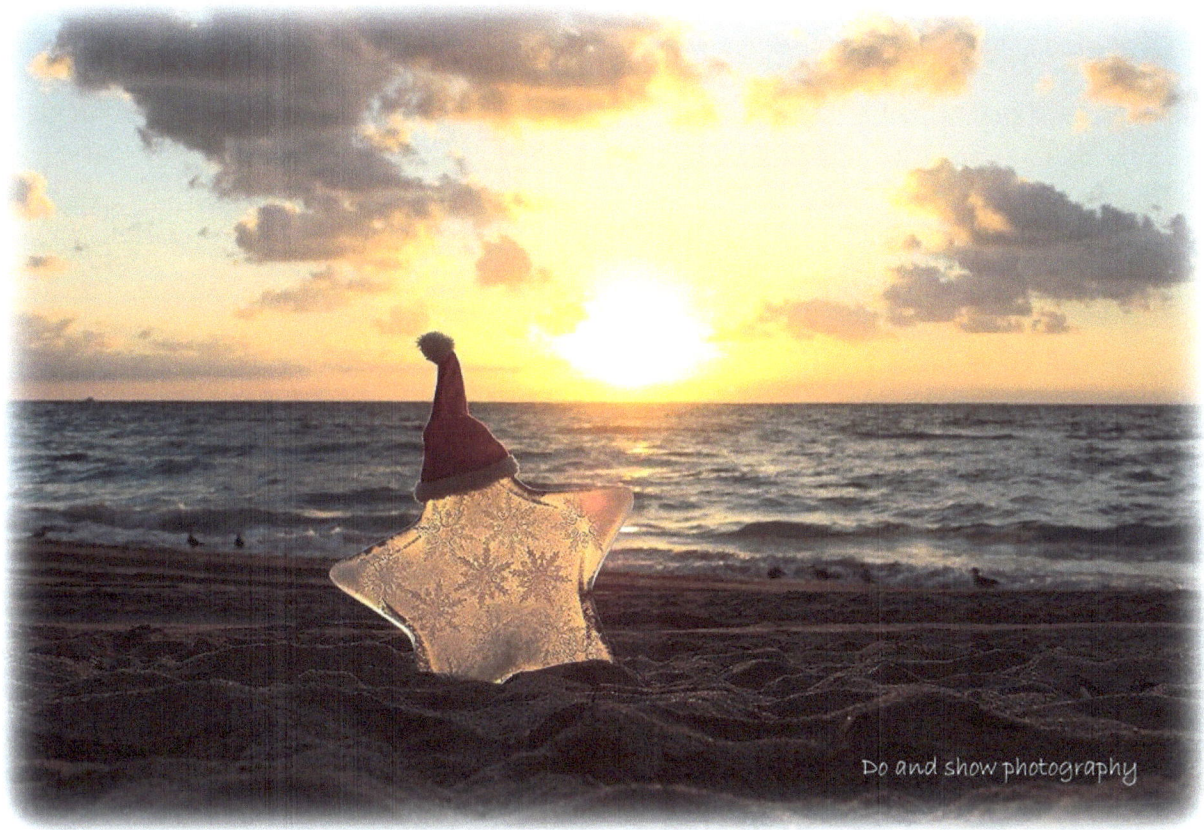

Christmas is my favorite time of the year besides summer. I am so very-very thankful for all the heartwarming memories I have gathered in my heart and mind throughout many holiday seasons. The music, the decorations, the great gatherings, the handmade gifts I create every single year ever since I was a little girl, … the scent of the pine tree. I've tried to figure it out what exactly, and I mean exactly Christmas brings me that mesmerizes me so very much that other holidays or events don't give me. I think it's the overflowing peace and love, knowing that I am cared for and loved, and I belong. All that. And of course, not needing to go to school or work, because in my case, I never had to, at Christmas time. I am not against studying and work, but we all need a break when we are allowed to just be, enjoy, create, love and have fun.

Gratitude-enhancing ideas: yes, I've known numerous people who don't get excited about the holidays or can't even stand them for various reasons. If you are one of those who feels this way, may I try to invite you to test out the idea of opening your mind again to find the beauty in this sparkling season beside the ugliness or sorrow you may have experienced in the past? It's not what happens with us but how we respond to it matters. Whatever sad or horrible thing has happened with you or your loved one on this holiday, you can disassociate it from Christmas, if you really want to. I don't say it's like walk in the park. It does take effort, determination and work, but doable. Humans, remember, are extremely powerful. I lost my father to a debilitating genetic disease, but I learned to understand by clinging onto his painful memory will not make my life or anyone's better in any way. I am sure he wouldn't have wanted it either. How to get then into the holiday mood? First, you need to be willing and open to do so. You must let go of the guilt or resentment you have been holding onto. If you believe you shouldn't celebrate or feel happy when that sorrowful time comes around each year, your subconscious mind will sabotage your efforts. Whatever has happened, it's in the past. It's done. It cannot be changed. What can be changed is how you look at it. As Dr. Wayne Dyer said, "when you change the way you look at things the things you look at change". Drop that heavy burden for good. You deserve to enjoy life, every day, every hour and every minute of it. Afterwards, you might want to start playing the holiday music a lot, make presents for loved ones, greeting cards, projects, science experiments and arts and crafts with your children, nieces and nephews. Brainstorm ideas regarding home décor and holiday dinner recipes. Make Christmas tree ornaments from wire and glass beads like on the picture below, or a big Christmas tree from felt with buttons sewn up to hang up laminated paper ornaments for your child like you see on the photo. Recycle old clothes by sewing the pieces together into a giant snake for your child to play with. Say "YES" to the happy holidays! These are just a very few ideas from the millions. I know from personal experience, it can be extremely heartwarming and captivating when you come up with a gift idea, you make it with your own hands, and pour your heart into it for your loved one. Enjoy!

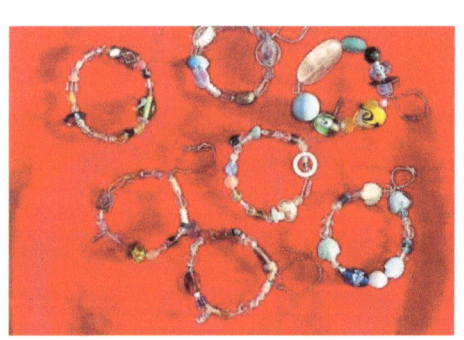
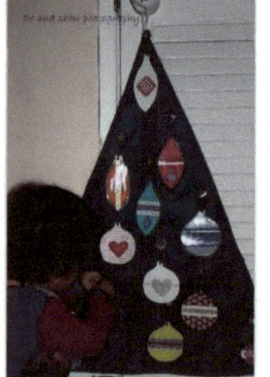
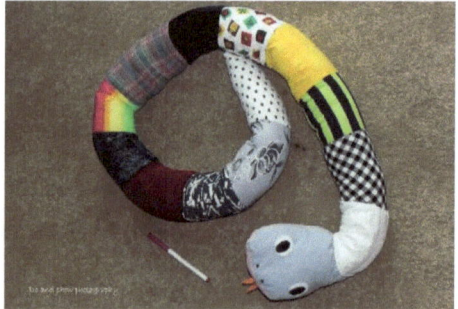

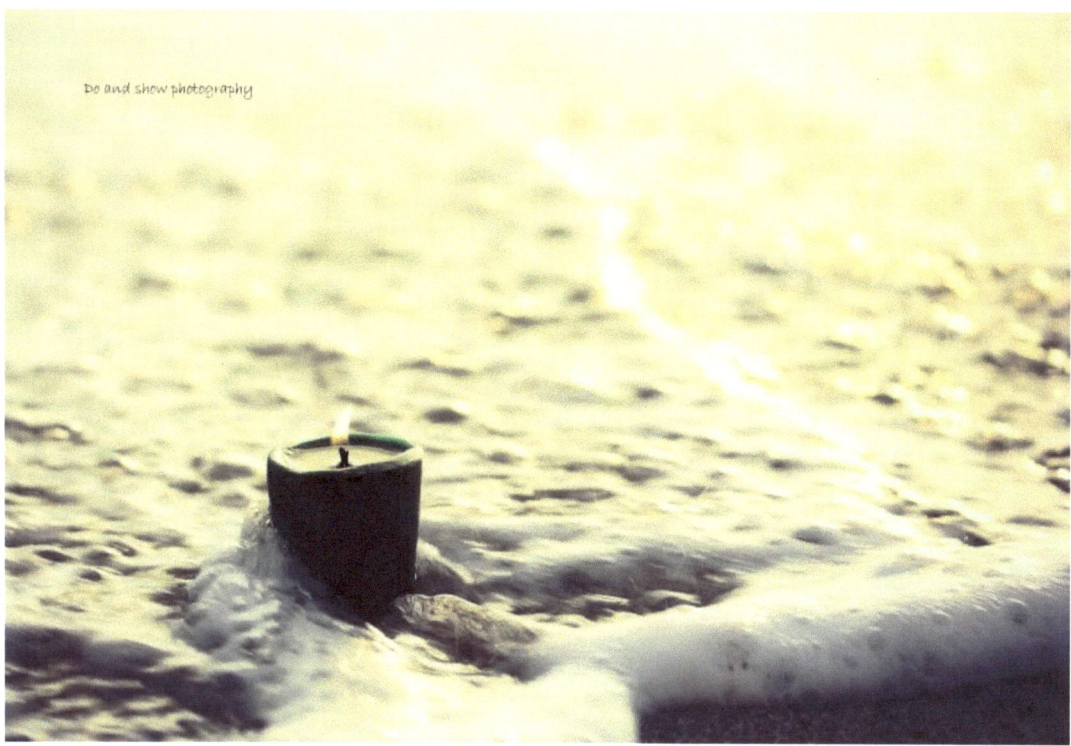

I used to have allergic reactions to candles as a young child. It's all gone now, but at any blackouts when we used candles, I developed fever and rash. Now, I feel very thankful for candles, especially the healthier kinds. They give off lovely scents, light up rooms to a very cozy degree, and serve a great purpose on a birthday cake. When my father passed away, I couldn't go to his funeral. I was living thousands of miles away, and it happened right after the twin towers collapsed. So, I lit a candle for him every day for a while. It made me feel I was doing something for his funeral this way.

Gratitude-enhancing ideas: my first thought would be for you is to use high quality candles, preferably from beeswax. According to benefits-of-honey.com, for example, beeswax candles are healthier, burn brighter and longer, environmentally friendly and nontoxic, hypo-allergenic, and a natural ionizer. Yes, they do cost more than common paraffin candles. Quality has its price. You can also make your own candles, involving your little older children, if you are up to it, and that can be real fun! Imagine using nontraditional containers for pouring the melted wax into like empty orange peel bowl, or coconut shell, or even a real sea shell. Carve some space out in apples or squashes where you can place tealights, for the November-December holidays. Enjoy candles around your relaxing bathtub. Here are some unconventional uses of candle wax. You can use it on your squeaky door hinges and stuck zipper. You can waterproof your postage stamp and address line on packages. I have used wax on fraying shoelaces as well.

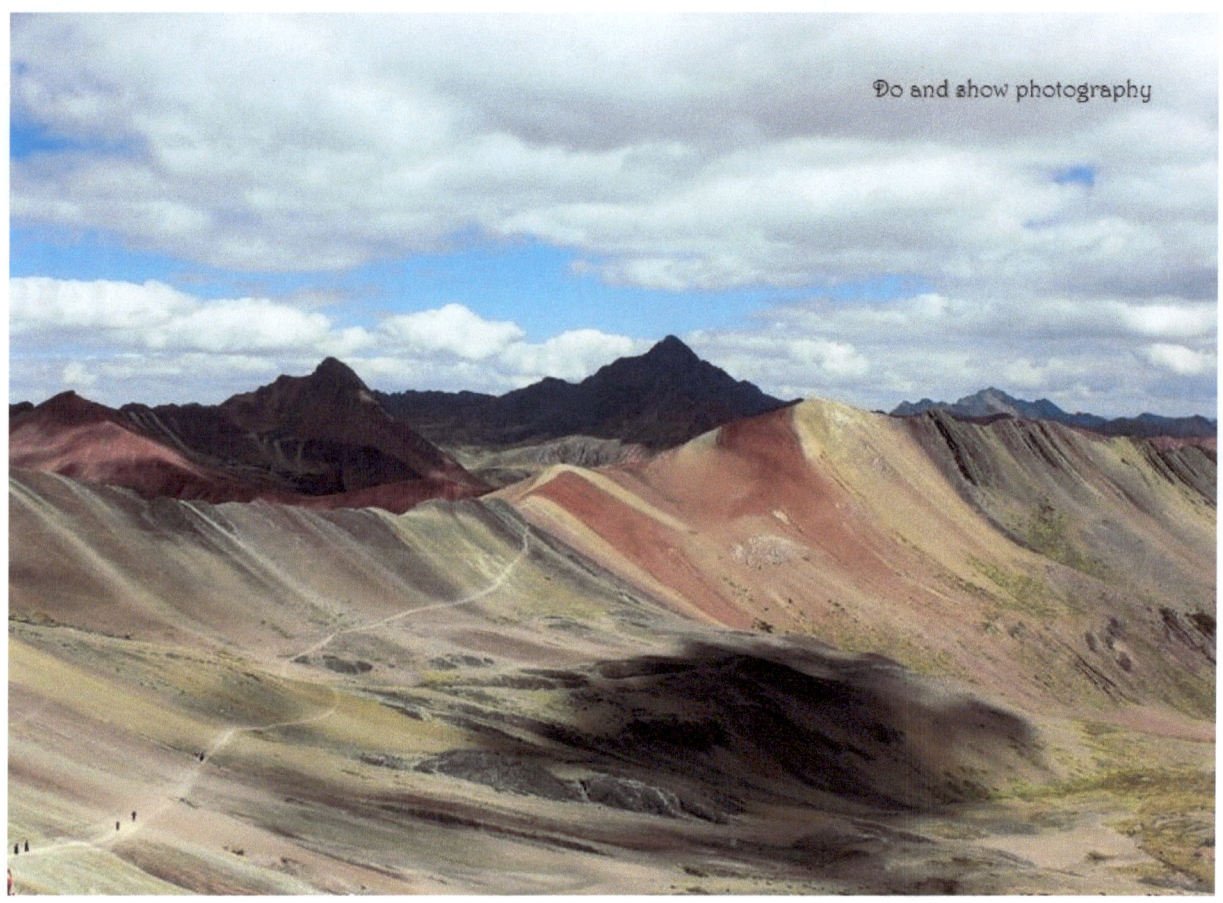

This is Vinicunca or Rainbow Mountain in the Andes, in Peru. Isn't it dreamy that we can see rainbows even in peaks of a mountain? I feel so very grateful for taking this absolutely strenuous, 6-hour-long hike to lay my eyes on this beauty. It's at a very high, approximately 17,000 feet high altitude which got me really altitude sick by the end of the day but it was all worth it. I went for it. I looked at it as a great challenge that I wanted to overcome as a passionate hiker but inexperienced climber. I also live at the sea level, so my body isn't used to high altitude at all. I feel we must have a great deal of gratitude for challenging situations. They are the only way to grow and improve skills. Just to sprinkle some more details: after the first few steps when we arrived with the bus from Cuzco, I felt short of breath already. The energy started to disappear from my legs. So, I rented a horse, as I was suggested. Many people did the same. Those who didn't, they were walking beside me silently and many of them didn't make it all the way to the top. Even riding a horse, it was extremely difficult and trying. The horse couldn't go all the way to the end, so I had to climb the last section myself. On the top, it was very freezing. On the way back, I began feeling lightheaded but managed to arrive back to the bus. Some people needed an airlift. I love hiking, but I am not a climber and I've never learned how to do it either. It was an amazing achievement and I have thought of it many times how grateful I feel that I made that decision instead of running or turning away from it.

Gratitude-enhancing ideas: aiming for a more active lifestyle generally tends to ensure a fitter and healthier body on a long run as long as we also pay attention to safety. I recommend starting hiking on a regular basis, or if you are already an avid hiker, then keep on doing it. On the other hand, I'd like to point it out how to approach challenges. From my own personal experience, I can tell you ever since I've been calling problems challenges and I am looking at them as such, I feel much more capable, stronger and smarter to deal with any situation. I place lots of focus on self-growth, therefore I appreciate challenges because I am very aware that without challenges I couldn't grow. I invite you to try the same and see how it feels for you, but also, give it some time. One of my positive affirmations is this: "I welcome challenges, self-discipline and discomfort in my life." When I welcome it, I can make it work for me. When I dislike it, I reject it, and that shifts the focus on the wrong things. What I resist, persists.

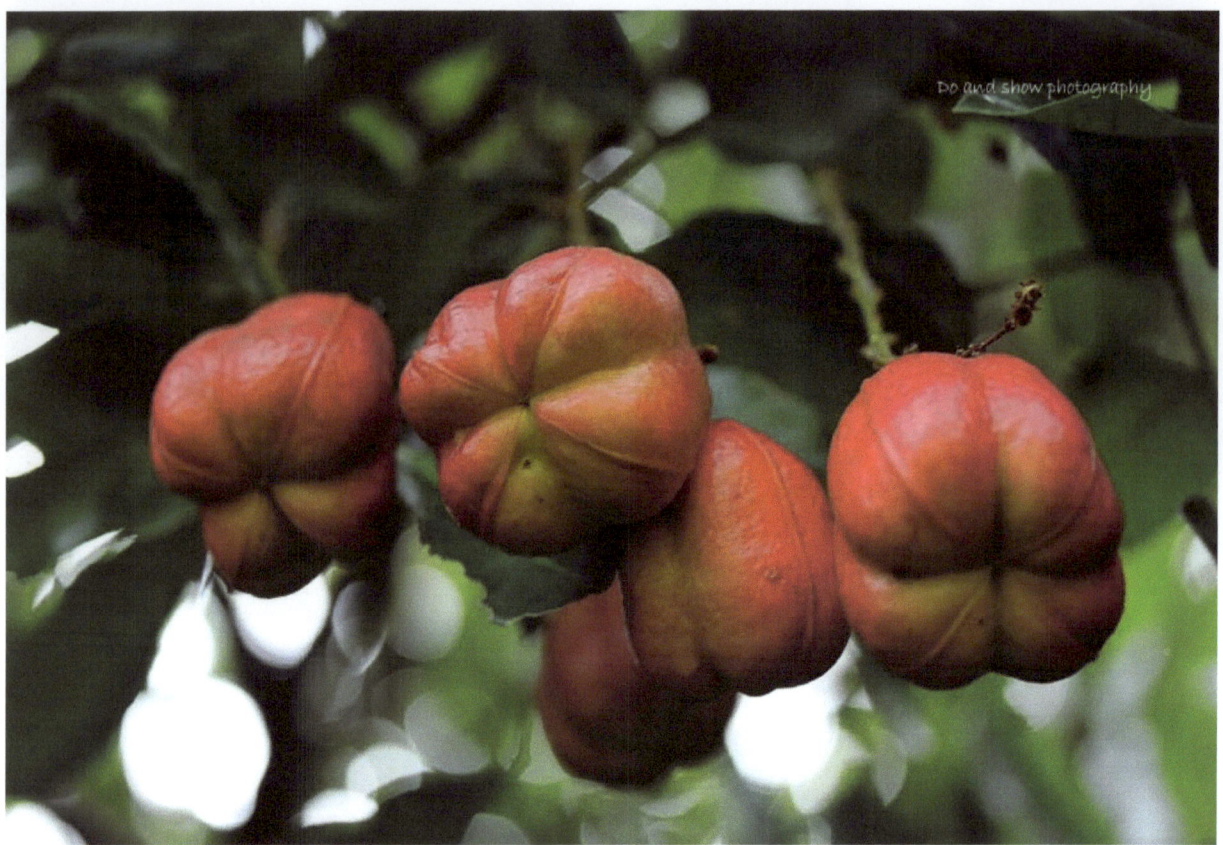

I am very thankful for living in these modern times for numerous reasons, and one of them is that now humans know most of the poisonous fruits out there and warn you with signs about them. The fruit above is a poisonous one, however, it looks very beautiful. I have always been extremely interested in exotic plants and fruits. I also love trying out new ones. Being curious is a great quality but it can come with risk, obviously.

Gratitude-enhancing ideas: I suggest you to practice open-mindedness. It could serve you very well on the long run. Try exotic foods but from reputable resources. Learn about poisonous plants and venomous animals, and take necessary precautions always. Besides, admire their uniqueness and beauty, their self-defense which is the main reason usually to evolve into poisonous and venomous living organisms.

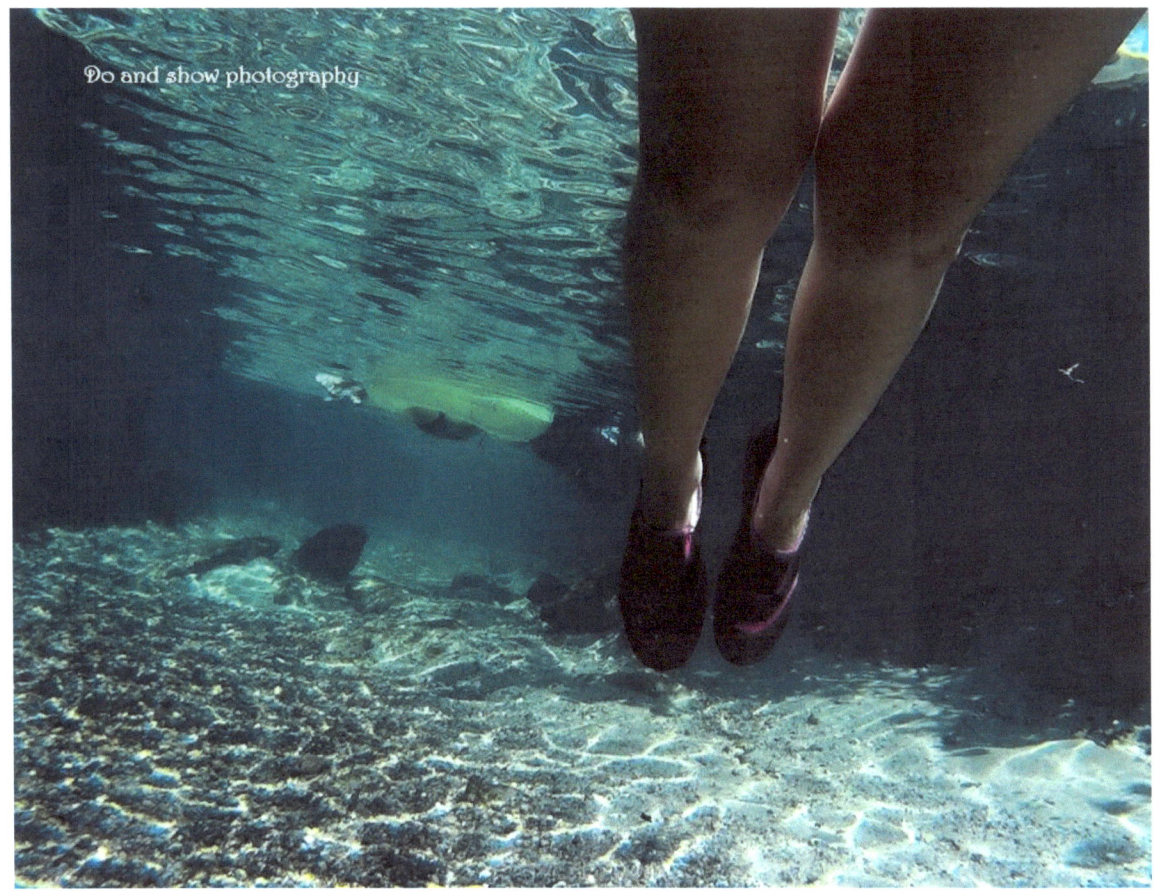

I have to express my endless gratitude for any clear bodies of water, and for my waterproof camera to capture all this beauty. Not many words needed, I guess to describe their wonderful advantages of crystal-clear waters. I've always been amazed by it. It also makes it much easier to see what is down there, of course, as well as feeling more secure regarding the water quality and hazards towards my health and safety. I often can't keep my eyes off of the unique patterns the sunrays create on the bottom of the waterbed. Just so lovely.

Gratitude-enhancing ideas: swimming is said to be one of the most beneficial exercises for any body type and for most health conditions. It's not about the actual swimming per se, but seek out gorgeous natural places where you can swim in clear waters and let your inner child be entertained by the waves and the sun's play on the water. Observe animals and plants living below the water level. Allow yourself to be in awe. I've met clients who feel sort of embarrassed to let others see when they are really enjoying something. They consider showing their amazement as a weakness. Do you think you are like that, too? How about trying to go the other way for once and see how it feels? It could be very freeing.

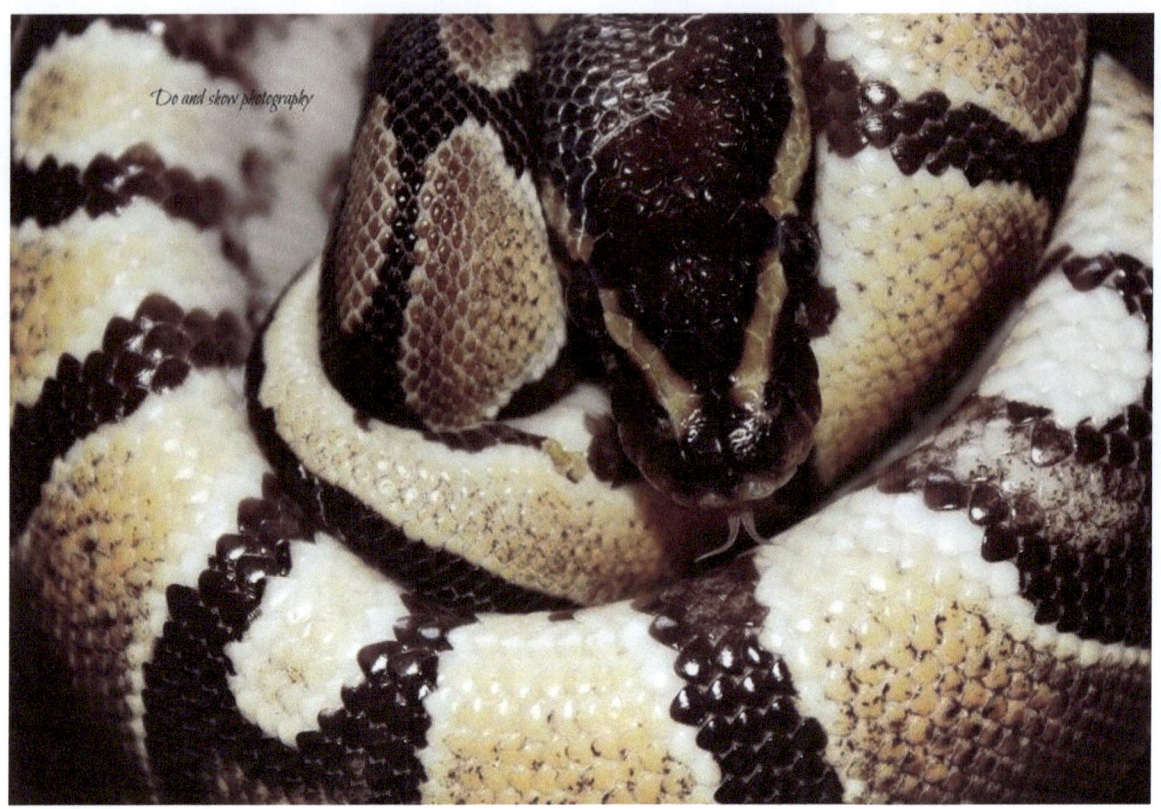

I know lots of people hate or dread snakes of all kinds. I used to be a girl who was very afraid of snakes or encountering snakes on my travels. To face my fear, I got myself a baby ball python. I kept playing with the idea for over a year, but in the end, I ended up buying one. It's been three years, and I have fallen in love with him. I feel so grateful for having him in my home, being able to watch him how he eats, sheds, moves around and flicks his tongue. I do play with him, too. It's a gorgeous animal with jaw dropping qualities. For instance, the way he sheds it amazes me each time. So smartly slithers around and about his enclosure rubbing his body and head against the wooden logs. He has taught me a lot. All animals do, actually. And while I really adore furry pets and animals, when I feed him the frozen, furry rat, I've learned to not feel sorry for the rat but completely switch my emotions and mindset into viewing it simply as food. Just to add, this kind of ability has been helping me out in other situations as well. Experiencing his wiggly-squeezing power on my body parts is a quite unique sensation. Snake-massage, anyone?

Gratitude-enhancing ideas: for one, look for ways to face your fears instead of running away from them or putting your head in the sand regarding them. Often what we fear it's because we don't know enough about it, and our imagination plays a tricky game with us. Get the facts and don't let your mind fool you. Your fear can actually turn into admiration like it's happened with me and my snake. For two, find value in the things you fear. No matter how hard it may be.

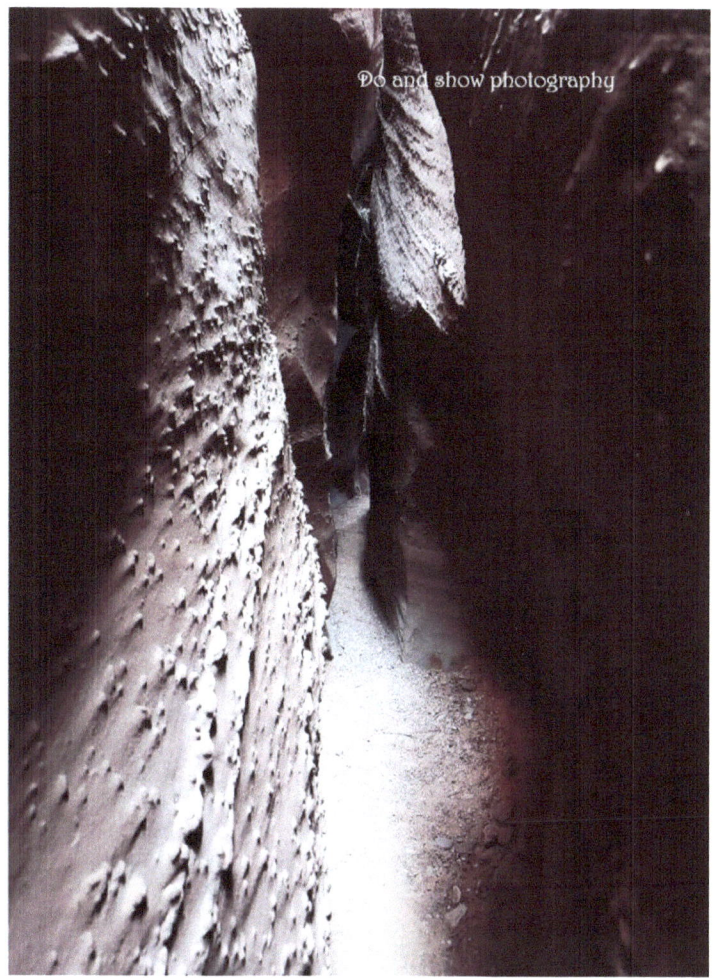

I've had a rather frightening experience going into this very narrow slot canyon in Utah. I didn't know I was claustrophobic till now. We just kept walking, squeezing through between the high walls, not knowing when it would end, and the panic struck me. Soon, we had to turn around. I am not sure if I'd ever go back, but I certainly am very thankful for this experience of a lifetime. I've found it captivating and stunning regardless my feeling of anxiety.

Gratitude-enhancing ideas: we learn more when we go through the experience. Why would I want to deny that to myself? I highly recommend you to put yourself through undesired experiences also, of course exercise caution always and know that you won't get hurt. When I hiked Rainbow Mountain, the same principles have driven me. I knew it would be great discomfort, but I wanted to try it anyway. I wanted to see how my brain responds to it. Great learning opportunities about myself. The whole life is about getting to know yourself, so don't hold back. Consciously don't pick only the joyrides. Have your ultimate goal to learn more about who you really are.

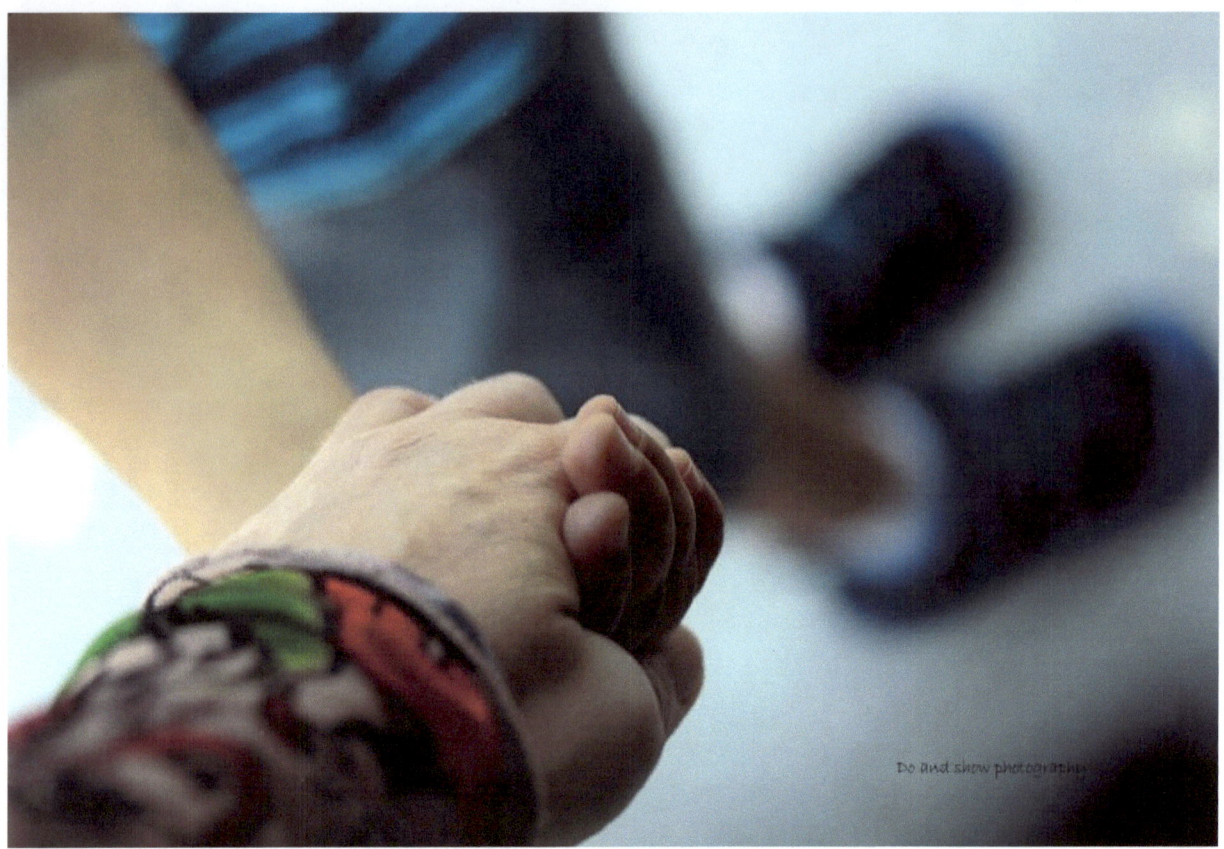

Gratitude shower! I feel so blessed for having my family and feeling their love every day in different forms. Love is energy that holds the world together, I believe. Being more physical with your loved ones is not only nice, and cute, but necessary for overall health, I believe. According to numerous sites, like thehealthy.com, hugging and physical touch reduce stress, build trust and feeling of appreciation, enhance self-esteem, boost immunity and could even be crucial for survival. Among animals, those that were patted compared to those that were neglected in this sense have shown signs of healthier appetite and behaviors. Children who are hugged a lot seem to develop more healthily as well.

Gratitude-enhancing ideas: you probably know that I will suggest you to begin hugging and holding hands more frequently. Don't feel afraid to show your feelings, your love and vulnerability. Let your loved ones know every single day how much you love them and care for them. You wouldn't want to wait to tell them when it's too late, would you? Show your love in various forms. By doing so, you'll feel so much better, and become a role model for them to copy you, and to realize it's a good way to live life. It's also the best way to create stronger relationships. Frequent hugs and hand-holding are acts of self-love as well.

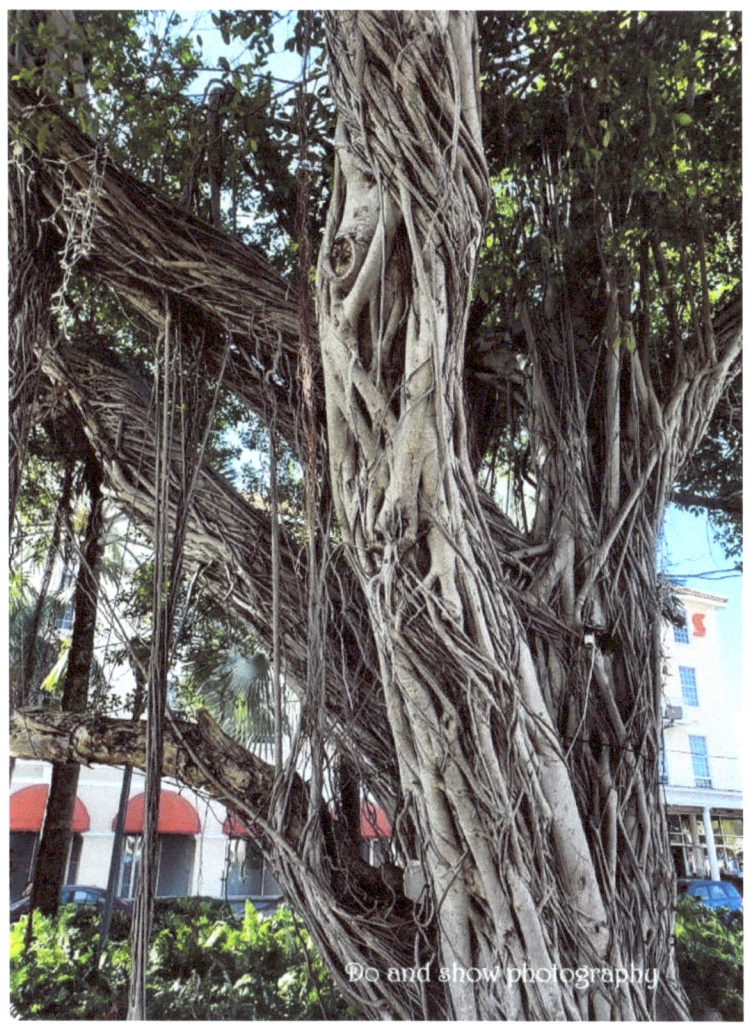

I feel so very grateful for trees, generally, and when I see trees like this one, I melt. All those roots woven across! Magnificent! It reminds me of being connected to everyone and everything. It also reminds me to always look for the root cause of issues. It's like nature keeps reminding us in countless ways how to live our lives more fulfilled. I am very thankful for these reminders, and inspirations. Life isn't easy, and we could use all the help we can get in order to create a fabulous life for ourselves.

Gratitude-enhancing ideas: I'd like you to ask yourself the question how often you think you go to the root cause of the problems. Are you a band aid-user-kind-of person trying to work things only at the surface? I've learned long ago to take time and effort to find the real cause of every issue in order to figure out a long-lasting solution. Try to recall how many times masking the problem has given you only a temporary solution, then things might have got even worse. Another thing is to remind yourself how connected we all are. Your actions will impact others.

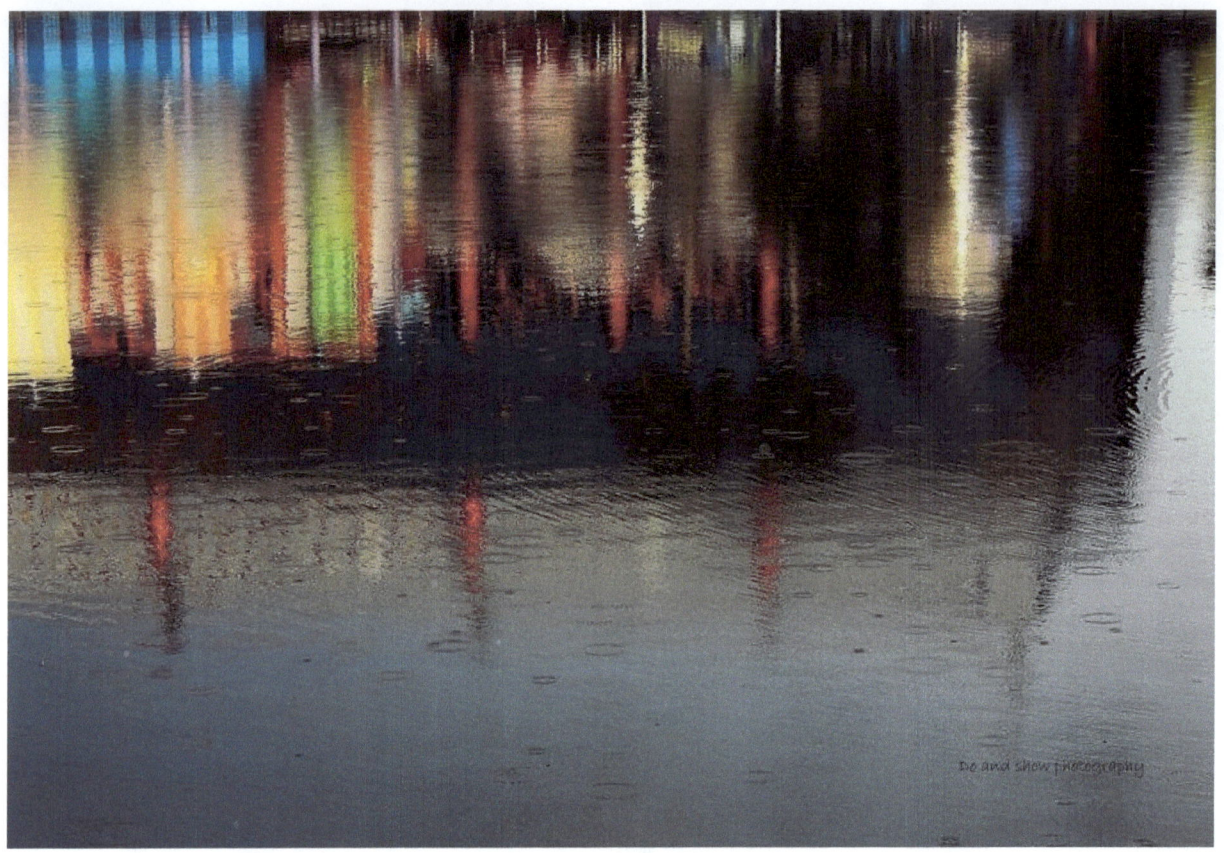

I am very thankful for all the colors around me and for my eyesight to be able to admire them all. Did you know the human eye can see about 7 million colors? According to colormatter.com. Huge! Who would've thought? Different colors make us feel different ways. The red color, for instance, is appetizing. Blues and greens are calming. There's a lot you can do utilizing colors to reach various goals. Think from how you paint your home, each room, and the clothes you wear to what colors you surround your children with.

Gratitude-enhancing ideas: it's worth doing research on how to play around with colors when you decorate your house. I'd like to invite you to try out color-meditation! Choose a place and time to avoid being interrupted. Sit comfortably. Close your eyes. Slow down your breathing and observe it first. Then start visualizing a chosen color, or place of a particular color depending on what you want to achieve. To relax your mind and heart, visualize green grass, or blue sky with white clouds. Light pink and purple also tranquilize. To feel more energized, bright yellows, red, neon colors work better. Imagine you are walking in a red tulip field and touching the flowers, or you are lying down on the sand looking up at dozens of yellow umbrellas. Just try it, and be amazed!

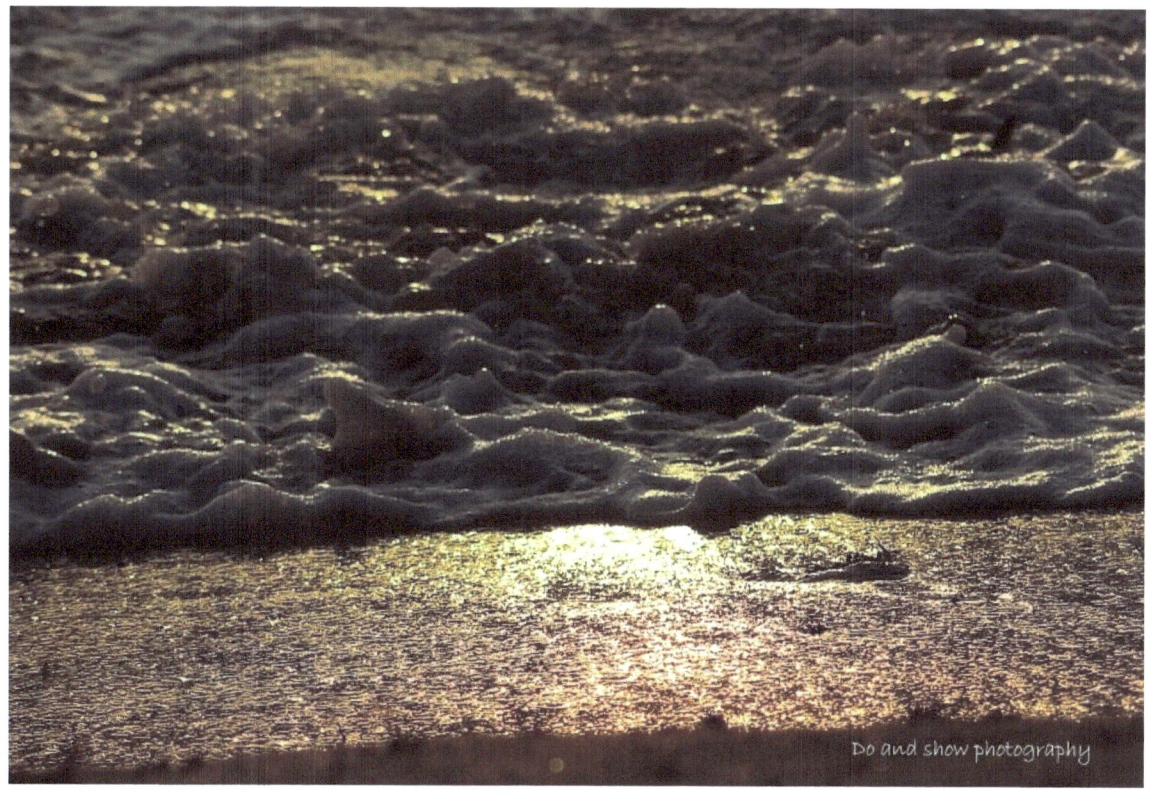

I am so very thankful for living by the beach as I've always wanted, and one of the reasons why it's very essential to my wellbeing is the practice of earthing or grounding. This means I get to walk barefoot on the sand and go through a special type of detox from electrical pollution via connecting with earth's energy directly. I feel so blessed I can do this every day! Hmmm, actually, I'd like to point out that we all can if we choose to devote a little time for it. It's always the matter of our priorities, and that is based on our understanding of the big picture instead of getting lost in or attached to the prompt gratification. According to barefoothealing.com.au, the cleansing happens because we get in touch with earth's free electrons that could be considered as excellent antioxidants due to their ability to neutralize harmful effects of free radicals that are known to contribute to diseases. Keep reading on, please, in case you are worrying about not living near the sea.

Gratitude-enhancing ideas: earthing isn't just walking on sand without shoes, it's also doing the same in grass, on dirt, or other natural materials. The larger skin surface you can connect with earth, the better or the faster you can cleanse. You can lie down wearing swimsuits or shorts and short sleeved shirt. Think of wading in shallow waters. Beautiful grounding experience! Can you imagine a week in wilderness, camping, without no electricity and cell phone coverage? What a priceless chance for the body to breathe up and detox!

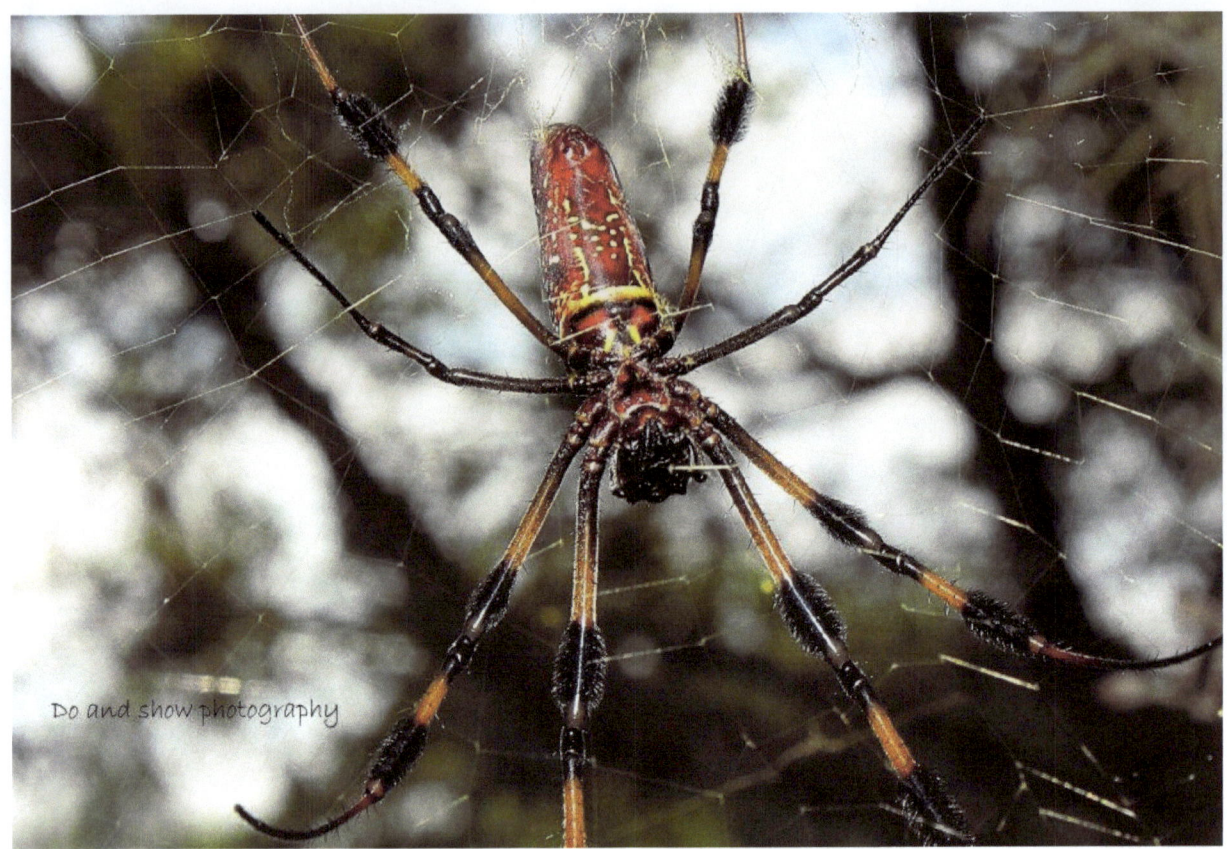

Looking at this photo, what's the first thought that pops into your mind? I wouldn't touch spider, either, like many other people, but I've learned to view them from a different angle. Many species are helping us to experience less of the annoying flies and mosquitoes. Yes, some are venomous, but the common house spiders are not. While long ago I used to get disgusted and scared of creepy-crawlies, now I know better. I understand it's always up to my mindset, my attitude how I see things. It's a wonderfully freeing experience, therefore, I am very grateful for spiders and what they do for our environments.

Gratitude-enhancing ideas: once again, it's time to repeat that turning disgust and fear around using curiosity and admiration can help a great deal. Learn more about these arachnids. Watch documentary videos. Consciously start focusing on their beautiful or interesting sides. Kids are naturally curious about nature and its living creatures. Take them out on nature walks. Gear up. Utilize magnifying glasses, cameras, nets, etc. but always with the intention not to harm animals and plants. Simply observe, record, and then release them if you caught them. Always exercise caution though. At home, make projects together about what you have seen. Brainstorm ideas. Let your kids come up with theirs. Another way to keep them away from constant tech-exposure.

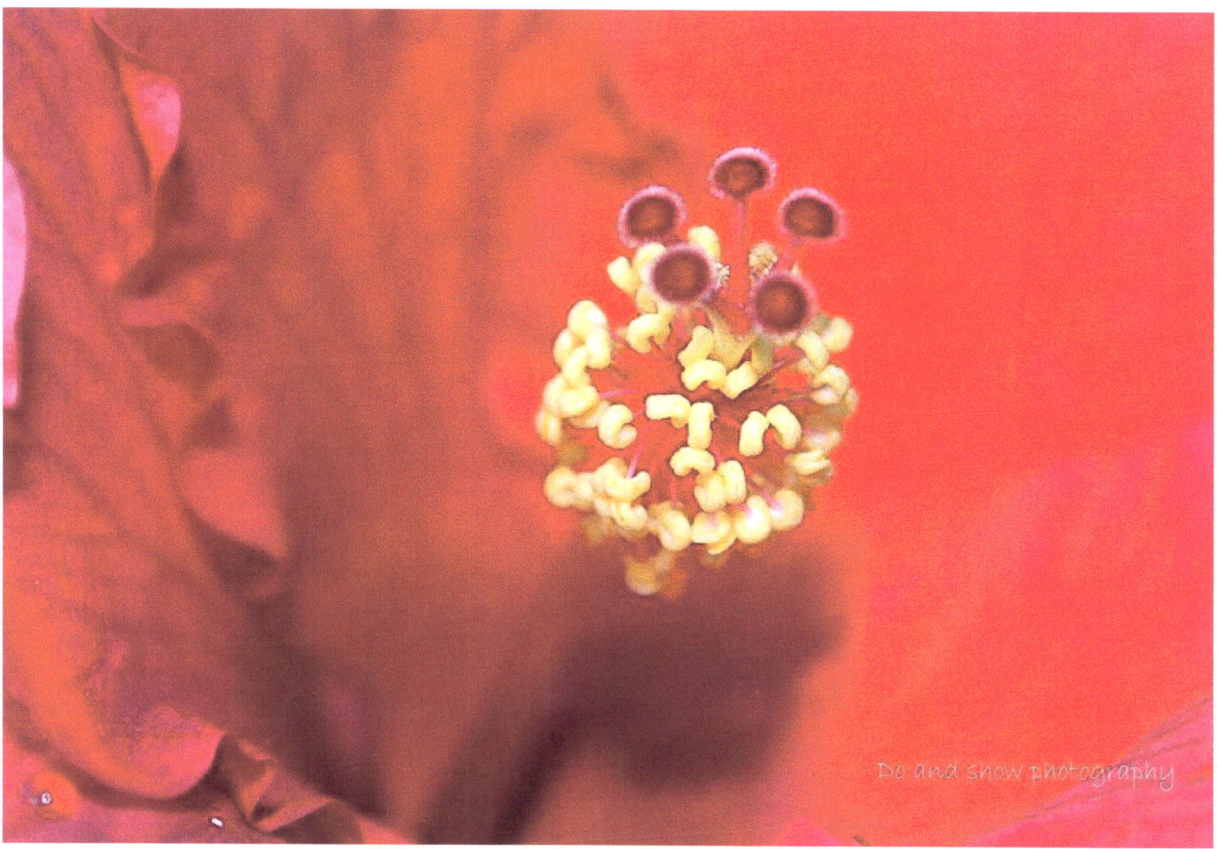

I feel gratitude for these tiny pollens in the flowers, and the busy bees and other insects that collect them, spread them, contribute to their survival and also make honey. What a fascinating system! According to getaway.co.za, at the last Royal Geographical Society meeting in London, the Earthwatch Institute declared the bees to be the most important living species on earth! Boom! Maybe you've heard that if bees disappeared from earth, men would die out within four years. Reading different resources, like forbes.com, it's thought to be said by Albert Einstein. I feel so thankful for those who have already recognized this and started taking steps towards protecting the bees.

Gratitude-enhancing ideas: observe flowers from closer too, and take close-up shots of them. Show them to your children, and discuss how pollination happens. Develop and help them to develop a healthy respect towards pollinators. You might want to consider planting flowers in pots for your balcony or yard that attract bees and they are good for them. Southrenliving.com listed flowers for this purpose, such as: poppy, sunflowers, mint, wisteria, lavender, honeysuckle, lilacs and more. Another interesting ingredient to add to your smoothies (I always do) is bee pollen for human consumption. Yes! It has so many kinds of vitamins, minerals, antioxidants. According to healthline.com, bee pollen has numerous benefits for health.

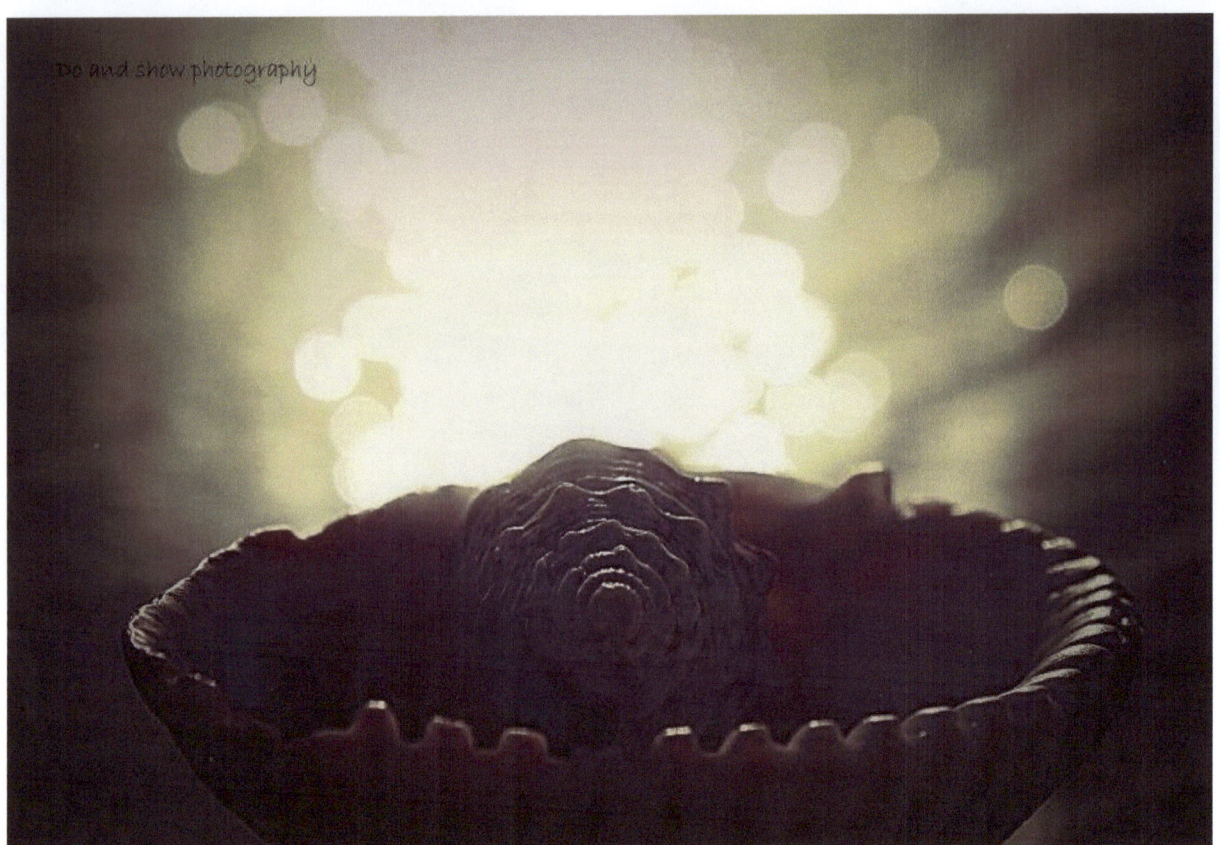

I am very thankful for the shells of all kinds. Coming from a beach-less country, I used to daydream about visiting the beach and moving there. I still feel those warm emotions I used to have watching a certain cartoon when the main character went to the beach and started collecting shells. It made me so happy every time recalling it. I have a big collection of seashells. I still admire them, and go into shell shops when traveling to tropical islands. Now I live on a beautiful, subtropical beach. One of my biggest dreams has come true.

Gratitude-enhancing ideas: even if you are not into collecting shells, take some time to look for them on the beaches you visit, and check them out in stores. Maybe you'd like to paint them or decorate them. Maybe you are open to create animals from different sized shells with your child. Think about photographing them in various backgrounds and light conditions to create framed wall art. How about wearing jewelry made of seashells? I'd recommend also watching short videos on the snails and clams, how they are born, how they grow their shells and what they eat. The point is to take a little time here and there to admire their beauty and diversity.

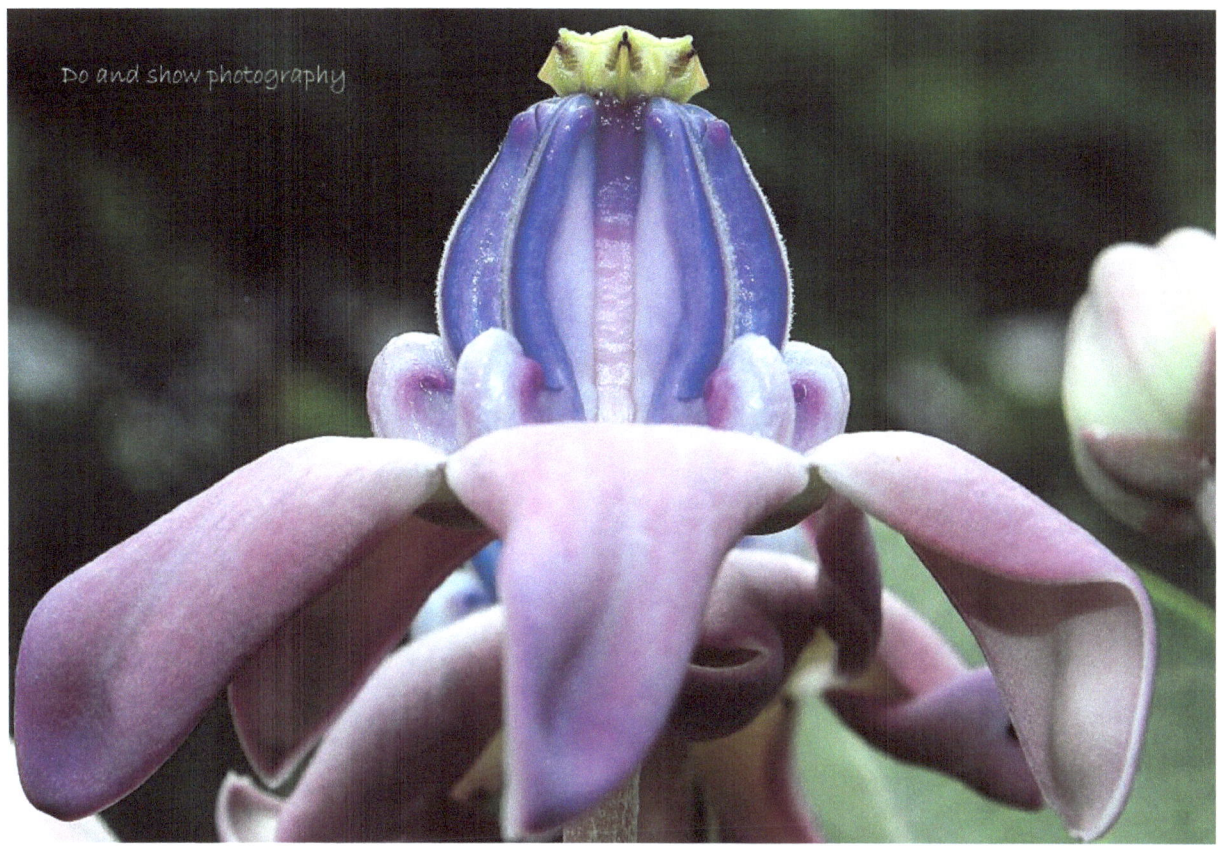

I did mention my gratitude for flowers before. Here I'd like to take the opportunity to talk a little about my gratitude for the unique things we encounter sometimes. There are those things that we see quite often and we get used to them. Then there are those, like this flower above, that maybe a number of people have never even seen yet. I spend a great amount of time to learn about nature, and when I'd think that I couldn't see another flower or fruit that I've never seen before, another unique image makes its way to my eyes. How exciting is that? This type of excitement and curiosity are qualities you would want to encourage in your child as well.

Gratitude-enhancing ideas: obviously, it's easier to get enthusiastic about something new than the old, usual things. Yet, I often meet people who pass by unique beauties without noticing them. Are you one of those people? Do you really want to be like that? Having your mind concentrated on the future possibilities – which are absolutely endless, therefore, it could take up all of your time and energy – or obsessed about returning to the past on and on, trying to dissect it what you could've done differently, both are pointless and futile. Being in the present, however, is what contributes greatly to a more balanced and more fulfilling life. That allows you to live in awe. That inspires you to enjoy anything and everything. That sort of pressures you to not miss out on things in the true meaning. That's what I like to call real living.

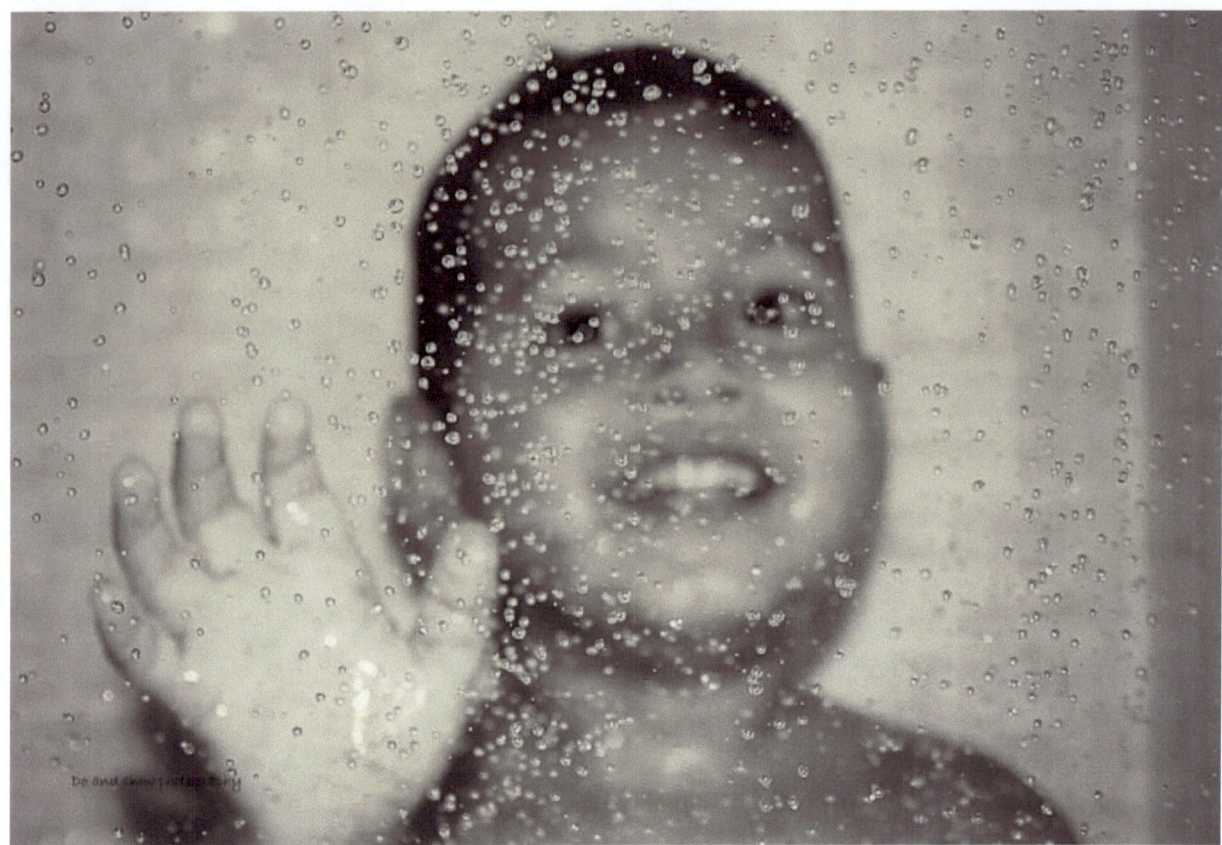

I must express my deep gratitude for being able to take showers and baths as I wish. Knowing that many people in the world don't have this luxury which for most people in developed countries are a normal part of life, I feel even more blessed by having access to clean, safe water. When we spend some time on the beach, or working in the garden, or standing on our feet all day, taking a hot bath or shower feels absolutely heavenly. I've also noticed long ago, that during shower, excellent and inspired ideas tend to flow into my mind. It's very exhilarating. Have you noticed something similar too?

Gratitude-enhancing ideas: bath isn't only about getting clean. It's also about relaxation, enjoying silence or calming music, spending quality time with our children, or even getting a little intimate with our partners. I'd suggest taking detox baths sometimes. I add a cup of baking soda and Epsom salt to the bathwater. You can also pour in Bentonite clay, essential oils (jasmine, chamomile, eucalyptus, etc.), lemon slices and sea salt. See it for yourself how it feels afterwards. Showers should be short to conserve more water. I love alternating hot and cold water in every 10-15 seconds. It's very invigorating, therefore, stimulates the removal of waste from the cells and supports the nutrient transport via the circulation system.

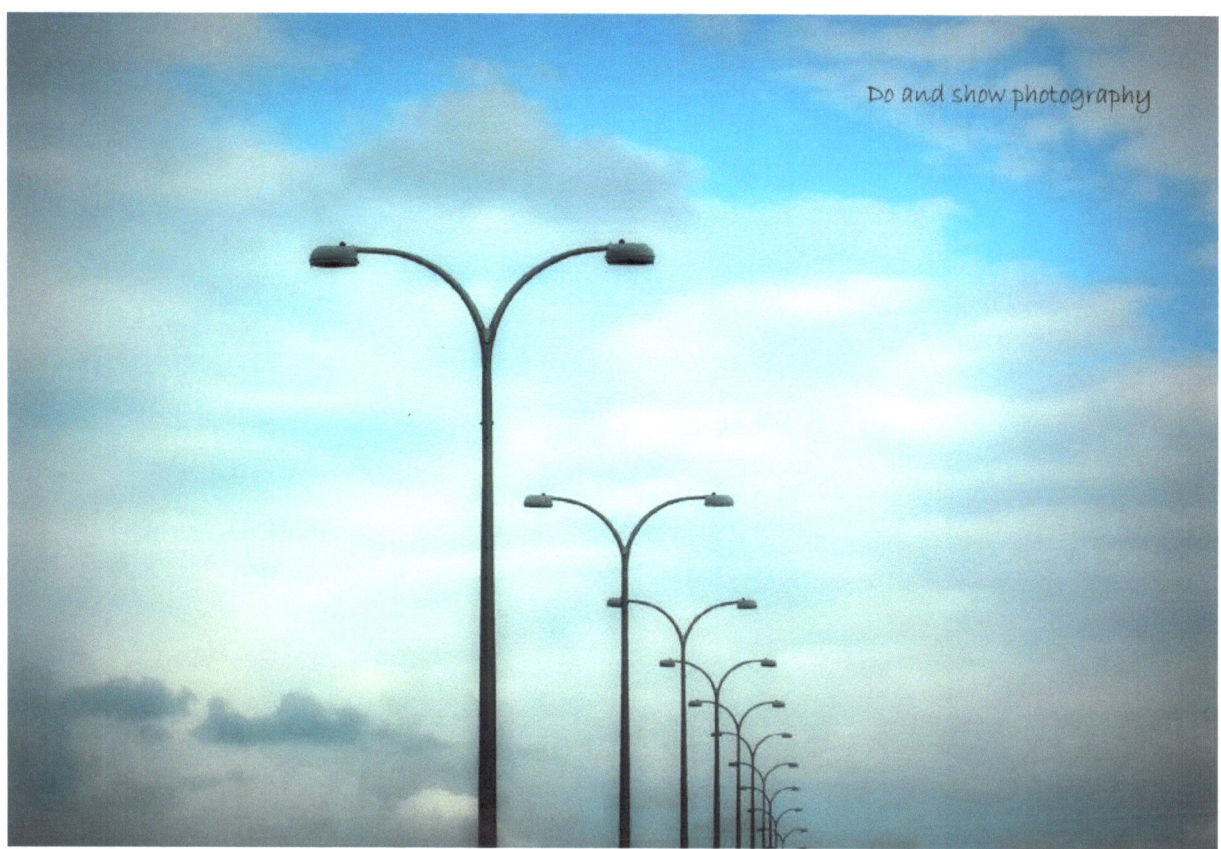

I feel absolutely grateful for the streetlights, and all the lights. I have thought of that too many times how lucky I am to be living in these modern times when we don't have to light a candle or a torch just to see better inside a building. When we drive at night, how important is to have streetlights, right? We have them even near highways in a lot of places. The cherry on the top for me is when I can take a great shot like this from an interesting angle. Very pleasing to my mind and my eyes, being a passionate minimalism photographer.

Gratitude-enhancing ideas: enjoying the comfort and practicality of lights and lamps is nice but it's essential to not waste resources like electricity. Educate yourself about the lifespan and energy-usage of various lightbulbs. Teach your kids about it too. Adjust your daily schedule to save more energy by needing to turn on the lights less. I have to share something with you here. Once we were wading and swimming in a cave, in Mexico. We all had helmets with built-in flashlights. The guide asked us to turn it off for a minute and listen to the water dripping. It was pitch dark. He explained that many cave divers die because of their flashlight battery running out. Without light it's practically impossible to find the way out in time. That makes one think, doesn't it? And how often we take lights for granted, right?

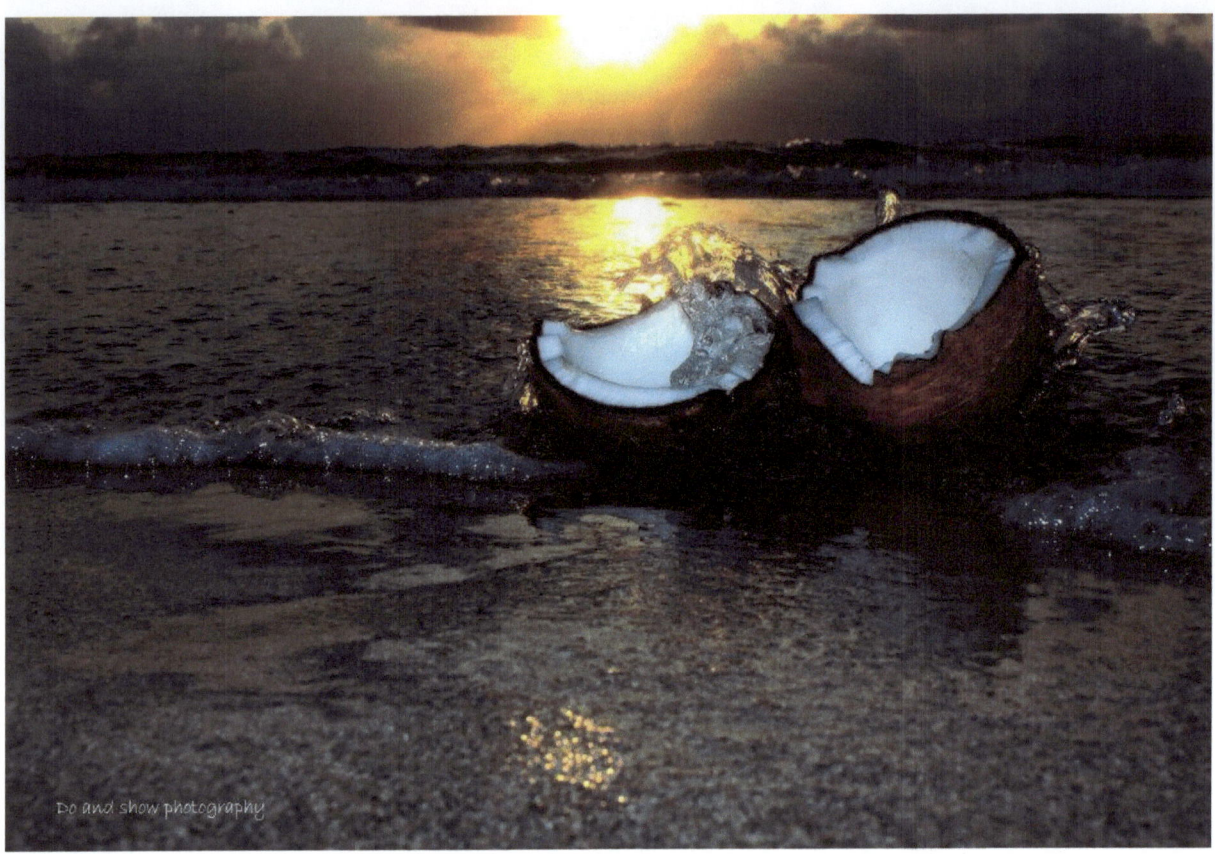

I must talk about my deep gratitude for coconut and coconut oil. I've always loved coconut in any form. Ever since I've learned a lot about the health benefits of cooking with coconut oil and using it for beauty, I don't have one day pass by without utilizing this wonderful tropical nut. I cook with its oil/fat, I drink its water, I eat its flesh grated or in chunks, I use its oil for my skin, and for my babies. It did amazingly for their diaper rashes.

Gratitude enhancing ideas: I am not asking you to believe me, but with an open mind, do some research. According to Dr. Axe's website, there are over 1,500 studies that show coconut oil's incredible benefits for health. It nourishes your skin. Try to apply it after bath. It has a high smoking point opposed to most vegetable oils which means it's much safer to cook with it because it doesn't oxidize like the other cooking oils. Oxidized oils and fats are linked to a wide variety of diseases. Try to bake with it more. Try it instead of diaper rash cream. It worked well for my babies. It's always good to make educated choices. Get real coconuts. You can crack its shell with a hammer after you removed the water from inside using a screwdriver and a hammer. Drill at least two holes, of course, to make sure the liquid can flow out when turned upside down. Strain. Dry the flesh pieces at the lowest heat your oven can do, or toast it a little. It's absolutely delicious. It can be added to numerous dishes and sweets, also, smoothies.

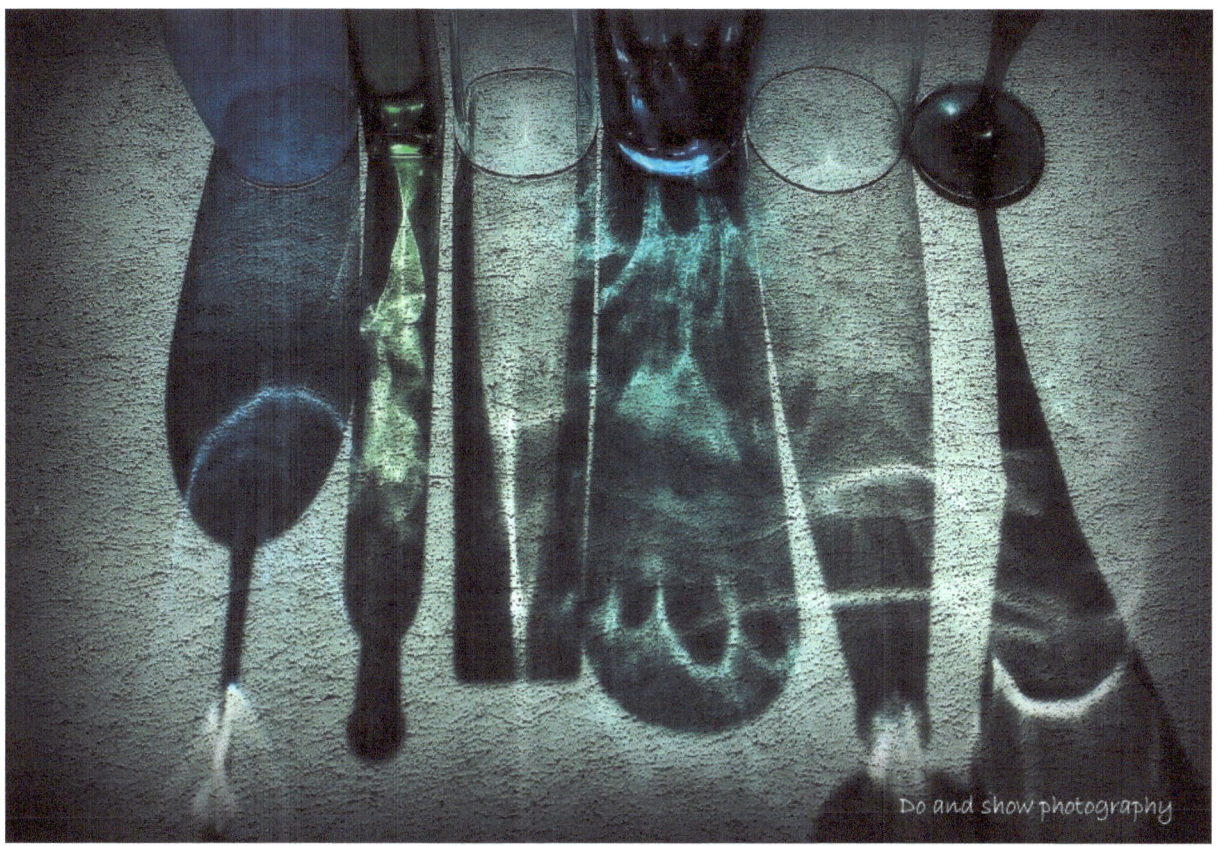

I am thankful for the glass and all the great things humans create from it. Although glass takes a million years to break down once it's discarded, according to greenlivingtips.com, it's a beautiful man-made material. Because of it, we can enjoy comfortable climate inside our homes and cars, we can see better wearing glasses, we can put food, drink, cut flowers and other items into glass containers to decorate and store, and much more.

Gratitude-enhancing ideas: simply admire glass objects and their qualities. Realize as you stand in front of the glass window that how amazing is to have that kind of protection from wind, cold, dust, flying insects and more. Appreciate how it can silence bothersome noises and sounds when you close your window. Applaud the marvelous glass vases, statues, and household items. Oh, and remind yourself that the mirror is made of glass too, and what a great invention that is! I've read on livescience.com that mirror was invented in 1835 applying a thin layer of metallic silver on the back. How cool is that? Maybe you'd like to visit a glassblower with your family and observe how they blow glass objects. Fantastic experience.

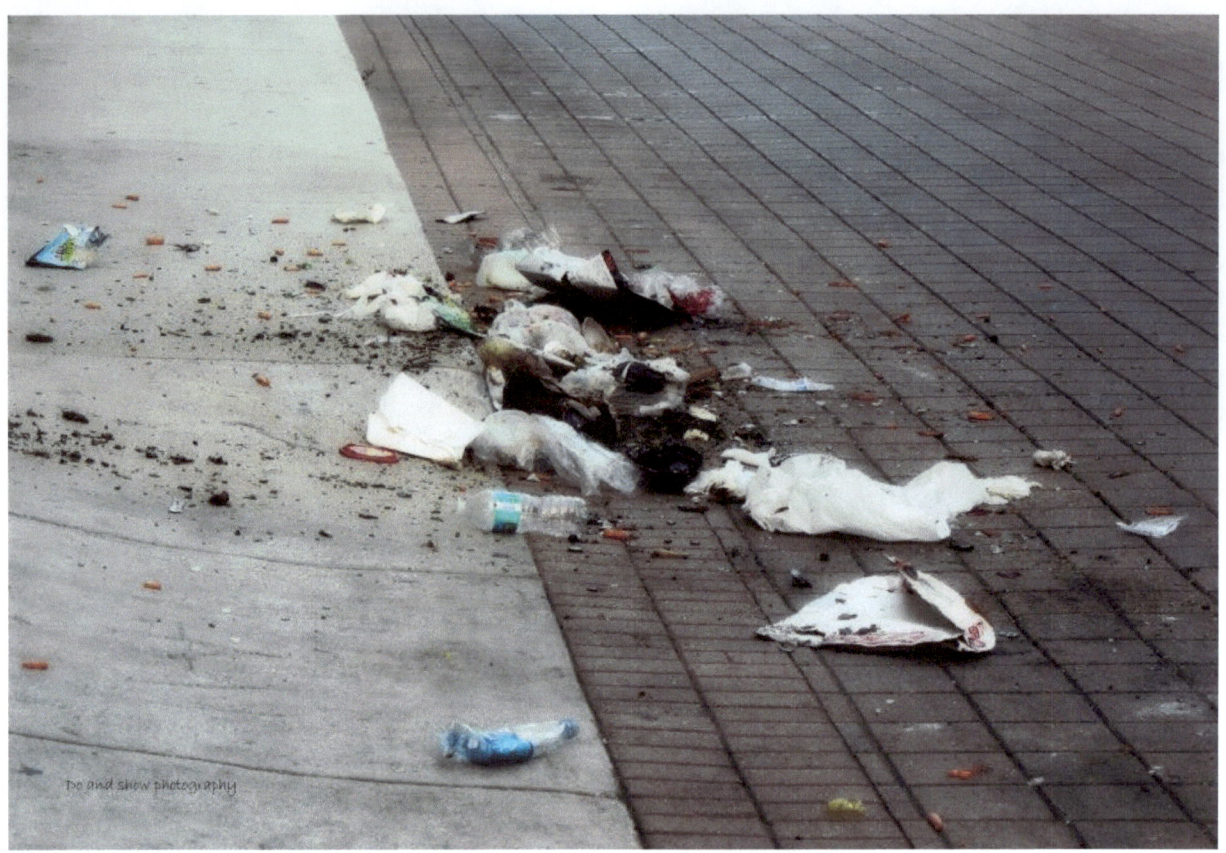

You may be wondering why I am showing you garbage and why I'd be feeling gratitude for it. When I was a teacher, and for a lesson, I had to read a book to the children about the garbage truck, it truly hit me what a super-duper important the garbage collector's job is (sorry for the language style, I am back in those times for a second). Even with their regular schedule of picking up trash from every neighborhood I see too much garbage lying around for my taste. Can you imagine how our homes and cities would look like in a month, in a year or a decade if there was no garbage-removal?! So, yes! I am absolutely and endlessly thankful for those who get up so early each day to drive to my street and take away the accumulated, smelly and germ-collecting trash bags.

Gratitude-enhancing ideas: I highly recommend participating in city's cleanups, and take your children with you! Talk about the importance of this. I got my boy a trash grabber tool, and we regularly go around the streets and our beach to do our part of the cleanup. It's a wonderful bonding experience otherwise, also. The breakdown time of various materials we, humans use daily is deeply shocking. Every family should get very serious about this topic because everyone's future depends on it. So spread these eye-opening numbers around. According to saveonenergy.com, an average American makes around 4 lbs. of garbage a day. USA has more than 3,500 landfills and that contributes to methane emission which is known to trap heat very effectively in the atmosphere.

So, how many years does it take for different items and materials to break down?

Apple core – 2 months

Paper towel – 2-4 weeks

Cotton shirt – 2-5 months

Cigarette filter – 1-5 years

Plastic bag – 10-20 years

Some other numbers from storage.neic.org's site.

Rubber boot sole – 50-80 years

Tin can – 50 years

Milk carton – 5 years

Batteries – 100 years

Sanitary pads – 500-800 years

Disposable diapers – 450 years

Tinfoil and Styrofoam do not biodegrade

Plastic items can take up to even 1000 years

Glass bottle – 1 million years

So, yes, do recycle and teach your kids to do it too, like religiously, whenever you and they can. I have other books that are filled with project ideas to reuse materials in the household. These books are also rhyming stories for young children with a long section to help parents to deepen their children's learning experience. Titles: Love me, Mommy, no matter what! And Love me, Daddy, no matter what!

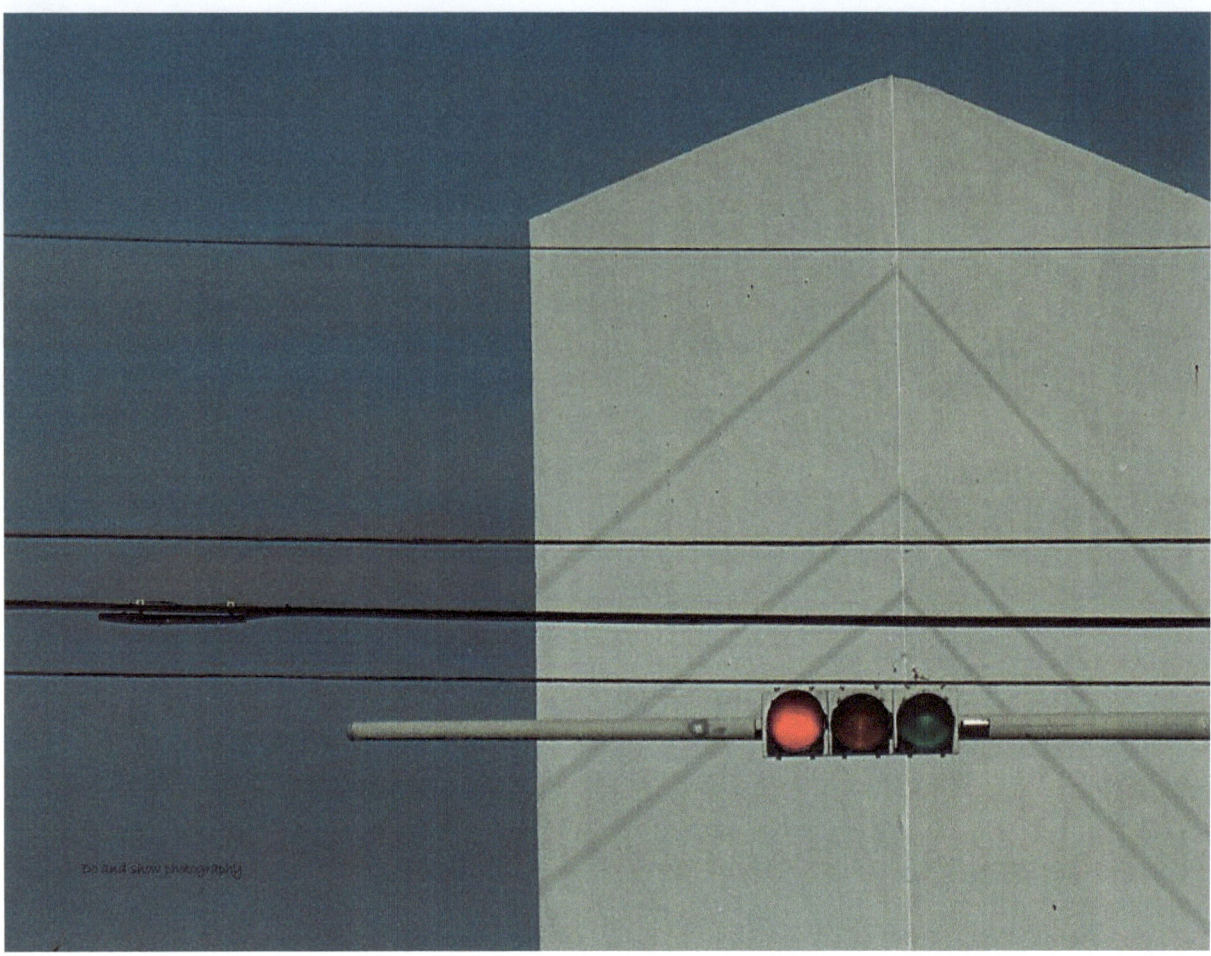

I love driving and I am very grateful for the traffic lights on the streets and roads. I've been in countries where there are fewer traffic signs and lights being established and used, and I recall my fear, my constant fear ... waiting to finally get to my destination each time. I believe traffic lights and signs are a brilliant invention.

Gratitude-enhancing ideas: while driving, pay more attention mindfully to these traffic signs and lights. Allow your mind to realize how many ways they can save your life. Feel the gratitude within. If your kids are with you in the car, point out signs, and educate them about what they are trying to prevent. At home, when they build from blocks and play with cars, suggest to them to create little street signs and utilize those too in their play. You need toothpicks or pipe cleaners for the pole, cut out shapes for the signs from cardboard (you can use pasta or cereal boxes as well, now that we've talked about recycling already), and they can stand these signs into a piece of playdough in a bottlecap, for instance. Get them involved. This way they can practice writing, spelling, cutting, exercising their creativity and more.

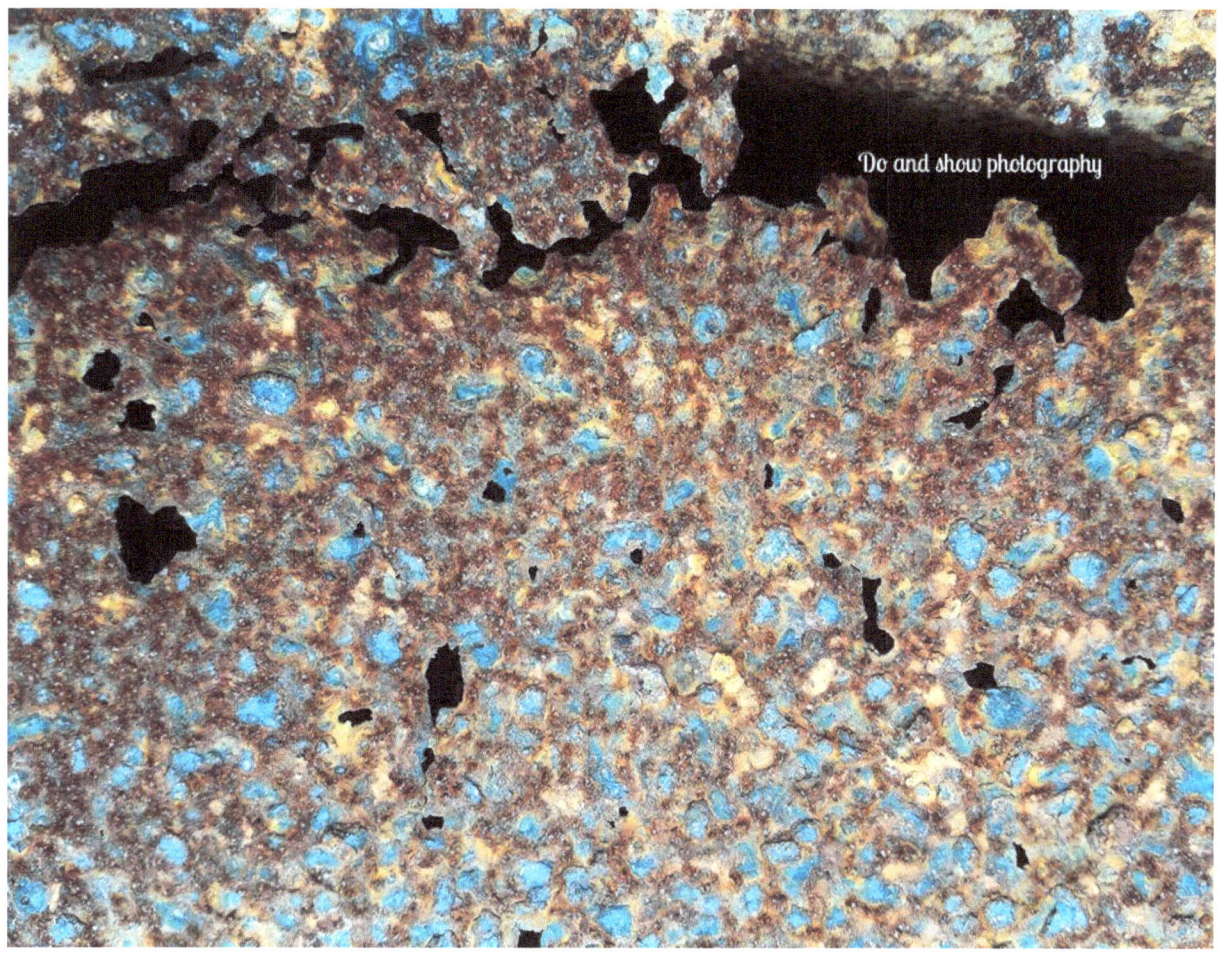

While we don't accept it happily that our metal objects can give into rusting, we can start seeing its beautiful side of it. As a passionate photographer, I find it very eye-catching to see all the discolorations of a rusty metal. What about you? Can you appreciate the other side of rustiness?

Gratitude-enhancing ideas: start viewing rusty items from an angle of admirable beauty. If they are rusty, there are some methods that can help in rust-removal. Use acidic liquids like vinegar or lemon juice to soak your mildly rusty items in it for a few hours, or sprinkle baking soda on it, and let it sit for an hour or two before you brush it with a metal brush. If that doesn't help, then do the next best thing and find what is good in it. Well, they certainly make a lovely subject for photographs, wall art, paintings and more. Let your creativity grow wings. Rustic rusty items look rather interesting and homey in a garden, yard or home. How about simply collecting them? I collect many items and it's a really lovely hobby. It makes my soul fly.

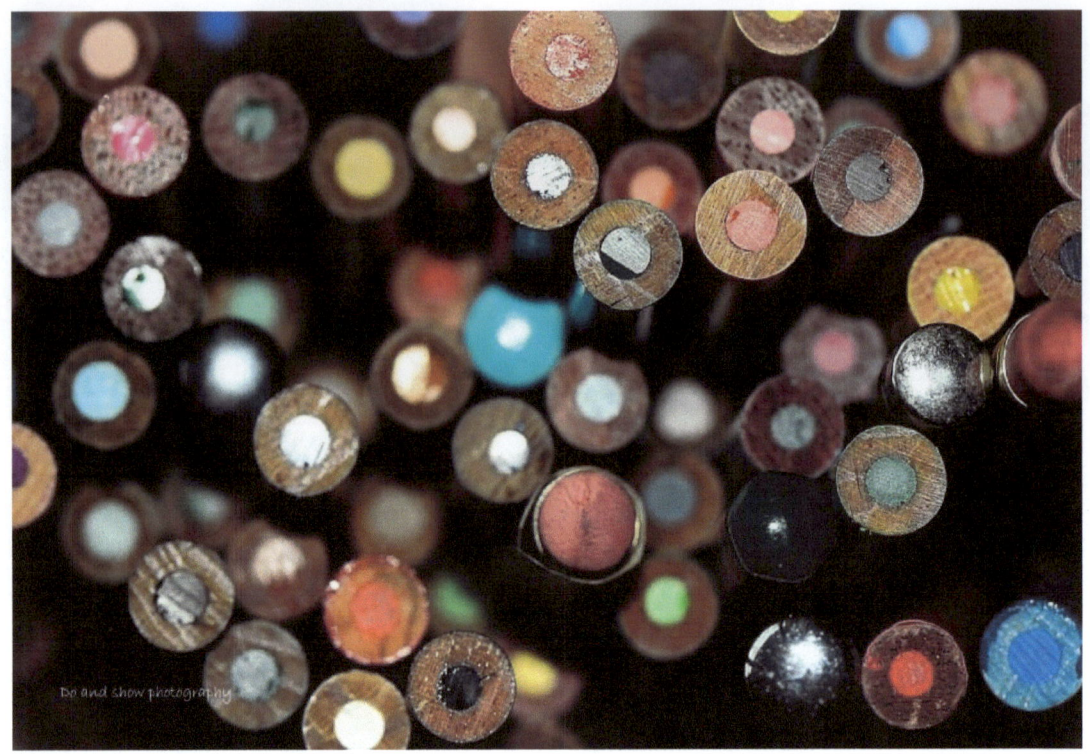

I am a very passionate writer since my childhood. This is one of the reasons why I write books, and not only on my native language. Hence, I feel very thankful for pencils and pens of all kinds. Writing and drawing go back, far-far back in time. It's pretty beneficial for our overall development, and even for our health. Just think of writing a journal and unloading those bothersome or harmful negative emotions. Drawing and writing can make you feel better, and I've experienced this countless times myself. Of course, I must add, without my hand and properly functioning mind I couldn't write, so I am very grateful for them as well. How many children dislike school and/or the endless practicing of writing of the letters and words. They don't realize it then what a wonderful ability it is to keep improving it.

Gratitude-enhancing ideas: bring yourself to the moment when you are writing down something and feel it, really feel it how blessed you are that you are able to write. Think of the pen or pencil as your fingers' extension. Different pens, pencils, crayons and markers convey a different feeling to our nerve endings. Some are really rolling smoothly, right? Others write kind of scratchily. I love personalizing everything about my life. It makes me feel even more unique and grateful. Begin writing a journal about your feelings and thoughts. It doesn't have to take more than a few minutes of your day. It does, however, go a long way towards your mental and emotional, therefore overall health. I know if from a personal experience. Make your special pen look even more special. Cover it with fabric, or glue gemstones or fur on it. Let your creative mind soar.

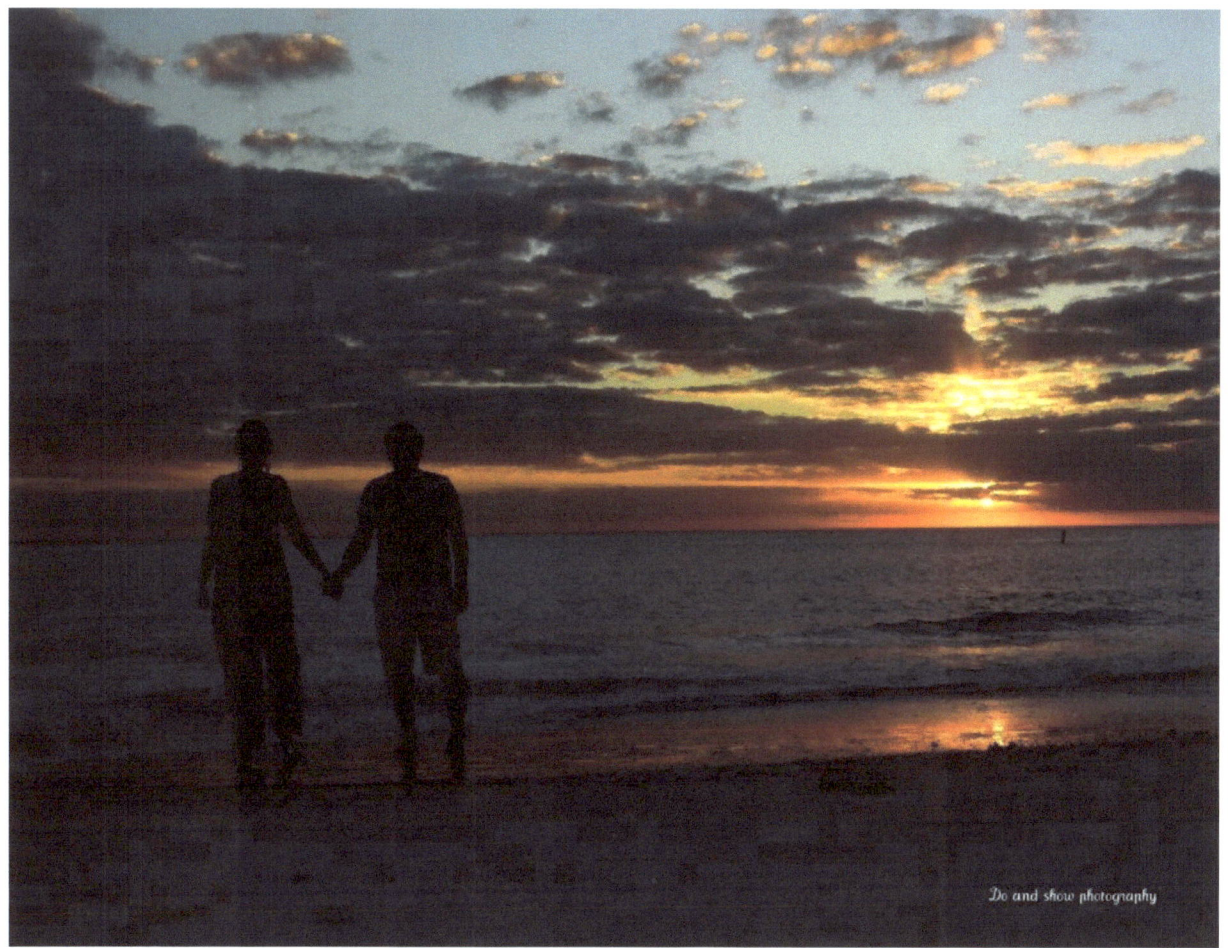

Ahhh, I feel absolutely blessed and grateful for finding love, and being able to keep it alive in my heart for many years. Yes, it does take tons of effort and time to make a relationship work, but, boy, it's worth it. I couldn't really describe the happiness I feel holding hands, hugging, kissing with my husband, looking into each other's eyes deeply, knowing we are there for each other, we belong together, we have been through marvelous and rough times, and we have created lives by joining. Wow! Isn't that incredibly, amazingly fascinating!?

Gratitude-enhancing ideas: take the time and energy every single day to show your love and care toward your partner. It does matter! It does matter a lot! I couldn't emphasize it enough. If you are already doing it, just keep doing more. Even on those days when you feel you'd rather run away and hide. Do a 5-minute foot rub. Hold hands while walking in the mall. Kiss good bye before you are off to work. Praise her/him in front of others. Tell her/him about your love. Share a breakfast in the bed. Go to the movies together. Giggle, hug and be silly sometimes. Chase her on the beach. …And, and, listen to her/him to understand, not just to respond something.

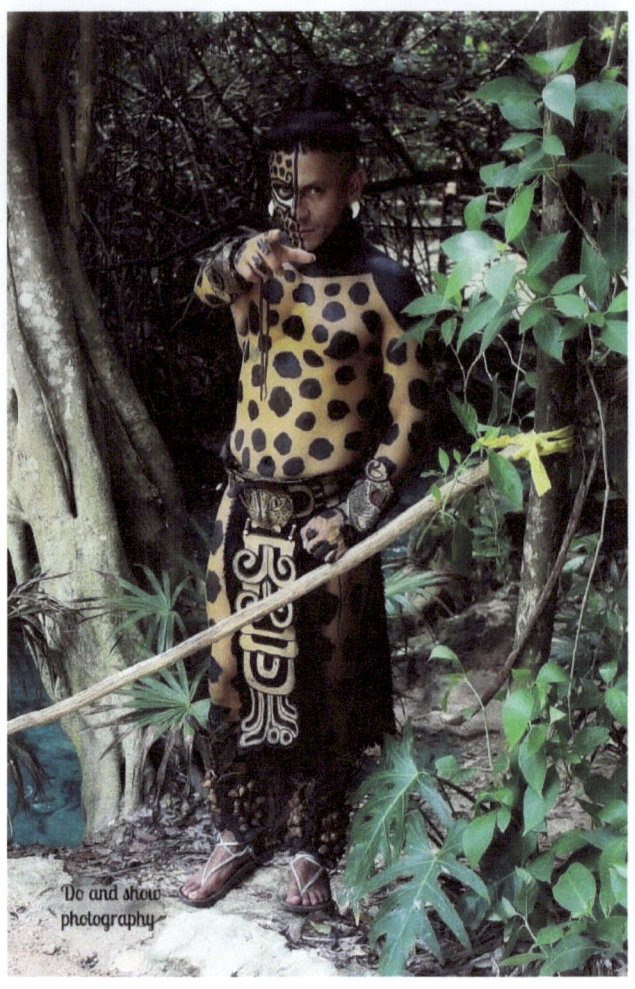

I am very thankful for our historians and other scientists who are involved in finding and figuring out our ancestors' past, how they lived, how they dressed, what they ate, built, how they behaved, etc. I've had the honor to watch live numerous groups of actors wearing authentic outfits and acting out dances and behaviors of natives who have lived hundreds of years ago. It's both intriguing and thrilling. This one above is from my trip to Mexico, viewing a show about the Mayans.

Gratitude-enhancing ideas: again, consciously find materials to get more educated about these topics. Create simple costumes and masks with your kids to get them familiar with ancient dress codes. Tell stories. Act it out. Watch shows together. When on a trip, ask information about programs that introduce the natives' or locals' lives. Try to imagine how it must've felt to live in those times.

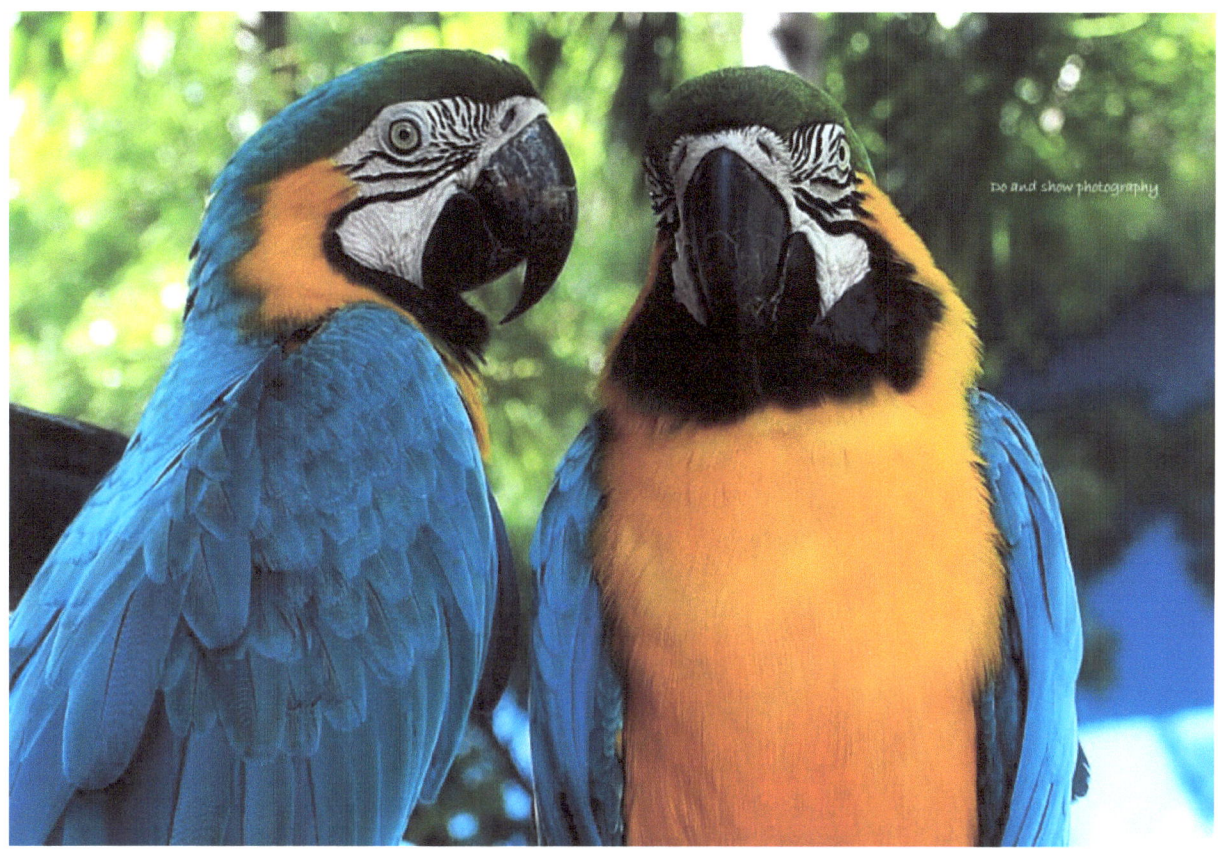

It's time to mention the birds, birds of all kinds I feel so grateful for. Their early summer songs fill my heart and soul with warm-cozy feelings. Their beautiful mating dances fascinate me. Their diversity in shapes, sizes and colors is very amazing. I recall having parrots as pets in my childhood years. It was a wonderful experience to see them interact, fly around, lay eggs and one learned to say good morning to us!

Gratitude-enhancing ideas: birds are living all around us, even in cities, so it's sort of easy to point them out to your children, and of course, lay your eyes on them too, to admire them. Remember, it's really the matter of training your mind to become more conscious, mindful, present and open to see beauty around. Becoming more mindful like this will lead to more appreciation towards them. More appreciation creates nicer feelings inside us. When you feel better on a regular basis, you're more likely to make more productive and more beneficial decisions for yourself. Maybe you'd like to consider to get a pet bird, finches, or lovebirds, or cockatoo, or macaw, just to mention a few. Make or purchase birdhouses, hang them outside, and watch the birds coming to eat the seeds you place in the feeders. Great bonding opportunity for family members.

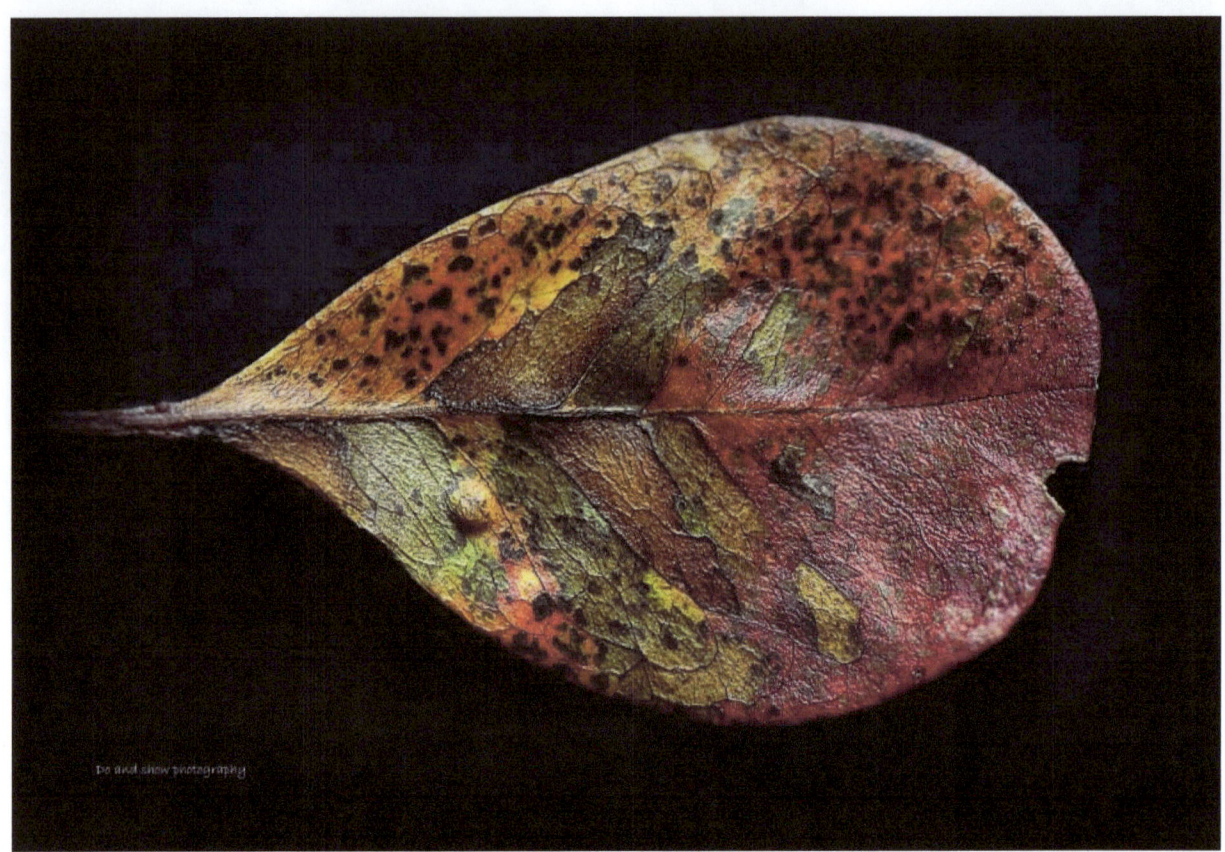

Although, I've talked about my appreciation for plants, leaves, and autumn leaves, I'd like to express my gratitude for the fabulous sight they create after the summer leaves. When I pick up a fallen leaf patterned with the hues of reds, yellows, browns, oranges and greens, I still find myself in awe. Not two leaves look alike! They are like nature's wonderful art pieces, all one-of-a-kind leaves. Some look sort of like a map. Autumn can feel a little depressing, at least to me, but these colorful leaves make me forget that.

Gratitude-enhancing ideas: instead of just raking all the dry leaves in the yard, gather some for art projects, like making an autumn leaf wreath, or center piece. It's easy to find Styrofoam wreath base or other geometrical shapes in craft stores. Using a glue gun, attach the pretty leaves on the Styrofoam. Add ribbons, nuts, beads or else, if you wish. Have your child create leaf-creatures by gluing them onto paper. Here's in interesting tip: using shape punchers, cut shapes out of sturdy leaves. You just made natural confetti! I wonder what you'd utilize them for.

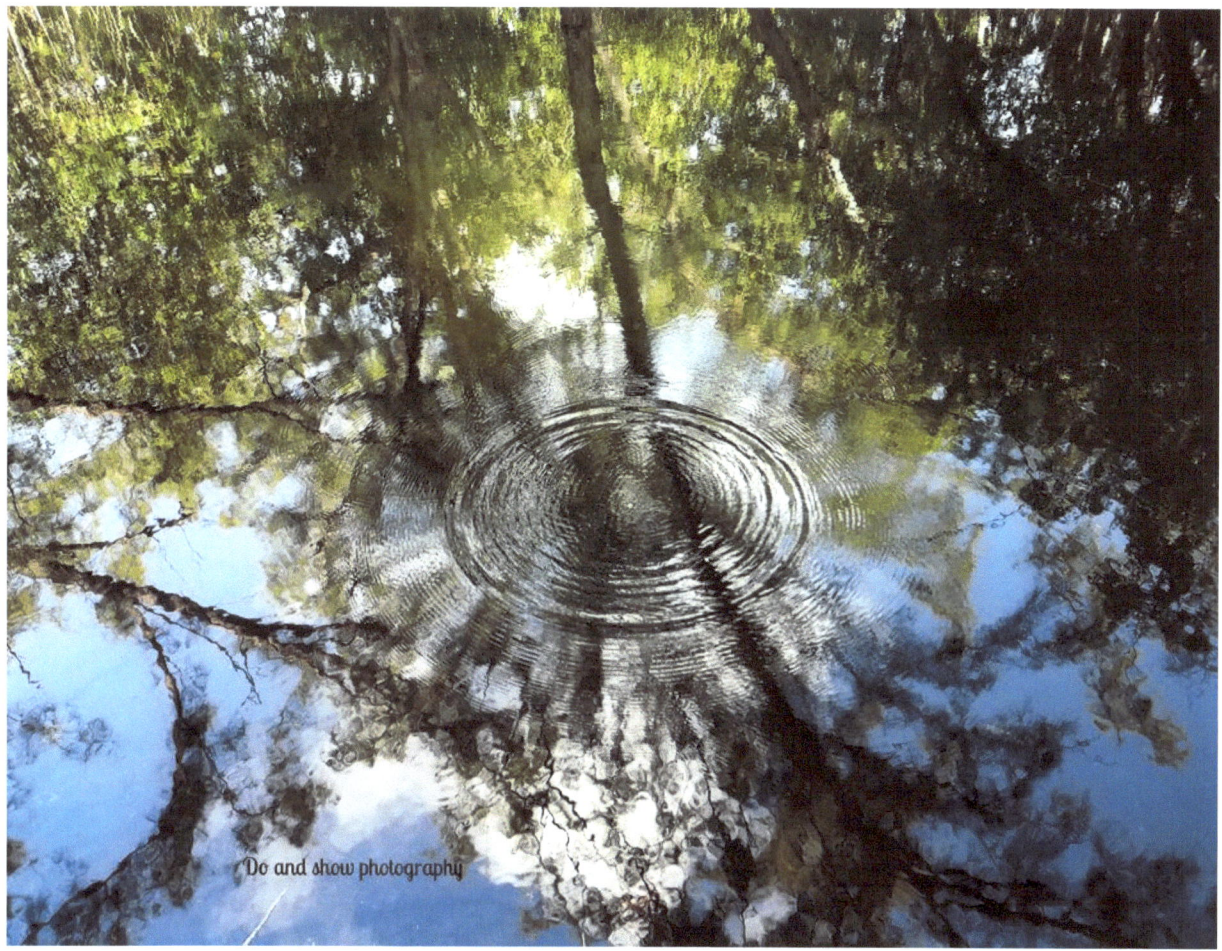

For a second, just recall memories when you were sitting or standing at a lake side or a pond, and you were throwing rocks into the water. I love photographing those water-rings on the surface of the water. They are not just lovely with the reflections of the nearby trees, but they remind me of something absolutely essential, that my decisions, my actions make an impact on my environment, on other people's lives, just like a ripple effect. Those people being influenced to some degree by my decisions also impact others as well. The ripples travel on and on and on and on…. I feel very honored, blessed, thankful and special to have this kind of power. On the other hand, I understand this can also be scary for some people due to exactly its profound nature. It does feel scary to me, too, from time to time.

Gratitude-enhancing ideas: now that you've read my thoughts on the ripples on the water, probably, you'll remember from now on your impact on the world. I recommend getting deeper into it. Feel the power in your hands, and let the feeling of the responsibility that comes with it tap you on the shoulder very often. That's how we can make a better world. I believe, we all are responsible for it. Now this is something crucial to teach to our children, right? As a holistic health and empowerment coach, I've observed and listened to countless stories about decision-making.

In a way, it's frightening to me how little people usually realize the weight of their choices. Including mine, too, of course. Many of us may have been raised to believe we don't have much power and our decisions don't matter much. I'd like to invite you to contemplate this topic a lot. It's that important in my opinion. Of course, occasionally, we realize that if I hadn't chosen this or that, this or that wouldn't have happened that way. Then again, how often do you really, I mean really grasp this concept and the end results? What about your children? Keep your mind focused on this domino effect because they can lead you to a totally different path and destination.

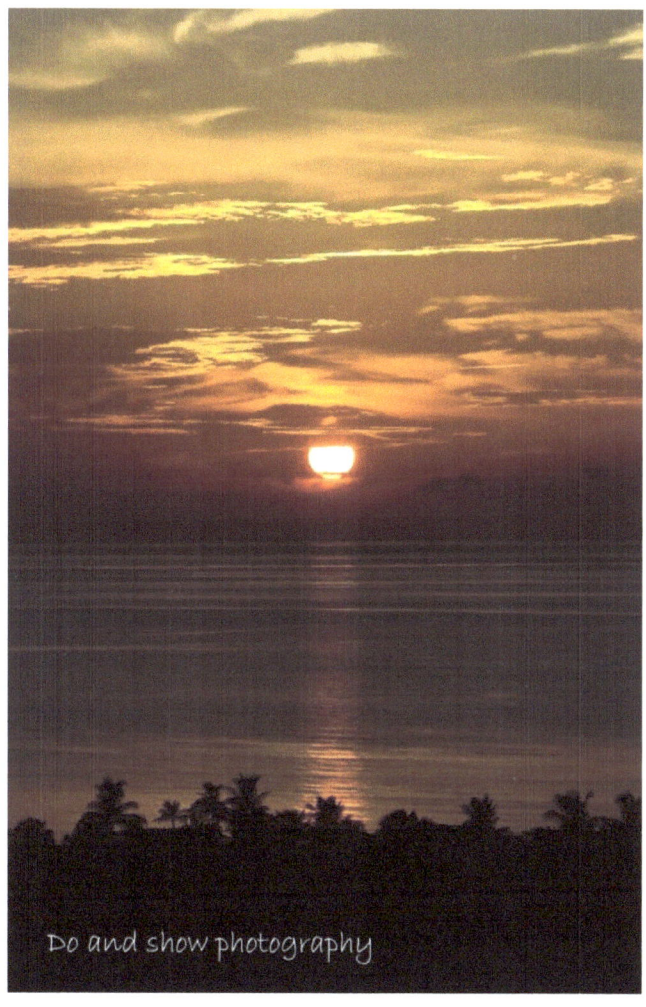

I am sure I don't need to elaborate on the beauty of a sunset over the ocean. It's easy to feel the gratitude for it. I've photographed hundreds and hundreds of sunrises and sunsets in the past few years. It's really hard to tell the difference between a sunrise and a sundown. They both can produce very similar effects on the sky and around. What I'd love to point out is the thoughts that the end of the day may bring. I feel deeply grateful for the sunset for its unique beauty and for the reminder that I've survived the day, I am still here alive and well, and I could say not only survived but thrived. Sunset tells me now the break is coming when my body and brain can relax. Isn't it incredible that we get to have a break from ourselves? It sounds funny but think about all the sort of abusive thoughts we allow to float around in our minds. When the majestic sun is going down, we know we can begin winding down too.

Gratitude-enhancing ideas: say thanks for going through the day, and realize it's still pretty amazing what you get to have and enjoy at the end of that day. Write it down! Yes! Share it with loved ones and encourage them to share as well. People will talk about (first) usually what matters to them the most. You can learn a lot new about your family and friends this way. I'd love to motivate you to make this a daily habit. Write down at least 3-4 of your achievements for that particular day. They don't have to be big accomplishments. Sometimes, remember, a small step means a lot. The key is to recall, acknowledge and celebrate them all every single day. Why? You want to feel capable and worthy, every single day. That's why. You want to be reminded of your talents, your abilities, your wins, your strengths. They will keep you going. It's a powerful habit to follow and teach your children as well. Right after you are done with your daily accomplishments, create a quick list of things to do the next day. This list should consist of those activities and actions that you need to do to keep your household running, related to your work, ensure your safety and health along with your family's, next small steps towards achieving goals and of course, something that simply lifts you up. When you've got a plan for the next day, you are less likely to forget any items on it, more likely to complete them all, and receive the sense of satisfaction. As you continue with this habit, you'll learn more and more how many items on the list can be planned for one day and how to play around with them. A so-called "to-do" list also helps you to feel less overwhelmed and more organized. This is actually part of stress management. There – in my personal and professional opinion – is no such thing as stress-free life. The idea is to manage or handle our stress better, or actually, the events we interpret stressful. Now, to do that, it's all about the right mindset but that'll be a whole other book.

Dear Reader!

I hope you've got inspired to start living your life more in the moment and begin taking the little and the big things in your life seriously lightly. Little things do matter, too, but the point is how we approach them. They need to be appreciated as well. Taking them lightly, I mean grab their positive and beautiful aspects of them. Become more playful and self-conscious. It's up to you! It's been always up to you. I'd love to hear from you regarding the improvements you were able to achieve in your life based on any of my books. Please feel free to contact me and share your experiences via email: meettherealyou@hotmail.com

Acknowledgement

I'd like to express my deep gratitude to my family who have been supporting me along my book writing and coaching journey. They have been so very patient with me when on our outings I have stopped countless times to wait for the perfect moment in order to capture beautiful images.

I want to express my gratitude towards all the other book authors and mentors I have been following and learning from.

I feel very grateful for you, dear READER, for choosing to get my book, giving it a chance, and taking the time to explore the pages.

About the Author

Beatrix Csinger has grown up in Hungary, Central Europe, witnessing her father losing hope little by little because of being struck with a genetic disorder called muscular dystrophy. Seeing someone she loved dearly to suffer from pain and the side effects of medications was a great contributing factor for her to start studying holistic health. Holistic or natural approach to health is when the person and his health are being viewed in the mirror of many-many details, especially the life choices being made. Beatrix has also been very interested in teaching young children. So, she has become a certified early childhood educator and has practiced over twenty years in classrooms. Meanwhile, she has begun conducting workshops and lectures to parents and families about various topics on the connections between lifestyle, diet, school work, behavior, focusing, etc. Her passion for helping others has grown greatly, hence, in the past year, finally, she has begun writing books. She is a holistic health and empowerment coach, speaker, published author, educator, passionate photographer, crafter and published poet.

You can write to her to schedule a free, half-hour-long phone session: meettherealyou@hotmail.com

Her website is under construction at the moment.

You can connect with her on Instagram @holisticbeatrixcsinger and @doandshowphotography

On Facebook: Meettherealyou holistic wellness, Minimalism by weekly themes and Do and show photography.

Upcoming books

Why me?

 - An interactive, holistic, self-discovery book for people who are willing to put in the work into learning about who they really are and into creating a shift in their mindset to produce better outcomes on the areas of overall health and happiness.

*

From My Beautiful Mind To your Beautiful Mind – Volume 2

- A holistic photo book with activities – Mind your self-talk

*

Your pets your holistic assets

- How can your pets help you to be healthier

*

And more children's books with a holistic approach.

www.ingramcontent.com/pod-product-compliance
Lightning Source LLC
Chambersburg PA
CBHW051152220526
45473CB00003B/745